C000212328

Minority Rights and Minority Protection in Europe

Minority Rights and Minority Protection in Europe

Timofey Agarin and Karl Cordell

ROWMAN &
LITTLEFIELD
INTERNATIONAL

London • New York

Published by Rowman & Littlefield International, Ltd.
Unit A, Whitacre Mews, 26-34 Stannary Street, London SE11 4AB
www.rowmaninternational.com

Rowman & Littlefield International, Ltd. is an affiliate of Rowman & Littlefield
4501 Forbes Boulevard, Suite 200, Lanham, Maryland 20706, USA
With additional offices in Boulder, New York, Toronto (Canada), and London (UK)
www.rowman.com

Copyright © 2016 by Timofey Agarin and Karl Cordell

All rights reserved. No part of this book may be reproduced in any form or by any
electronic or mechanical means, including information storage and retrieval systems,
without written permission from the publisher, except by a reviewer who may quote
passages in a review.

British Library Cataloguing in Publication Information Available
A catalogue record for this book is available from the British Library

ISBN: HB 978-1-78348-190-3
ISBN: PB 978-1-78348-191-0

Library of Congress Cataloging-in-Publication Data

Names: Agarin, Timofey, author. | Cordell, Karl, 1956– author.
Title: Minority rights and minority protection in Europe / Timofey Agarin and Karl Cordell.
Description: London ; Lanham, Maryland : Rowman & Littlefield International Ltd, 2016. | Includes
    bibliographical references and index.
Identifiers: LCCN 2015047658 (print) | LCCN 2016010044 (ebook) | ISBN 9781783481903 (cloth :
    alk. paper) | ISBN 9781783481910 (pbk. : alk. paper) | ISBN 9781783481927 (electronic)
Subjects: LCSH: Minorities—Government policy—Europe. | Minorities—Civil rights—Europe. |
    Europe—Ethnic relations.
Classification: LCC JN34.7 .A43 2016 (print) | LCC JN34.7 (ebook) | DDC 323.14—dc23
LC record available at http://lccn.loc.gov/2015047658

∞™ The paper used in this publication meets the minimum requirements of American
National Standard for Information Sciences Permanence of Paper for Printed Library
Materials, ANSI/NISO Z39.48-1992.

Printed in the United States of America

Für Tante Lise
Dein Karl

Für Jörg
Dein Timofey

Contents

Abbreviations

BDI—Democratic Union for Integration
CEE—Central Eastern European
CoE—Council of Europe
EC—European Commission
ECJ—European Court of Justice
EMRR—European minority rights regime
EU—European Union
FCNM—Framework Convention on National Minorities
HCNM—High Commissioner on National Minorities
IO—International organization
LLRA—The Electoral Action of Poles in Lithuania
NATO—North Atlantic Treaty Organization
NGO—Nongovernmental organization
NPD—People's Democratic Party
NRIS—National Roma Integration Strategies
OSCE—Organization for Security and Co-operation in Europe
OSI—Open Society Institute
PDPA—Democratic Prosperity of Albanians
PHARE—Programme of Community Aid to the Countries of Central and
    Eastern Europe
SDSM—Social Democratic Union
SMK-MKP—Party of the Hungarian Community
SNP—Slovak National Party
TEU—Treaty on European Union
TFEU—Treaty on the Functioning of the European Union
UDMR—Democratic Union of Hungarians in Romania
UK—United Kingdom

UN—United Nations
VMRO-DPMNE—Internal Macedonian Revolutionary Organization—
    Democratic Party for Macedonian National Unity
WWII—World War II

Acknowledgements

We wish to thank Anna Reeve for her encouragement and, indeed, her infinite patience with regard to the production of this volume.

Introduction

Talking the Talk?

Since the collapse of 'really existing socialism' in the late 1980s, the political complexion of Europe has undergone a number of fundamental changes. In general terms, these changes may be subsumed under the heading of the 'return to Europe'. They involved the dissolution of not only the Soviet bloc but also the entire ideological apparatus upon which it rested. In addition, the aforementioned 'return to Europe' spurred a transition towards liberal democracy, a system of rule that had shallow roots in the entire former Soviet bloc. Nascent political elites, in concert with established actors drawn from the West, embarked upon a process of system design, aimed at establishing and entrenching liberal democratic structures and norms in societies where historically they had been marginal to the conduct of politics. As a result, we find that within the context of wider socio-economic and political transition, the doctrine of the separation of powers was introduced, alongside regular competitive elections, and the growth of civil society was encouraged and capitalist free market principles were introduced as a means of aligning post-communist economies with those of liberal democracies.

Another important area that saw considerable change, and one with which our book is directly concerned, was that of minority rights. Interested West European policymakers, politicians and civil society activists were all aware of post-communist Europe's ethnic diversity and legacy. Indeed, the example of the disintegration of Yugoslavia was to serve as a reminder that the situation with regard to ethnic minorities, disputed borders and memories of past political legacies was highly combustible. We take the view that West European (and North Atlantic) policy decisions towards 'the East' have resulted from a mixture of historical fears, contemporary experience and, indeed, misunderstandings of both, as well as uncertainties about the direction of future developments. Given the consensus that emerged in the early 1990s across the post-communist area that the 'return to Europe' was paramount, desirable and best achieved by means of accession above all to the North Atlantic Treaty Organization (NATO) and the European Union (EU), inevitably a broad (cross-continental) consensus had to be reached on how best to fulfil the necessary conditions in order for this 'return' to be accomplished.

So, during the 1990s, post-communist Europe engaged in what many have described as a 'pedagogical process', whereby such states experienced a procedure that may be best understood as a 'teaching experience' with regard to democratisation and liberalisation. This was apparent in a number of policy areas, and in particular, within the field of minority rights. We contend that much of what happened in this policy area was governed as much by requirements set by West European governments as by states that wished to 'return to Europe'. In other words, a kind of political curriculum was devised (and internalised by post-communist states) during the period of accession to the Council of Europe, NATO and the EU.

Naturally, the rhetoric put forward by emergent post-communist elites was that of a genuine commitment to change, with policies being implemented as a reflexive response to formal requirements, which needed to be met in order for the 'return to Europe' to be accomplished. It is our contention that in the process, form has been confused with content. To be sure, all EU member-states now have an impressive array of guarantees that are designed to prevent and punish ethnically based discrimination. Yet just as established West European democracies have flaws with regard to the implementation of minority rights norms, it is equally clear that in post-communist Europe the transposition of minority rights provisions into legislation often has been grudging, haphazard and uneven. Paradoxically, although the EU's post-communist member-states actually have more comprehensive regulations on minority rights than do the majority of its more established members, EU membership and the adoption of 'common values' do not necessarily appear to have changed attitudes and behaviour in the manner expected in the 1990s. Even less so, political institutions of new member-states have changed little to facilitate minority protection. In light of this gap between expectation and reality, this book adopts a novel approach to explain this disjuncture, as elaborated further in this proposal.

First and foremost this book seeks to assess the underpinnings of minority rights protection in post-communist Europe and to evaluate the impact of the domestic institutions on the operation of the European minority rights regime. We do so because there are indications in a range of countries—for example, in Hungary, Romania, Bulgaria and Latvia—that the European minority rights regime operates in a manner that is non-equitable. This fact is of significance not only to the academic community but also to practitioners with regard to the future harmonisation of norm implementation in Europe—specifically, the EU.

Such a turn of events is also of obvious importance to members of (ethnic) minority communities themselves. As we pointed out when commenting upon the political context within which these reforms took place, the common goal shared by newly emergent post-communist political elites and wider civil society was that of the 'return to Europe'. Stripped down to its essentials, this desire was articulated as a demand for admission into the EU and NATO as an objective of identity politics. Whereas consideration of NATO and minority rights is not central to this volume, evaluation of the role of the EU is of primary importance. Precisely because EU membership was made conditional upon post-communist states proving their prior fitness for membership by undertaking sweeping reforms and designed to eradicate past practice, our book focusses upon the institutional context of the EU. Self-evidently, the accession process involved post-communist states acceding to the EU's (and Council of Europe's) pre-existing minority rights regime. Given the implementation gap that exists between theory and praxis, we argue that the practice of minority protection in the wake of EU and NATO accession these countries have not followed the path anticipated by the 'old' member-states. Thus, one of our central points of investigation is the examination of the process by which the effectiveness of formal minority rights instruments that have been installed in post-communist Central Eastern European (CEE) EU member and candidate member-states has undermined the normative logic of supranational European political and security organizations' involvement during the European integration process.

Such an investigation is important for another reason. NATO and the EU are set at some point to expand further into the Western Balkans and are already holding talks with a number of states that in the recent past witnessed ethno-national violence—for example, Serbia and Bosnia and Herzegovina. It was precisely this occurrence of mass violence that prompted European organizations' explicit interest in the nature of inter-communal relations in these states and in establishing missions aimed at preventing a further erosion of inter-communal trust, as in Kosovo and Macedonia. If these countries are to join either the EU and/or NATO in the near future, it is essential that the academic and policymaking communities assess the impact of post-communist domestic institutions on the implementation of the European minority rights regime in post-communist Europe.

Further, given the intricate connection between social and political institutions in the diverse case studies utilised in the book, we highlight the powerful dynamic that domestic policymaking and institutional developments brings into forums of international security organizations and privileging the EU. We discuss the structural conditions that resulted in changes of minority rights provisions in 'new' member-states. In the past, providing minority protection regionally, domestically and at the level of European institutions was perceived to be both conceptually and practically the only feasible avenue for conflict prevention and post-conflict reconciliation. In this volume, we re-examine that premise and discuss the extent to which this goal has *not* been achieved due to constraints of domestic political institutions.

Throughout the book, we employ case studies and comparative approaches. The cases selected have been chosen in such a manner that the full spectrum of policy issues and outcomes available to the governments of post-communist Europe can be revealed in a systematic manner. Moreover, both single and comparative case studies are embedded within an overall methodological framework that isolates three levels of analysis and exclusively draws upon examples and cases taken from those post-communist states that have in recent years acceded to the EU. The three levels are the sub-state politics; domestic/national policymaking; and European norms, fixed in international agreements, laws and policy blueprints. Distinguishing these levels allows us to isolate the impact of structures on actor choices under conditions found in post-communist societies and track the reasons for which international organizations sought to grant minorities some form of *protection*. Through the analysis of differential structural impacts on actor preferences, we seek not only to identify the causes for policy implementation throughout those regions where the minority is the de facto majority/plurality but also to emphasise how European legal frameworks have consistently enhanced state capacity to govern societies resident on their territories regardless of the congruence between the 'nation' and the 'state'.

By employing different levels of analyses, we will establish how domestic policymakers follow the logic of appropriateness when conforming to normative pressures from 'above', while at the same time, exercising pressure upon subordinate agents to comply with and accept policy and legal blueprints verbatim. Identifying similarities in the underlying logic that spans all three levels of analyses allows us further to make sense of a range of legal directives, policies and opinions pertaining to dynamics of minority protection. Therefore, we examine the impact of European initiatives at the national level, and the impact of national policy upon regional levels of policymaking as exercising pressure upon actors at subordinate levels to comply with the content/letter of law. At the same time, policymakers respond by emphasising the compliance in form when explicating their decisions and communicating bottom-up from the regional to the national and ultimately to the European level. While measures of minority rights protection are bound to distinguish policy spaces, such as regions within states and states within the EU, we see policies as indicators for differential preferences actors hold at each individual level of analyses and reflecting upon respective structures of opportunity understood here as nation-state political institutions.

Existing studies of the common European policy framework—specifically, those focussed on minority protection and non-discrimination—have explained changes in nation-state institutions in terms of influence exerted from the European institutional environment. Emphasis on the 'exogenous' has left analysis and theory of the role domestic institutional dynamics play in dynamics of the European minority rights regime neglected. We aim to close that gap by investigating how nation-states input into and diluted European institutional oversight of minority rights issues since the 'big bang' enlargement of 2004.

STRUCTURE OF THE BOOK

In effect, we have split the book into two related sections, each of which is in turn comprised of thematically linked chapters investigating the relationships between international/domestic and domestic/regional levels of policymaking in post-communist nation-states. As and where appropriate, we complement the theoretical analysis with empiric discussions of various policy frameworks and policy outputs in conjunction with case studies drawn from a range of countries in post-communist Europe. In turn, the case studies draw from post-accession states together with examples from states that are to one extent or another in the pre-accession phase. The cases chosen also reflect internal variance in legislative and institutional frameworks employed in these two groups of states. Our analysis involves the consideration of issues surrounding historic indigenous minorities and the position of more recently arrived migrants.

The opening chapters introduce the overall factual context for minority protection in the enlarged EU, offer an overview of the academic debates on interactions between states on issues pertaining to minority accommodation and scrutinise the dynamics in relationships between the EU and its member-states that privilege certain interpretations of minority rights protection over others. We engage in detailed discussion of each of these issues in the first section of the book, comprising three chapters.

Chapter 1 assesses the extent to which members new to the European minority rights regime have extoled the development of said regime, whilst often only reluctantly and selectively providing the guarantees stipulated by such norms underpinning its functionality. We adopt this approach because we firmly believe that although European integration has somewhat challenged the Westphalian conception of state sovereignty, national political institutions have retained the capacity to influence the dynamics of the emergent European institutional framework. Therefore, this chapter focusses upon those institutions of member-states tasked with the implementation of policies in order to analyse their 'lock-in' effects upon the European minority rights regime. This chapter emphasises the bottom-up impact of domestic institutional dynamics on the evolution of norms and standards of European minority rights' protection and will contribute to the analyses of constituent institutions' path dependency on the European minority protection framework. Navigating this complicated set of interrelated contexts allows us to conclude that while at the level of European and national norm setting we can identify principle agents of policy change in nation-states and sub-state/regional policymakers, respectively, sub-state policy changes reflect societal institutions maintaining ethnic community boundaries.

Having established the overall framework, chapter 2 examines the interaction between the European and the EU member-state institutions and the 'lock-in' affects the latter exercise upon the European minority protection regime in post-communist Europe. This approach allows us to isolate the under-researched impact new member-states have had on the development and trajectory of European organizations' norms in minority protection and the impact of the domestic policy environment upon the European minority rights regime itself. It achieves this through the examination of the role institutionalisation of ethnic identity played in politics of nation-state building (e.g., political institutions and territorial arrangements, the existence of minority parties) in a range of post-communist EU member-states, thereby throwing into sharp relief the spectrum of formal (ethnic) minority arrangements in post-communist Europe. We pursue a diachronic assessment of minority protection/non-discrimination policies and practices in post-communist EU states before and after EU accession while treating them as reflecting domestic policy dynamics. Working backwards from regional to national, and then from national to European levels of policymaking and norm setting, we are able to conclude that the political institutions found at these diverse levels of analyses all reflect the societal foundations that define societies as ethnically diverse. We contend that political institutions built to manage ethnically diverse societies not only structure domestic publics' interactions in terms of an ethnic/language community but also export 'best practice' from regional to national policymaking and from national to European levels of norm setting. In so doing, political institutions at all three levels of our analysis confirm and rehash ethnic identities as fundamental principles to account for in policymaking and norm setting and, as a result, lock in minority rights protection into a rhetoric of formal compliance with European norms that are themselves vaguely defined.

Following from our detailed study of the impact domestic policy outputs have upon the European minority rights regime, we will be in a better position to consider the reverse process in chapter 3. While the majority of scholars studying the impact of the European minority rights regime on member-states analyse the relationship as one of inequality between the more powerful actors (international organizations) and the less powerful actors (the states), the core claim of this chapter is that it is states that hold the most power in this relationship. This chapter provides an analysis of domestic institutional environments that have produced codes for best practices that the international organizations have incorporated into the European minority rights regime and project upon other member-states as blueprints for resolving domestic issues in minority rights protection. As a result, these experiences of institutional steering of domestic conflicts have entered the pantheon of international organizations' possible solutions for securing minority rights and have, with varying degrees of success, been disseminated within and without the EU. However, such an approach also demonstrates that institutional evolution at the nation-state level is a process that reflects actor preferences and institutional opportunities specific to a domestic context and therefore is a process of endogenous change that cannot be effectively applied in all cases of minority rights accommodation. To illustrate this point, we will investigate the impact on minority policies and practices in post-communist EU member-states on overall regime development. We will analyse change in international rhetoric and communicated norms in European institutions (EU, OSCE, Council of Europe) before and after EU enlargement, particularly that of 2004. We achieve this by examining the policy outputs of a representative sample of countries drawn from across the region and comparing those policies and outputs to the international norms to which they correspond.

So far we have dealt with a subject matter that, as our review of competitor literature shows, has provided the main focus and thrust for earlier studies in the field. The strength of our book lies in its approach combined with detailed consideration of other 'objects' of the European minority rights regime. Therefore, the book's later chapters apply our analytical framework as outlined above to specific policies of minority protection and non-discrimination as developed throughout post-communist Europe that deal with two different, sometimes under-researched groups: indigenous minorities that have no readily identifiable kin-state, and migrant communities. Given the unprecedented migrant flows into the EU that occurred in 2015 and show no signs of abating, this latter theme is of particular importance. It is so for two reasons: The first relates to the overall scale of migration and the attendant pressures it places upon the receiving societies. The second relates to the differentiated responses of European governments, which in broad terms corresponds to the pre-1989 political configuration of the continent.

Chapter 4 has two aims. The first is to familiarise the reader with the overall factual context within which the overall work is framed. The second is to outline the detail of our theoretical and methodological approach, which blends the comparative method with levels of analysis approach. The central claim of our book is that post-communist states have learnt to 'talk the talk' of respect and protection of human and minority rights, and yet they neglect the very norms to which they subscribe through their membership of a range of international organizations. In light of that, we argue that the general impulse towards democratisation in the post-communist area was important and broadly speaking virtuous; these states' participation in the European minority rights regime should thus be seen as genuine. However, we add the caveat that during the 1990s within post-communist Europe there was also a wider recognition based on *Realpolitik*—namely, that incorporating European minority rights regime norms within the domestic legal code was sine qua non with regards to accomplishing the 'return to Europe'. As a result, the *Realpolitik* aspect of joining the European minority rights regime has undermined the quality of minority rights implemented on the ground. Moreover, twenty-five years after the collapse of communism and ten years following 'big bang EU enlargement', minority and majority communities across the region continue to claim that nation-states offer the best bulwark of protection against the tyranny of the 'other', despite consistent evidence to the opposite. Precisely for this reason, our book balances a levels of analysis approach with comparative political analyses in order to allow us to focus on the interplay between national and sub-national domestic institutions and policy with its supranational counterpart in order to assess future perspectives for minority protection in Europe.

The conventional approach to the study of this topic is to identify design flaws in the legislation and policies as proposed by institutions such as the Council of Europe and the EU. To that end, the influence of the European institutional environment on minority protection and non-discrimination policies in nation-states has been studied extensively, but studies of the reverse aspect of this relationship are so far lacking, and it is this key aspect that underpins this book. This point is crucial to our argument, as it is our contention that in order to better understand the contemporary situation, it is necessary to focus upon the states of post-communist Europe as autonomous actors and not as mere recipients of directives and initiatives from 'the West'. Our book aims to correct this imbalance by studying the effect domestic institutions of nation-states have upon the development of European minority protection and non-discrimination. As stated, we will achieve this goal by combining comparative analysis with levels of analysis approach that focusses upon the supranational and national levels.

Having introduced the reader to the overall approach, we deal with the causes specifically in chapter 5, which is dedicated to the discussion of post-communist Europe's largest ethnic minority, the Roma. Past research has argued that the policy focus on the Roma has been negligible: either because they are to all intents and purposes irrelevant to the priorities of domestic policymakers or because the Roma rarely possess the means and structures to enable them to lobby in an effective manner. We regard such 'judgements' as being methodologically and intellectually flawed. Our analysis seeks to provide an alternative explanation by consideration of how and why the Roma continue to suffer exclusion by once again examining the interplay between domestic outputs and the European minority rights regime. We argue that Roma fall through the cracks of the said regime not despite but because no member-state is compelled to support and accommodate this socially stigmatised group that is often portrayed as politically expedient with regards to nation-state building.

In chapter 6, we illustrate that such flexibility in norm interpretation is not limited to post-communist European states but has wide purchase in countries on the continent. We analyse policies states have applied towards minorities who do not settle on a state-bounded territory by tracing overall developments in this sphere since the late communist era. Our book differentiates between the ethnic minorities that are territorially settled and those that are not for two main reasons: First, the different challenges for political institutional accommodation that arise from the different circumstances in which these two groups find themselves require differentiated institutional and policy arrangements. Secondly, although non-territorially concentrated minorities find themselves marginalised throughout the region, few post-communist governments have embarked upon strategies that have resulted in such marginalisation having been in any way eased. Here we conclude that resident minorities reach out to their kin-states, rather than to their states of residence, for protection of their cultural, linguistic, and increasingly social interests challenging the principle at the heart of the European integration related to subsuming traditional ethno-national identities in favour of their civic European counterpart.

Our study of minorities and the European minority rights regime in post-communist Europe concludes with chapter 7, which examines the minority rights regime with regard to so-called migrant communities. Given continuous migratory flows from the less-developed world to the EU, this is another important and under-researched area, with significant ramifications for the entire European minority rights regime, especially for those states whose citizens are unused to such migration flows. Although inward migration of non-titular nationals is on the whole a novel experience for post-communist Europe, the examples of Estonia, Latvia, Slovakia, Hungary and Romania show the politics of immigration is no more absent than it is contentious. The majority of post-communist European states have until very recently hosted neither (large-scale) communities of migrant workers nor non-kin refugees from outside Europe. The examination of the domestic reaction to such changes is of particular importance, focussing our attention on the limits of EU member-states talking the talk without walking the walk of minority protection.

In addition, this chapter elaborates our key point that the often neglected dynamics of domestic institutions also prevent change in the international regime and, as such, have a (negative) impact upon the European minority rights regime. Having observed how states as actors impact on regime dynamics as a whole, we will be able to make specific predictions about (candidate and otherwise) states' expectations and behaviour once they become full members of international regimes.

The conclusion of our study identifies the interaction between states and the international regime as those of two distinct agents setting and pushing their individual agendas, at all times in pursuit of their individually perceived payoffs in the context of the opportunity structure they encounter. In addition, the application of our analytical framework to these cases and others will ascertain whether any departure from 'European norms' in praxis provides a salutary lesson in terms of assessing wider perceptions of 'The Other' by majority communities in European states, East and West. In the aftermath of unprecedented inward migration flows, our book argues that 'international regimes', nation-states and domestic political actors talk the talk of minority rights while increasingly walking out on minority protection.

Chapter One

The Workings of the International Regime

The big bang enlargement of 2004 saw ten post-communist states joining the EU, completing the accession process just ten years after having applied for membership. In these countries, EU accession has also marked the end of formal conditionality processes, assuaging concerns about post-communist states' ability to fully respect the corpus of EU legislation transposed into domestic law and implementation capacity. In attempting to explain political and social change in candidate and later, member-states, much of the literature, however, treats a range of actors operating in domestic politics as if they form an homogenous whole, who possess a shared set of goals and domestically promote agendas set in the international arena, in the absence of individual input, achieved through either participation or consultation. While such analyses help us understand the dynamic of the policymaking process domestically, assess the response rate of domestic policymakers to international incentives and ascribe certain decisions to individual actors in domestic politics, they emphasise *change* over *stability* in political processes. Our main concern in this book is with issues that have remained little changed over the past twenty-five years of transition in the post-communist political space. This is why in this chapter we introduce the theoretical framework that will allow us to identify the underlying fundamentals of the contemporary minority rights regime in Europe and in later chapters illustrate how—despite the changes—many contentious issues pertaining to the policies of minority rights protections remain unresolved.

A wide array of process tracing and descriptions of policies/situations/ outcomes of the Europeanisation process posit causal relations between and empirical evidence in support of the view of 'games political actors play' without taking into account the background conditions that lead up to and determine actor choices that are of crucial interest for political analyses. This chapter introduces the core argument of our book, that attention to opportunity structures is largely absent from (much of the) research on the impact of Europeanisation processes on domestic change. This view precludes a systematic assessment of reasons for which attention has been granted to polities, politics, and policies, which have changed over time, but it has not assessed what has *not changed*. In our view, in order to explain the deficits of minority protection mechanisms in Europe, the origins of institutional stasis warrant greater attention.

This is important for several reasons. First, if our analyses were to offer a systematic assessment of interactions between actors at different levels of policymaking (international actors versus domestic actors), these would point directly to perceptions of opportunity structures as experienced by political actors, rather than as identified by researchers. Secondly, institutional contexts, in which political actors perceive choices of policies as realistic and desirable, would facilitate analytic distinction between anticipated outcomes that are declared and those that are realistically expected, allowing more specific predictions about the maximally effective behaviours.

As has been suggested in much of the literature to date, the changes in domestic policy dynamics were rational and in keeping with structural opportunities offered by domestic institutions.[1] However, when domestic political institutions did not allow domestic political elites to toe the line on offer from the international community, the rationale for spurious change in policies was indeed legitimised only to reap the short-term benefits of EU accession. This distinction allows us to identify the sources of (lack of) change in domestic policies as sitting with the institution of the state. This helps us consider the expressed versus the covert compliance of domestic actors with institutional rules of the international cooperation game, as during the accession process.

1. THE INTERNATIONAL REGIME AS
THE BACKGROUND FOR POLICY CHANGE

Across Europe, issues pertaining to minority protection are regulated by member-states and require nation-states to identify groups that may be eligible for minority protection on their sovereign territories. As such, this chapter argues that we ought to pay greater attention to the dynamics of policy changes in *national* institutions, as these are the drivers of policy innovation domestically and as such also are able to input international organizations' attention to specific issues, identities and interests. However, one must be extremely cautious as to the origins of domestic policy changes in nation-states and focus on institutions of that state as socialising and determining permissible and desired patterns of action that domestic actors choose to follow. Domestic political institutions are therefore primary points of reference for domestic political actors when they decide on policies best suited for their domestic situations, as well as those on which they should lobby international organizations. As a result, despite the fact that international organizations (such as the EU, OSCE or Council of Europe) outwardly project a set of internally agreed-upon norms, such norms reflect closely the values and perceptions that domestic political actors see as desirable and possible. With regard to issues related to minority populations across European member-states, these sets of norms constitute what has become known as the European minority rights regime.[2]

The European minority rights regime provides a comprehensive agenda for identifying and recognising minority groups that find themselves in a situation requiring attention and perhaps in need of protection from the tutelage of the state where these groups reside. However, the European minority rights regime lacks autonomous capacity as it does not have the ability to engage with its constituent members (states) beyond the capacity to promote and leverage change with the reference to shared interests and rationale of its participating parties, and only as such legitimising its existence as a principle agent in resolving a collective action dilemma for participating countries.[3] Thus, the European minority rights regime only has the capacity to act on the basis of the embedded reasoning and follow the rules agreed upon by its constituent parties.[4] The regime exists as a complex actor established as a result of member-states' engagement in jointly solving collective action problems in pursuit of their collective interests.[5]

Norms for and rules of minority protection as upheld and overseen by the European minority rights regime therefore rest on the rationale of cooperation between actors within member-states to establish an arbiter for regulating issues relevant to minorities. As a result of inter-state negotiation (and presumably agreement), the European minority rights regime plays a role of interest mediation between actors within and between its constituent states to avoid conflict and ensure peace and stability on their territories.

The focus of research on actors engaged with minority rights and their protection in new EU member-states prior to accession has led to considerable soul searching since EU accession: with the focus on domestic political actors responding to international pressures during the accession process, attention was steered away from domestic institutions facilitating the transposition and implementation of minority rights.[6] As a result, many issues relating to the international regime/domestic actor interface are often seen as challenging the pre-existing structural conditions, allowing both sides to engage constructively with one another in order to implement change in practice.[7] Our claim is that if scholars take a parsimonious approach to the issue of minority rights protection as practiced, one also needs to identify those preferences that shape institutional frameworks and opportunities of the agents promoting minority protection in its own right.[8]

Conceptually, actor choices regarding the anticipated outcomes are embedded in an institutional framework within which principle actors operate, define and calculate long-term interests. It is therefore surprising that past research on interactions between the European minority rights regime and domestic actors emphasises actorness rather than institutional opportunity structures framing actor choices. Much of the research on this interface presumes that these actors are acting rationally while failing to determine the source of this rationality lacking the interest in institutions.[9] Actor calculus follows prior experiences and is made in accordance with auxiliary interests that have been formed within the dominant institutional context or within the context into which the actor has been socialised previously.[10] In a competitive game of interest entrenchment, our actors input into domestic political institutions in order to shape institutional design and increase returns for themselves.

With regard to agents active at supra-state (regime) and sub-state (political elites, minority actors) levels, we may note that agents' engagement and exchanges are different within respective contexts of interaction. At regime level, actors cooperate in order to ensure peace and stability across the set of member-state territories, while at the domestic level individual actors negotiate terms of access to resources in order to likewise maintain stability.[11] At both levels of actor interactions, the origins of interests' formation and their dynamics take place within the extant framework of political institutional structure. Therefore, at both levels political institutions of a state precede actor choices in policy preferences and thus exercise the steering impact on international regime and domestic actor dynamics.

Thus, the European minority rights regime as an individual actor facing resilient state institutions would be just as likely to push for reform that benefits the regime as a whole as would domestic political actors involved in institutional redesign in order to enhance their interests.[12] In both cases, those options on the menu of change that are likely to bring comparatively less advantage to principle agents at both levels of interaction are unlikely to be their preferred choices.[13] In short, mapping agents' interaction requires analyses of institutional frameworks, which either are responsive to exogenous pressures for change from the regime down the scale or mitigate the impact of endogenous actors' pressures further up the scale.

Whereas pre-accession scholarship focussed on what is clearly an international structure of incentives for domestic policy change, post-accession scholarship has widely engaged country-specific analyses of the environment within which social and political actors find themselves, and how these actors interact with segmental institutions and translate institutional pressures into policies.[14] This also explains why since the EU enlargement of 2007, there has been a perceptible decline in scholarship comprehensively analysing minority issues in post-communist states. Much greater focus has been placed on institutional adherence to and implementation of previously passed legislation, deepening policy integration and options for policy backsliding. Conceptually comparative analyses of state *compliance* prevail in analyses of dynamics in actor responses to policy suggestions by international monitors. Where generalisations were once common in pre-accession analyses of regional trends, we now see cases of comparative studies in the coordination of policy, legislative *adjustments* and, broader, institutional redesign. So the focus of analysis is placed squarely on the process of interactions and mutual updates between actors at two levels: international regimes as actors influencing domestic policy/law-making actors' choices, or the reversed impact of domestic political actors on dynamics of international regimes.[15] In both cases, however, interactions between the two are mediated through the prism of domestic political institutions.

Domestic political institutions, therefore, cut both ways: first, in terms of the balanced impact domestic actors have on an overall regime dynamics in the long run, and, second, pressures exercised by the regime upon domestic political actors to comply as delayed investment into future gainsay. The relevant scholarship has dealt in some depth with how domestic actors impact on dynamics in state policies domestically and how this triggers other states to anticipate either cost or rewards accruing from membership.[16] Much of the scholarship on accession conditionality, democracy promotion and impact of international organizations on domestic policies has investigated the top-down and bottom-up processes involving actors. However, how domestic political institutions, as lens-coordinating actors, prioritise each option has been insufficiently addressed. Interestingly, it seems that two assumptions underlie these broader strands in theory development here: First is that there can be no unexpected consequences of states' action post-accession because all options available to them would fall into either/or logic (compliance/backsliding), shutting down routes for policy development outside the framework of top-down cohesion.[17] However, background expectations invested into rationalising policy choices to different audiences by principle agents of change are rarely appreciated for what they are: the negotiation of structural constraints by sentient agents.[18]

Rewarding as these analyses are, it is our contention that such approaches mix up the levels of study considerably. While identifying actorness in processes, many such analyses forego identifying institutional context, which not only determines the dynamics and direction of possible changes but also socialises political actors (domestically and internationally) as to appropriate types of behaviour. Thus, and for good reason in the past, countries seeking EU accession were analysed en masse as their options were structurally (and similarly) constrained by an institutional framework from which the states as actors could pick options, and contemporary research focusses more often on differential political dynamics inside countries as a result of incurred institutional changes pre-accession.

Past research has conceptualised externally projected normative standards (such as, for example, minority protection norms) onto domestic political arenas by analysing the response of political actors domestically to conditionality pressures (i.e., as actors), but could hardly discern same-scale effects from regime level to old member-states. This is because the relationship between the international regime and states have been conceptualised as a structure-agent relationship, not as an interaction between two distinct agents capable of setting their own agendas and pursuing their individual and distinct goals. In the wake of EU enlargement, it is time to set these assumptions aside and view the international regime/domestic political actors' interface as following the shared underlying logic. Both the international regime and domestic actors operate in an environment following a normative assumption about the crucial role of institutions as structures reducing voluntaristic action by agents, and thus allowing actors to increase returns while embedded in the structure known to them.

2. AGENTS OF POLICY CHANGE

Though often perceived as operating independently of one another, following different (at times, conflicting) logics and submitting to exclusive reasons for maintaining existing interactions, the actors who populate the international and domestic policymaking communities continuously engage with one another. Actors who act seemingly independent of one another might appear to be undertaking independent decisions, but it is generally agreed that they find themselves locked into a field where they must play by the shared set of rules. Ultimately, decisions about political directions at the national level involve relational ties between competing groups of political actors for voters' attention, where competitors follow the same set of rules even if they disagree with one another about policy issues.

Similarly, decision making in an international arena is not so much a deliberate action of states' representatives involved in an international community's stabilisation. Rather, parties to international political decision making follow tested mechanisms designed to ensure domestic stability by means of reaching inter-state agreements and maintaining order the absence of destabilising political processes happening outside the domestic arena.[19] In their interaction, the EU and domestic decision makers, much less concerned with the stability of other actors (international organizations or states in inter-state relations, staffing of political parties and the role of personas in domestic politics) as opposed to the stability of institutional arrangements opening the proverbial window of opportunity for an individual person or a state, continue with practice as usual and thus avoid adjustments to changes in structures determining limits and options.[20]

Complex actors such as international organizations and domestic actors operate in an institutional environment where their own chances for success are predicated upon cooperation with other actors in the field. Importantly, both types of actors face similar challenges from less complex actors (member-states in the case of an international organization, opposition political parties in the case of policymakers in government) who seek changes to the rules of the game and question the effectiveness of the coordinative power of superordinate actors located in structurally more advantageous positions. However, the complexity of relationships between member-states in the forum of international organization, or between parties during policymaking processes, indicates that all of these interactions are relational. As such, actors at all levels of political interaction and decision making assess the costs of adjustment to changes in the institutional framework taking place without these actors' involvement against the costs of investing in institutional change at an early point and as such exercise greater leverage in the institutional redesign process.[21] In the process, all actors thus find themselves in a position whereby they need to negotiate pressures from political institutions that make up for an opportunity and challenge to existing policy change.

Curiously, both international organizations and domestic actors interact with their constituent actors in a way that entrenches their pivotal position in linking up constituents (such as actors represented by minority groups, community's member-states, etc.) through institutionalised mechanisms (such as community rules, state institutions, etc.) into a compound whole. In so doing, international organizations as well as domestic actors raise the costs for collective actions to lower-level actors and prevent them from challenging the effectiveness of the established institutional structures. In both cases, superordinate actors do so to ensure that their coordinating capacity outweighs the impact lower-level actors could have on the institutional setting, and thus prevent the restructuring of existing role allocations. This appears to be a shared way for superordinate actors to manage interactions with actors at the lower level of organization (international organizations with the national political actors, domestic political actors with minority activists). These are at all times attentive to the structure of domestic political institutions that both international organizations and domestic political actors experience as ratchets preventing revisions of previously formalised patterns of interaction.

Removing actors such as the EU and domestic policymakers from explanations of political change allows us to take institutions into account as a lens through which actors appraise available opportunities. In so doing, we avoid the reductionist view of political actors as impulsively driven, reactive bots exempt from socialisation processes and hence are able to swap preferences at ease and make economy-based decisions. Actors operate in different institutional environments that define sets of desirable and feasible potential actions and exercise differential pressures on persons who assume different roles in distinct context. One, possibly the same person, could be subject to a distinct set of institutional pressures when operating as a representative of a state in an international arena, but would need to respond to and communicate the experience of international pressures on the country they represent differently when in the domestic context, when operating under different set of constraints that determine context-specific sets of preferences.

It is from this perspective that domestic institutions exercise their ratchet effect: institutions are not actors in their own right; yet they critically impact upon actor perceptions of options and opportunities for changing patterns of actions in reflection of, first, community capacity to accommodate and, second, the domestic public's ability to communicate policy changes effectively.[22] Overall, domestic institutions managing policies on the territory of a nation-state have no input in their own right. They largely operate as a lens adjusting the perceptions of both domestic and international actors on the horizon of what is desirable (top down) and possible (bottom up).

A focus on domestic political institutions as a corrective lens on international politics as well as domestic policies allows us to separate rules of policy change from the reasons for which they occur. Though these are related, they must be kept separate if we want to use analytic advantage and identify origins of policy/behaviour change. On the one hand, EU and domestic policymakers are bound by shared understandings that national sovereignty limits all actors (international actors, domestic political elites and challenges of cooperation between the two—for example, advocacy NGOs) in their exercise of potential for change. On the other, it is widely acknowledged that the EU seeks to maintain stability, prompting cooperation as an early conflict-prevention mechanism for its member-states. However, while research on conditionality and monitoring habitually speaks of individual states or at best of state dyads as targets of intervention, it is domestic policymakers who choose to respond (or not) to international interventions.

Domestic political actors, however, negotiate and craft pre-existing institutional commitments of their states in order to maintain domestic peace and stability, fending off intervention by appeasing domestic assent to institutions of the state and thus legitimising the lack of institutional congruence between domestic and international institutional design. They assume leadership only because they maintain certain rules and cannot operate outside the narrowly defined mandate sketched around them by domestic political institutions. Changes in national policies are only possible where there is a clear mandate for implementing change as a way of maintaining social stability—

either by allowing gradual change or by stalling changes until the breaking point—in order to ensure the stability of domestic political institutions as a way of sustainable engagement with agents of the EU. Political actors follow the logic appropriate to the modus operandi of political institutions within which these actors can operate only insofar as they perform a certain function—that is, assume the role *as a political institution*, such as 'the leader of the party' or 'the president'.

3. THE RATCHET EFFECT OF STATE INSTITUTIONS

The crucial role played in the process by domestic political institutions in setting the framework for action of domestic political elites is of essence here. While domestic political institutions are a valuable resource, allowing political elites to achieve their objectives either to effectuate or to subvert changes in any one policy area (e.g., minority rights), actors make their choices about optimal policy preferences, keeping in mind the context of state. It is this actor-specific rationality that is being formed by the institutions of the state and accounts for dynamics in short-term policymaking as well as in the long-term change of political institutions themselves. We contend that state institutions act as mediators and indeed agenda setters for domestic political elites who have been able to promote minority rights at some point, whilst at others thwarting change.

Let us review this theoretical discussion with reference to the dynamics of minority protection policies in post-communist countries during the EU accession process. As we have established, though domestic political elites have considerable leverage to initiate policy change at home, whether and which policy changes they are likely to advocate is wholly determined by the institutional setting of the nation-state. As such, domestic institutions exercise a twofold ratchet effect upon goal rationality of actors at the domestic level as well as at the level of international regime, thereby mediating the influence of (short term) rationality of both on domestic policymaking.

First, domestic political institutions shape political elites' incentives to engage with policies and should be seen as the primary causes of domestic policy change and stability. Most scholars of minority protection in Europe see international regimes as the primary source of change in choices of domestic actors in accession and post-accession countries. It is often argued that the European minority rights regime prompts domestic political elites to undertake changes to legal and political order in their states to increase the 'fit' with the structured regime environment. This view points to the existence of distinct coordinating capabilities on the part of the international regime upon domestic actors to change internal policies and, as a result, export norms of minority protection from the 'old' Europe into 'new' EU member-states. Thus, while political actors in West European states are seen as being in agreement with and following the rules of the international regime, political elites in the accession states followed externally set rules and engaged in restructuring their domestic institutions to 'fit' with those stipulated by the European minority rights regime. Yet, in the absence of domestic political elites in accessions states seeing the externally stipulated changes as feasible, pressures to redesign and re-engineer their domestic policy institutions could have been successfully implemented. Therefore, domestic political actors had already perceived the necessity of changing domestic policies as a result of the perceived inefficiency of domestic political institutions, as well as opportunities available within those institutions to change in order to increase the 'fit' with the internationally stipulated norms. ↙ ↙

Secondly, analyses of institutional and policy changes in accession countries focus on the impetus for domestic policy change as occurring as a result of the international regime's steering such change. Political elites in acceding countries, therefore, unsurprisingly perhaps are expected to comply with externally set norms, while assessing how far their domestic publics would be able to bear with the changes. The preoccupation with domestic policymakers' capacity to 'sell' intangible policies to their electorates is certainly worthy of investigation. Yet thus far it has been done at the expense of focussing on constraints domestic policymakers experience from public opinions expressed through the ballot box, rather than from state institutions as framing expectations of these publics in relation to the sovereignty of domestic policymakers over their decisions. If nothing else, such a view leaves no room to appreciate inconsistencies in domestic communication between political actors and their electorates about the rationality of norm transposition as well as the negotiations between domestic political actors and actors of the international regime following the abatement of conditionality after the accession.

These two points of research on conditionality and compliance remind us of historical institutionalism. They indicate that political change in any one particular policy area is largely dependent on the configuration of domestic political institutions and is caused by institutional tradeoffs to avert exogenous shocks to state functionality.[23] Interestingly, however, nonsticky institutionalism posits that agents, capable of adjusting rules learnt to conditions in domestic and international institutional environments, are but accidental products of institutional configuration and as such are severely restricted in their choices.[24]

So, unlike research that muddles through the issues of actorness, we posit that it is those agents implementing change who have envisaged opportunity for gradual alterations in the institutional designs. This allows us to focus on one level of analyses throughout, suggesting that domestic policy changes are at all times originating in a domestic institutional opportunity structure.

We are also able to identify policy innovation as a result of domestic actors operating through the institutional framework already in place in their nation-states. Thus, we should see domestic political actors' choices as pursuits of maximising returns yet unpredictable in their normative orientations, whereby the worldview of these agents is fundamentally a product of domestic political institution design.

Far from positing that domestic actors as well as those of the international regime are 'locked in' the dynamics of domestic institutions, we believe that they are acting rationally albeit on the basis of limited information available to them about potential outcomes of their decisions. At all times, domestic and international actors operate within the institutional structure they know best and seek to amplify its effects for themselves with limited investment in change, as these very actors have but a limited capacity to cope with situations unknown and therefore opt to conform to rules of the game existing in the extant institutions. It is the domestic political actors' affirmative interaction with domestic institutions that warrants our specific attention.

According to such logic, domestic political actors are 'locked in' only insofar as the institutional settings within which they operate correspond to normative expectations they have developed about the fundamental modus operandi of the international regime they seek to join.[25] If, as the scholarship on post-communist states concludes, during the accession some form of democracy was already in place across the region, we must assume that the European accession process has exposed post-communist political elites to novel strategies—rather than to the novel objectives—of consolidating their existing political institutions. Therefore, the extent to which we can confirm the democratic credentials of the CEE states before the beginning of the accession process need to be measured against the Copenhagen Criteria of 1993, which themselves were set as standards by Western European member-states as a novel mechanism to benchmark the limits of permissible and desirable behaviour on the part of pre-accession states.

Since the late 1980s, European engagement with the new and re-established states in the post-communist area followed two principles, informed by the Helsinki Declaration of 1975 that confirmed Europe's (then) post-war political boundaries: first, that the borders of reconstituted and newly emerging states were sacrosanct and would not be revised, and second, the pre-existing and newly emerging minority groups would be protected as part of the sovereign obligation of the nation-states.[26]

By opening accession negotiations with post-communist states, therefore, the agents of the international minority rights regime affirmed the shared principle of state sovereignty and the central role played by domestic institutions in steering and socialising actors of incipient change. Actors from an international regime engaged in concerted action towards accession states only briefly allowed new member-states to maximise their input potential and leverage over policymaking outside of their sovereign domain—that is, on the territory of further candidate states post-accession. In turn, these states traded in future benefits of membership for temporary compliance with externally set requirements, making temporal compliance and institutional engineering not so much a matter of a choice, but rather a matter of ensuring domestic stability.

Post-accession, the political elites became 'locked into' their action patterns by institutional design as well as by choices by earlier regimes in response to pressures exerted by then existing political institutions of international regimes. Whilst reflecting on their own perceptions of necessary accommodation to external pressures, the main source of their compliant behaviour, however, was in neither the external regime's pressures nor their predecessors' choices of policies, but rather in the clearly limited opportunities for change available in the context of political institutions. In practice, this meant that nation-state political actors in the accession states followed two competing logics: that of compliance with pressures from international regime actors and those that resulted from the initial state building and democracy consolidation in their own countries. Although these appear to have differential goals, they both assert the capacity building of domestic institutions and seek alignment of domestic institutions with the normative standards, however set, of the international regime.

Overall—and again—although logics of domestic and international regime actors might appear distinct here, they are not. Both seek to maximise their returns in the long run by undertaking a minimal change of their institutional set-up while accepting costs of (monitoring/compliance) in the short term.

Such findings highlight the need to consider the deeper importance of democratic—that is, open to contestation—political institutions as opposed to the importance of the commitment to democracy or democratisation as such for the management of post-conflict societies.[27] Indeed, differentiated forms of external democracy building that enforced societal peace while weakening long-term state cohesiveness and future prospects for state functionality hindered most post-communist states we have analysed. This reflects the conditions under which the post-communist states were consolidated for and by the nationalising titular elites, albeit at different points and under different institutional circumstances. All were set to build state institutions that infused ethno-national design, social service provisions and devolved administration with a neo-liberal economic rationale in response to de facto states' inability to play a strong role in maintaining social cohesion.

In this context, research on newly established post-communist states privileged an extensive focus on actors rather than on the structures facilitating European integration. Formerly belligerent ethnic groups and the parties representing formerly hostile communities are scrutinized in terms of their en-

gagement with one another. Yet because the study c
facilitating these groups' emergence, preference forn
physical, moral or financial support are hard to d
groups of individuals with shared ideas and ideals, p
have been often lumped into a single category of stud
nationalism. Yet one of our primary concerns here is v
ment in the region during the process of state buildin
communism over the past two decades. It has been
concerns over identity and emphasised that the EU men......p would facilitate state building across the post-communist area. Formally, concerns about
the identity of the group that 'owned' the state overlapped with the priorities
of the EU in promoting accession states' democratic governance. The extent
to which equal participation of all their residents in democratic consolidation
in the light of European accession was considerably limited by the original
design of domestic political institutions. The next section of the chapter,
therefore, turns to limitations experienced by national societies in candidate
states when accessing and updating governance mechanisms in the wake of
the EU accession.

4. THE IMPACT OF STATE INSTITUTIONS ON POLICY CHOICES

The dominant view found in the scholarship on post-communist states' engagement with norms prescribed to them during EU accession emphasises
the role of agents in the process of restructuring political, economic and
social institutions. In so doing, much has been written on how political elites,
national communities or citizens lacking in experience of new institutions
negotiate and interpret new constraints to their distinct advantage. There is a
wealth of studies analysing how actor understanding of possible and desired
changes interact with the institutional capacity for endogenous change. Un-
tangling actors' perceptions about and their real capacity to achieve desired
outcomes would greatly increase both the interest in focussing the impact
community has on domestic actors in general and the lack of policy dynamics, especially in policies beyond the points when structural constraints are
perceived to have withered away.

The issue of actors' perceived capacity to engage with and effectuate
changes in a coordinated opportunity structure has been clearly identified in
research on accession compliance and adherence to norms in the cohort of
the post-communist member-states.[28] Building upon discussions reflecting
on combined legacies of pre-communist, communist and pre-enlargement
institutional dynamics, one should account for actors' expectations invested
into institutions that delivered state services during the communist era and as
such provided an experiential background for political actors to identify the

their actions as regards to engagement with such issues during the of the EU accession.[29]

Much of what remained the same is said to have been 'ingrained' in cultural practices, determined by an environment of compound social and economic transformation and constrained by political institutions, which themselves barely coped with the complexity of transition.[30] Much scholarship on post-communist states often frames institutional challenges in sectoral and issue-area analyses as behavioural and attitudinal 'legacies of communism'.[31] Karl Jowitt claimed that three character-defining features distinguish relationships between actors and structures in communism, all of which posit coordinative—rather than communicative—relations between policymakers and wider society.[32] Little surprise, therefore, that the institutional capacity to coordinate actions between agents of change with conflicting (and partially exclusive) interests during the communist era has been reproduced during the accession period and remained in place after the 2004 to 2007 enlargements.[33] These practices continue and shore up the sense of continuity. A perception of the need for protection and informed stewardship maintain institutional practices that perpetuate modes of social interaction based on compliance rather than on negotiation in domestic decision making.

EU conditionality has 'locked in' political actors' choice of strategies within domestic institutional structures legitimised as 'the only game in town'.[34] These factors have allowed state institutions to steer political actors away from the politics of contention and antagonistic group interests towards cooperation within the given EU framework. With the target of EU integration at hand, post-communist political elites could well claim that tutelary guidance of publics by means of rigid political mechanisms would induce security in the short term, whilst producing side effects of enhanced national sovereignty within the EU in the long run.[35] As such, therefore, it is essential to query the institutional underpinnings of political elites' practices that set policies and rationales domestically in reaction to conditions tied to their states' participation in the international community.

States' participation in the international playing field links choices of domestically embedded and internationally pressured actors to opportunities perceived as feasible and advantageous at both domestic and international levels. While the constraints of the international community act upon domestic agents through the structure of domestic political institutions, these are then the structures providing background knowledge to domestic actors as to the appropriateness and feasibility of their agentic abilities.[36] Hence, discussion of and analyses of contemporary political realities has 'a natural affinity between historical institutionalism and legacies explanations, based on their shared attention to historical factors as a cause of current [policy] outcomes'.[37] Although 'in the legacies paradigm' these persist throughout periods marked by critical junctures, domestic policy dynamics across post-com-

munist EU member-states have been shaped by sets of exogenous institutional factors, such as most prominently sticks of EU conditionality and carrots
of EU membership.[38] This type of scholarship primarily (re-)introduces the
perceptions of states as being unitary, anthropomorphic actors operating in
the field of—and therefore responsive to pressures from—external actors. As
a result, this perception of institutional constraints as being located outside
actors' choices suggests that other actors rather than political institutions
form the background to individual experience and emphasise the short-term
impact of minute actor-centred calculation—rather than the long-term impact
of institutional socialisation—on agents of change.

The analyses of domestic change in post-communist states' policy dynamics have suggested often enough that 'the role pre-accession institutional
change carried out in *response* to conditionality [plays] for post-accession
compliance'.[39] If anything, this points to structures of political institutions
playing the central role in explanations of compliance whether in terms of
general factors, such as institutional design or administrative capacity, or in
specifics, such as the timing of institutional change and adjustment of actor
strategies to deal with novel institutions.[40] It is these structural conditions
that allow the international community to input change into domestic policies, on the one hand, and facilitate domestic actors' access to international
structures in order to legitimise policies that might appear impalpably domestically, on the other.

Although actors operating in an international context (such as political
elites negotiating on behalf of the state in an international forum) can easily
access both the domestic forum (which they represent) and the international
arena (where they need to hammer out agreements), they always appear as
actors with their individually defined priorities. However, they are naturally
constrained by opportunities offered to them in the context of nation-state
institutions. Thus, although political actors appear on our radar as actors who
we perceive as causes for political institutions' change, they have indeed
rather little of their capacity to act in situations where they find themselves
facing an unstructured set of opportunities.

Let's take an example of domestic political elites following the advice of
international organizations and, as in the process of complying with, say,
accession monitoring, thereby increasing their country's chances of joining
the EU. In the past, analyses often suggested the focus on the individual
calculus of political actors who aspired to maintain domestic popularity by
delivering what the majority of the electorate aspired to—that is, EU accession. However, we should pay attention to opportunities available to these
individual political actors. Their calculation is limited by the potential benefits they can claim for themselves *individually* as a result of being in the
office at the right time, offset against the spoils other actors will receive
stemming from joint action within an institutional framework. Domestic po-

litical elites, therefore, would need to gather considerable support for either a wider set of goals, such as joining an international organization with a longer-term goal (and also costs spread over a longer term), or a much narrower but much more costly decision about policies that would demonstrate compliance with international norms in the short term (but has a considerably higher adjustment cost on the domestic population).

As this example demonstrates, at each point of political decision making—domestic political actors reacting in one case to the international organization's incentives and, in the other, to appeasing the electorate at the domestic political arena—change in policies is envisaged and the ousting of political elites from their office in the case of unsatisfactory performance is likely. It is the stability of domestic political institutions that remains the main priority of actors at all three levels of analyses: political elites are concerned with the stability of political institutions because they form the background for individual functional identities *as* political elites. The electorate is equally concerned with the maintenance of political institutions as a way to ensure the stability of the polity's functions and by extension of political service offered to citizens. Finally, international organizations are equally interested in maintaining the stability of political institutions at the nation-state level because these are actors that qua their existence guarantee legitimacy to the international organization's interaction with all other member-states.

While interactions between international organizations, domestic political actors and their electorate form the focal point for analyses of processes as they develop, those structures shaping interaction are the precondition for different actors' perceptions of their ability to assume responsibility and make decisions as actors in the first place. Hence, despite the welcome contribution made by many studies to understanding pathways of change and the role individual and collective actors play as both facilitators and saboteurs of the process, what they lack is perspective on the background against which opportunities for such changes occur—specifically, the impact political institutions have on choices and behaviours of political (alongside social) actors during the process of interaction between actors with various weights in the context of interaction (that is, states in the process of European integration).

As such, state policies provide reasons for participating actors to ensure stability and facilitate top-down cohesion, affirming the central role of domestic political institutions as constraints upon actor choices. Usefully, this perspective on political actors' choices of action can be seen not only in circumstances when outcomes are advantageous but also in those cases when policy outcomes are from actors' points of view and are counterproductive. It is here that the role of domestic political institutions becomes clear as an interface of international organizations and domestic actors. First, domestic political institutions lock both types of an actor into the path of maintaining stability. Actors opt for the pre-existing institutional setup and thus exercise coordinate action in order to avert comprehensive change and instead effectuate—only where necessary—gradual change. Secondly, both types of actors reflect upon their past experiences of operating within the given institutional context in order to anticipate the potential outcome of their (in-)action. In the process, the set of communicated preferences and patterns of actions individual actors choose to pursue in whichever political circumstances they find themselves in are all determined against the institutional background that makes clear the challenges and opportunities available to actors at each specific point.

All actors are locked into a domestic institutional dynamic that raises the cost of collective action ultimately geared towards institutional change. This is how domestic political institutions extoll negative impact on change. Domestic political actors do not experience political institutions because they form a backdrop for actors' experiences and perceptions of the possible. International organizations, however, do not experience domestic political institutions as institutions, because these are inputting existing decision-making processes in the international forums and appear primarily as actors, though, as the discussion above has demonstrated, they are not. Overall, we have shown that institutions of the state ratchet up the benchmark for change and thus can hamper policy, actors and identity preferences, precluding the development of more inclusive political agendas in the long run.

CONCLUSION

The theoretical discussion in the chapter has tangible practical application. Though it is widely acknowledged that *prima facie* new EU member-states perform better than their Western mentors when it comes to minority rights provisions and non-discrimination legislations, state institutions slow down the application of such provisions and penalise non-compliance with the letter of policy by actors at both levels of analyses, of regime and of member-states. Institutions exercising a ratchet effect are therefore performing what they are expected to do: hamper changes in practices by actors on the ground—that is, of new member-states within the regime where they have outperformed their mentors, within an overall regime whole that makes it difficult to overcome the dilemma of collective action for new member-states in relation to old ones.

The focus on state institutions as ratchets for change goes a long way to explaining why some changes trickled down from international- to domestic-level legislation while others have not. The very reason for suggesting that the implementation of new and changing old policies is a response by political actors to real and perceived challenges to their legitimacy presumes a constant political institutional structure that socialises competing political actors and allows them to negotiate their mutual interests effectively. In the scholarship on economics, the ratchet effect refers to situations in which actors choose to limit their output, rationally anticipating a linear positive relationship between rewards and outputs. Higher levels of flexibility in levels of performance result in either raised output requirements or sanctions. [41] This chapter introduced the concept in order to identify state institutions as structural conditions providing agents with an *opportunity* to develop and implement policy innovation.

In contrast to overtly agency-centred approaches that study policy dynamics as resulting from the input of behaviourally predictable acting agents, this chapter suggests looking at an institutional opportunity structure as opening options to agents yet not determining these. Throughout the chapter, we have treated institutional structures as resources, allowing actors to see ways for their own empowerment, sustaining equilibriums and thus maintaining stable relations between domestic institutions and different-level actors externally pressing for change. The key argument of the chapter is that a more balanced—and we argue, a more realistic—approach to policy change and stasis at both domestic and EU levels needs to query agents' ability to operate outside the context of previously known political institutions. Any pre-given set of choices that actors can pick from has been inculcated into them and can be appreciated only by accounting for the institutional environmental impact on actors. Therefore, actors have a choice of paths to take, but they cannot ignore the circumstances in which they find themselves and must be seen as agents only within the given institutional context. This primarily explains agentic interaction with institutions by both confirming and changing these domestically and at the level of international community, while at all times being constrained by sets of domestic political institutions that actors find *before* formulating action strategies.

The above also suggests the importance of differentiating between the effects of internalised European norms in the validation of external demands in light of local opportunities *and* the strategic use of reference to European pressures as a convenient instrument for legitimising changes to domestic publics. It is essential to understand these three differentiated dimensions as respective functions for states as actors concerned with minority issues post-accession. They are actors tapping into the resources of nation-states; projecting potential outcomes of policy changes upon institutions of their state after accepting community norms; and restructuring the processes of minority protection norm validation balancing domestic institutional constraints in their own, as well as in other, member-states. This differentiation brings an important analytical benefit for understanding the effects of European integration on states as independent actors in domestic policies in general, and in ensuring the continuous relevance of minority issues in a dynamic that involves interactions between actors of different levels, all of which are locked in their respective domestic institutional frameworks.

Domestic policymakers are locked into a zero-sum game of power redistribution within the structure of domestic political institutions that meets with challenges from closely knit minority communities, residing compactly and (often) having a powerful broker in domestic policies such as minority parties. However, it is worth considering the fact that political institutions regulating relations between minority and majority players domestically do not operate on their own and require policies that follow, if not extend, the logic of domestic sovereignty and primacy of domestic over international decision making. Domestic political actors are often perceived as oscillating between minority recognition and minority co-optation. Yet they always reflect upon institutional opportunity structures and as such promote the consolidation of the dominant legal understanding of the state/society relationship.

As we discuss in the following chapter, seeing state institutions as ratchets for international regime impact on domestic policymakers and policies related to minority participation, as well as for domestic actors' agendas on international regime dynamics that allows cross-sectional analyses of relations both pre- and post-accession. Furthermore, bearing in mind that domestic institutions are comparatively stable allows us to avoid the principal-agent problem with regard to changes in actors' priorities and facilitates the study of the robustness of change at both international and domestic levels throughout the remainder of the volume.

NOTES

1. David J. Galbreath and Joanne McEvoy, 'European Integration and the Geopolitics of National Minorities', *Ethnopolitics* 9, no. 3–4 (2010): 357–77; Gwendolyn Sasse, 'Tracing the Construction and Effects of EU Conditionality', in *Minority Rights in Central and Eastern Europe*, ed. Bernd Rechel (London, New York: Routledge, 2009), 17–31; Ulrich Sedelmeier, 'After Conditionality: Post-Accession Compliance with EU Law in East Central Europe', *Journal of European Public Policy* 15, no. 6 (September 2008): 806–25, doi:10.1080/135017 60802196549.

2. David J. Galbreath and Joanne McEvoy, *The European Minority Rights Regime: Towards a Theory of Regime Effectiveness* (Basingstoke: Palgrave, 2011).

3. Wolfgang Zellner, *On the Effectiveness of the OSCE Minority Regime: Comparative Case Studies on Implementation of the Recommendations of the High Commissioner on National Minorities of the OSCE* (Hamburg: Hamburger Beiträge zur Friedensforschung und Sicherheitspolitik, 1999).

4. Andrew Moravcsik and Milada A. Vachudova, 'National Interests, State Power, and EU Enlargement', *East European Politics and Societies* 17, no. 1 (2003): 42–58.

5. Andrew Moravcsik, 'The Origins of Human Rights Regimes: Democratic Delegation in Postwar Europe', *International Organization* 52, no. 2 (2000): 729–52.

6. Heather Grabbe, 'How Does Europeanization Affect CEE Governance? Conditionality, Diffusion and Diversity', *Journal of European Public Policy* 8, no. 6 (2001): 1013–31.

7. Claudio M. Radaelli, 'How Does Europeanization Produce Domestic Policy Change? Corporate Tax Policy in Italy and the United Kingdom', *Comparative Political Studies* 30, no. 5 (1997): 553–75.

8. For a notable exception, see Ulrich Sedelmeier, 'Is Europeanisation through Conditionality Sustainable? Lock-In of Institutional Change after EU Accession', *West European Politics* 35, no. 1 (2012): 20–38.

9. Tim Haughton, 'Half Full but Also Half Empty: Conditionality, Compliance and the Quality of Democracy in Central and Eastern Europe', *Political Studies Review* 9, no. 3 (2011): 323–33, doi:10.1111/j.1478-9302.2010.00220.x; David J. Galbreath, 'European Integration through Democratic Conditionality: Latvia in the Context of Minority Rights', *Journal of Contemporary European Studies* 14, no. 1 (2006): 69–87; Tina Freyburg and Solveig Richter, 'National Identity Matters: The Limited Impact of EU Political Conditionality in the Western Balkans', *Journal of European Public Policy* 17, no. 2 (2010): 263–81.

10. Tina Freyburg et al., 'EU Promotion of Democratic Governance in the Neighbourhood', *Journal of European Public Policy* 16, no. 6 (2009): 916–34.

11. Sonja Grimm and Okka Lou Mathis, 'Stability First, Development Second, Democracy Third: The European Union's Policy towards the Post-Conflict Western Balkans, 1991–2010', *Europe-Asia Studies* 67, no. 6 (3 July 2015): 916–47, doi:10.1080/09668136.2015.1055237.

12. Aimee Kanner Arias and Mehmet Gurses, 'The Complexities of Minority Rights in the European Union', *The International Journal of Human Rights* 16, no. 2 (2012): 321–36; Karen E. Smith, 'The European Union at the Human Rights Council: Speaking with One Voice but Having Little Influence', *Journal of European Public Policy* 17, no. 2 (2010): 224–41.

13. Heather Grabbe, 'European Union Conditionality and the "Acquis Communautaire"', *International Political Science Review* 23, no. 3 (2002): 249–68; Lynn Tesser, *Ethnic Cleansing and the European Union: An Interdisciplinary Approach to Security, Memory and Ethnography* (Basingstoke: Palgrave Macmillan, 2013), especially chapters 4–8 for case studies of CEE countries.

14. Geoffrey Pridham, 'The EU's Political Conditionality and Post-Accession Tendencies: Comparisons from Slovakia and Latvia', *JCMS: Journal of Common Market Studies* 46, no. 2 (2008): 365–87; Diana Panke, 'Good Instructions in No Time? Domestic Coordination of EU Policies in 19 Small States', *West European Politics* 33, no. 4 (2010): 770–90; Thomas Risse and Kathryn Sikkink, 'The Socialization of International Human Rights Norms into Domestic Practices: Introduction', *Cambridge Studies in International Relations* 66 (1999): 1–38.

15. Bernard Steunenberg and Mark Rhinard, 'The Transposition of European Law in EU Member States: Between Process and Politics', *European Political Science Review* 2, no. 3 (2010): 495–520; Tobias Böhmelt and Tina Freyburg, 'The Temporal Dimension of the Credibility of EU Conditionality and Candidate States' Compliance with the *Acquis Communautaire*, 1998–2009', *European Union Politics* 14, no. 2 (2013): 250–72.

16. Heather Grabbe, *The EU's Transformative Power: Europeanization through Conditionality in Central and Eastern Europe* (Basingstoke: Palgrave Macmillan, 2006); Tanja Börzel and Thomas Risse, 'When Europeanisation Meets Diffusion: Exploring New Territory', *West European Politics* 35, no. 1 (2012): 192–207.

17. Jeffrey T. Checkel, 'Why Comply? Social Learning and European Identity Change', *International Organization* 55, no. 3 (2001): 553–88; Rachel A. Epstein and Ulrich Sedelmeier, 'Beyond Conditionality: International Institutions in Postcommunist Europe after Enlargement', *Journal of European Public Policy* 15, no. 6 (2008): 795–805.

18. Venelin I. Ganev, 'Post-Accession Hooliganism: Democratic Governance in Bulgaria and Romania after 2007', *East European Politics & Societies* 27, no. 1 (2013): 26–44.

19. Tim Haughton, 'When Does the EU Make a Difference? Conditionality and the Accession Process in Central and Eastern Europe', *Political Studies Review* 5, no. 2 (2007): 233–46; Haughton, 'Half Full but Also Half Empty'.

20. Antoaneta Dimitrova and Geoffrey Pridham, 'International Actors and Democracy Promotion in Central and Eastern Europe: The Integration Model and Its Limits', *Democratization* 11, no. 5 (2004): 91–112; Thomas Gehring, Sebastian Oberthür, and Marc Mühleck, 'European Union Actorness in International Institutions: Why the EU Is Recognized as an Actor in Some International Institutions, but Not in Others', *JCMS: Journal of Common Market Studies* 51, no. 5 (2013): 849–65, doi:10.1111/jcms.12030.

21. Arild Underdal, 'Strategies in International Regime Negotiations: Reflecting Background Conditions or Shaping Outcomes?' *International Environmental Agreements: Politics,*

Law and Economics 12, no. 2 (2012): 129–44; Tom Delreux and Bart Kerremans, 'How Agents Weaken Their Principals' Incentives to Control: The Case of EU Negotiators and EU Member States in Multilateral Negotiations', *Journal of European Integration* 32, no. 4 (2010): 357–74.

22. James Mahoney and Kathleen Thelen, 'A Theory of Gradual Institutional Change', in *Explaining Institutional Change: Ambiguity, Agency, and Power*, ed. James Mahoney and Kathleen Thelen (Cambridge: Cambridge University Press, 2010), 1–37; Giovanni Capoccia and R. Daniel Kelemen, 'The Study of Critical Junctures: Theory, Narrative, and Counterfactuals in Historical Institutionalism', *World Politics* 59, no. 3 (2007): 341–69.

23. Jan-Hinrik Meyer-Sahling, 'Varieties of Legacies: A Critical Review of Legacy Explanations of Public Administration Reform in East Central Europe', *International Review of Administrative Sciences* 75, no. 3 (2009): 509–28; Mahoney and Thelen, 'A Theory of Gradual Institutional Change'.

24. Shu-Yun Ma, 'Taking Evolution Seriously, or Metaphorically? A Review of Interactions between Historical Institutionalism and Darwinian Evolutionary Theory', *Political Studies Review*, 1 July 2014, doi:10.1111/1478-9302.12059; Peter A. Hall and Rosemary C. R. Taylor, 'Political Science and the Three New Institutionalisms', *Political Studies* 44, no. 5 (1996): 936–57.

25. Sedelmeier, 'Is Europeanisation through Conditionality Sustainable?'; more specifically, on minority issues in post-communism, see Timofey Agarin, 'The Dead Weight of the Past? Institutional Change, Policy Dynamics and the Communist Legacy in Minority Protection', in *Institutional Legacies of Communism: Change and Continuities in Minority Protection*, ed. Karl Cordell, Timofey Agarin, and Alexander Osipov (London: Routledge, 2013), 14–30.

26. Geert-Hinrich Ahrens, *Diplomacy on the Edge: Containment of Ethnic Conflict and the Minorities Working Group of the Conferences on Yugoslavia* (Baltimore: Johns Hopkins University Press, 2007), 86; more generally on the Helsinki Accords, see Richard Davy, 'Helsinki Myths: Setting the Record Straight on the Final Act of the CSCE, 1975', *Cold War History* 9, no. 1 (2009): 1–22.

27. William Easterly, 'Can Institutions Resolve Ethnic Conflict?' *Economic Development and Cultural Change* 49, no. 4 (2001): 687–706.

28. Paul A. Sabatier, 'Top-Down and Bottom-Up Approaches to Implementation Research: A Critical Analysis and Suggested Synthesis', *Journal of Public Policy* 6, no. 1 (2008): 21–48.

29. Gerardo L. Munck and Carol Skalnik Leff, 'Modes of Transition and Democratization', *Journal of Democracy* 29, no. 3 (1997): 343–62.

30. Wendy Slater and Andrew Wilson, *The Legacy of the Soviet Union* (Houndmills: Palgrave, 2004).

31. Karl Cordell, Timofey Agarin, and Alexander Osipov, eds., *Institutional Legacies of Communism: Change and Continuities in Minority Protection* (London: Routledge, 2013).

32. Ken Jowitt, *New World Disorder: The Leninist Extinction* (Berkeley: University of California Press, 1993), 259.

33. Frank Schimmelfennig and Arista Maria Cirtautas, 'Europeanisation Before and After Accession: Conditionality, Legacies and Compliance', *Europe-Asia Studies* 62, no. 3 (2010): 421–41; Melanie H. Ram, 'Legacies of EU Conditionality: Explaining Post-Accession Adherence to Pre-Accession Rules on Roma', *Europe-Asia Studies* 64, no. 7 (September 2012): 1191–1218, doi:10.1080/09668136.2012.696813.

34. Geoffrey Pridham, 'Securing the Only Game in Town: The EU's Political Conditionality and Democratic Consolidation in Post-Soviet Latvia', *Europe-Asia Studies* 61, no. 1 (2009): 51–84; To-Ch'ol Shin and Jason Wells, 'Is Democracy the Only Game in Town?' *Journal of Democracy* 16, no. 2 (2005): 88–101.

35. Timofey Agarin and Ada-Charlotte Regelmann, 'Which Is the Only Game in Town? Minority Rights Issues in Estonia and Slovakia during and after EU Accession', *Perspectives on European Politics and Society* 13, no. 4 (2012): 443–61, doi:10.1080/15705854 .2012.731934; Simonida Kacarska, 'The Representation of Minorities in the Public Sector in the EU Accession Process', in *Institutional Legacies of Communism: Change and Continuities in Minority Protection*, ed. Karl Cordell, Timofey Agarin, and Alexander Osipov (London: Routledge, 2013), 217–31.

36. Tine Hanrieder, 'Gradual Change in International Organisations: Agency Theory and Historical Institutionalism', *Politics* 34, no. 4 (2014): 324–33, doi:10.1111/1467-9256.12050.

37. Jody LaPorte and Danielle N. Lussier, 'What Is the Leninist Legacy? Assessing Twenty Years of Scholarship', *Slavic Review* 70, no. 3 (2011): 650.

38. Ibid., 652; See also Anna M. Grzymala-Busse, *Redeeming the Communist Past: The Regeneration of Communist Parties in East Central Europe* (Cambridge: Cambridge University Press, 2002); and somewhat more sceptical, Laszlo Csaba, 'From Sovietology to Neo-Institutionalism', *Post-Communist Economies* 21, no. 4 (2009): 383–98.

39. Sedelmeier, 'After Conditionality', 22.

40. Aneta B. Spendzharova and Milada Anna Vachudova, 'Catching Up? Consolidating Liberal Democracy in Bulgaria and Romania after EU Accession', *West European Politics* 35, no. 1 (2012): 39–58; Gergana Noutcheva and Senem Aydin-Düzgit, 'Lost in Europeanisation: The Western Balkans and Turkey', *West European Politics* 35, no. 1 (2012): 59–78; Maria Koinova, 'Challenging Assumptions of the Enlargement Literature: The Impact of the EU on Human and Minority Rights in Macedonia', *Europe-Asia Studies* 63, no. 5 (2011): 807–32, doi:10.1080/09668136.2011.576023.

41. Yoshitsugu Kanemoto and W. Bentley MacLeod, 'The Ratchet Effect and the Market for Secondhand Workers', *Journal of Labor Economics* 10, no. 1 (1992): 85–98.

Chapter Two

Nation-State Building in the Transition from Communism

In the previous chapter, we argued that by distinguishing levels of analyses we are in a much better position to identify the origin of policy innovation when considering cooperation between international organizations, nation-states and domestic political actors. By so doing we can trace the background against which domestic political actors, nation-states and actors in international regimes identify certain policies as being sensible in their own right—as congruent with the normative expectations of other state actors in their respective interactions; and ultimately, contribute to regime stability at the international level. Such a distinction makes it clear that both types of interactions—between international regime actors and domestic political elites, as well as between the domestic political elites and the societies they govern—determine policy development.

As we argued in the previous chapter, this distinction facilitates understanding of not only the rationale for policy change but also often neglected—because masked in communication between actors—ultimate policy objectives, both domestically and internationally. More fundamentally, we have pointed out that although policymakers have distinct and identifiable preferences, they are guided by their prior expectations from and experiences of domestic political institutions. They serve as a framework for reference for all actors, at domestic and international levels of decision making. Identifying the constraining role of domestic political institutions makes it much easier for us to assess whether the objectives of policies stated by political actors challenge or maintain prior institutional guidelines to ensure the stability of state institutions. The discussion in the preceding chapter suggested that only a very limited space is available for political actors at any of the

aforementioned levels to challenge the institutions of statehood as the legitimising core of international cooperation.

In this chapter, we will move from a more abstract discussion of actors of
international regimes, domestic institutions and society to our case of the
minority protection in post-communist member-states of the European Union. This allows us to consider the impact of Europeanisation with regard to
the accommodation of ethnic diversity in post-communist member-states in
general and on the relationship between resident minorities and institutions
of nation-states specifically. In keeping with our interest in the impact of
political institutions of the state upon domestic political actors to alter policies in the realm of minority protection, at the end of the chapter we underline how new member-states constrain the existing commitment of the EU
towards joint diversity management.

1. POST-COMMUNIST STATE BUILDING: NATIONAL IN FORM, EUROPEAN IN CONTENT

Since the demise of communism in Central Eastern and Southeastern Europe
and despite the emergence of new (re-)established states on the ruins of the
socialist federations of Czechoslovakia and Yugoslavia, the borders of nation-states have remained the same across much of the European continent.
However, an increasing number of sub-state regions (for example, in Spain,
the UK and Belgium) strive for greater regional autonomy. This begs the
question whether citizens today turn towards ethno-political agendas coupled
with a simultaneous demand for government to be brought closer to 'the
people'.

Set in the context of wider issues that European societies face, we need to
note the coincidence in the rise in preferences for the ethno-territorial management of diversity and the increased sense of citizens' agency in political
decision making.[1] As state capacity to deliver services at the level previously
known to publics has been compounded by the economic instability resulting
from the ongoing Euro crisis, similar cause-and-effect relations can be easily
observed across the entire continent. Indeed, ethnic mobilisation in regions
such as Scotland, Catalonia and Flanders showcases the close connection
between the levels of concentration of ethnic groups on 'their' designated
territories allowing us to identify similar perceptions of ethnic ascendancy to
state institutions across time and space.[2] Yet all such comparative analyses of
the role (perceived) ethnic solidarity plays in mobilisation, restructuring
state/society relations and the redefinition of state institutions require first
and foremost analyses of mechanisms through which ethnicity—rather than
any other marker of identity—becomes the central rallying point in the absence of expressed ethnic grievances.

It is instructive to compare contemporary ethno-territorial mobilisation across the EU with the initial period of destabilisation in Eastern Europe that became markedly more noticeable from the mid-1980s. In parts of the communist bloc, socialist regimes sought to facilitate the management of ethnic difference by creating ethno-federal units for significantly large ethnic groups in order to facilitate (tenuous) access on the part of such groups to the state bureaucracy and avenues of participation in decision making at the level of 'their' ethno-territorial unit. There is a commonly shared perception among both the political establishment and academia that an important factor in the collapse of communism in Central and Eastern Europe was the overall destabilisation in centre-periphery relations.[3] Though the socio-political and economic restructuring of socialist regimes has been often seen as a trigger for transformation in the region, we believe that all things being equal, claims of state-bearing, titular nations dealt the ultimate blow to fragile state-society relations during the late communist period. As has been suggested in the widely available scholarship on post-communist states, debates and concerns with regard to national identity were never absent in communist-ruled Europe during the period of communist rule.[4]

In effect, communist policies of nation building led directly to political mobilisation along ethnic lines by fostering the cohesion of ethnic communities. Whether the state was in effect ethnically defined as in the case of Poland or officially multi-ethnic with a guiding role being played by two (Czechoslovakia) or more (Yugoslavia) groups at the expense of non-Slav groups (e.g., Hungarians in Czechoslovakia; Albanians and Roma in Yugoslavia), all socialist states bore clear traits of ethno-national homelands for their dominant ethnicity. Such a situation sustained the hierarchical pyramid for negotiating power relationships between ethnic groups in everyday communications. They also raised the symbolic stakes of titular versus non-titular nations/nationalities based on their perceived roles of such communities within the state.

Broadly similar processes of explicit and implicit nation building took place across the communist area, although the intensity varied significantly depending on the state. Poland, Romania and Czechoslovakia all lost territory to the Soviet Union in 1945. Forced to turn a blind eye to these territorial losses and related processes of flight and expulsion, the communist elites in these countries sought to legitimise their rule through a mix of social reform and hypernationalism.[5] So throughout the communist bloc, a wave of forced migration took place, principally in 1945, but stretching into 1949. The explicit aim was to ensure greater congruence between nation and state. Remaining minority populations were either silenced or heavily circumscribed in terms of their political capabilities. In turn, having sponsored this process, successive communist regimes presented themselves as the only effective bulwark against 'revanchism' in all its forms.[6] The communist regimes boasted political institutions designed to protect the culture and language of the titular ethnic group. Institutionalising ethnic identity as a major criterion for the selection of political elites in ethnically defined (communist) states provided post-communist political elites with an opportunity to claim and maintain ownership over institutions of the state whilst excluding or limiting access to resident non-titular populations.

As communist rule lurched towards oblivion, ethnicity remained a central reference point for the political mobilisation of majorities throughout the region.[7] However, ethnic groups that found themselves on the territory of the 'wrong' nation-state lacked the requisite institutions to enable them to mobilise without reference to communist ideology and thus were ever more reliant on perceptions of ethnicity as a means by which they could attempt to assert claims upon distinct political institutions for self-government and possible independence.[8] The success of ethno-political mobilisation across the former communist bloc countries immediately before the 'official' end of communism has thoroughly entrenched the view among post-communist citizens that while political institutions faltered together with the communist regimes, ethnicity remained an important and galvanising reference point in political discourse.[9] It was both a rallying point in protest movements and an effective tool with which to assert (ethno-)national ascendancy, in the case of Yugoslavia, even to the point of civil war. If anything, loosely defined but omnipresent ethnicity, or, in the communist parlance, 'nationality', emerged as the only persistent form of communal bond amidst the multitude of transitions.

It is unsurprising, therefore, that given the salience of ethnicity during the period of communist rule and its central role as a tool to make sense of social transformation after communism's collapse, the 'triple transition' of the early post-communist years only amplified the importance of ethnic identity for the design of state institutions.[10] The question of state ownership constituted one of the core issues on the agenda of democratising states. The majority of the post-communist polities emerged as de jure mono-ethnic states, serving primarily, if not exclusively, the members of an ethno-cultural core nation whose name these entities bore.[11] Yet, despite World War II and post-war expulsions, only a handful of post-communist states were ethnically homogeneous and most hosted significant numbers of national minorities, many of which boasted an ethnic kin-state just across the border.

In effect, between 1988 and 1990, the hollow communist promise of national self-determination became real and each ethno-national community across the region sought to claim greater rights, even to the point of the creation of new states—for example, Croatia and Slovakia. The leadership of majority groups attempted to maintain institutions of communist quasi nation-states on the territory of countries they 'owned'. At the same time, representatives of minorities sought to internationalise their grievances and appealed in particular to kin-states to seek external protection and advocacy in dealing with 'renegade' political elites of their states of residence, who also played the ethnic card to their own advantage. [12] In this instance, the cases of Hungary and the Hungarian diaspora and Serbia and the Serbs are particularly instructive.

Offering a neat and accessible perspective on social interaction between ethnic groups, communist political institutions channelled claims on economic resources, political representation, recognition of cultural distinctness and tools of maintaining cultural difference in ethnically diverse post-communist societies. During the transition, political elites maintained institutions of the state that favoured individuals of one ethnicity over all others. [13] In so doing they sponsored the further politicisation of ethnic identity on the part of both majority and minority communities on their territories.

The resultant failure of post-communist states to ensure equal access of all residents to the political process in the early post-communist phase only further polarised interpersonal and inter-group relations. The distinction ran particularly deep between the dominant, majority communities who could lay legally sound claims to state ownership. Non-dominant groups often found themselves to be the object of policies tasked with managing ethnocultural diversity. [14] Whereas attention to different ethnic markers had never yielded its central place under the communist regimes, it has now been taken to new heights as states have now been implicitly 're-imagined through the prism of nation'. As a result, post-communist nation-state building has generated perceptions of cultural homogeneity within polities' borders while at the same promoting the view that polities bear an inherently different character due to the difference of cultural communities they serve. As we shall discuss in chapter 5, the preoccupation of political elites in the early post-communist years with shoring up domestic sovereignty against external meddling and internal challengers has destabilised interstate relations as well as domestic state-society relations.

During the entire process of institutional consolidation in post-communist Europe, ethnic identity remained an unchallenged and central marker for delimiting groups from one another and in identifying individuals' potential allegiance to the state and, as a result, eligibility for accessing scarce resources. The crucial importance of ethno-political mobilisation and nation-state building in post-communist Europe has given rise to a wide-ranging scholarship on tensions between 'nationalising states', 'national minorities' and their 'external homelands'. [15]

In context, the lasting contribution made by Rogers Brubaker in his *Nationalism Reframed* has guided analyses of post-communist politics for a generation since its publication in 1996, calling for—but regrettably not causing the—'reorientation in the study of nationalism'. [16] On many occasions Brubaker has claimed that the focus on political process should privilege the relations between political minorities and the states only if they impact upon actors' own perceptions of selves as able and potent actors of/ for political change. In his earlier work, Brubaker indicated that domestic political actors derive their perceptions of desired political behaviour from often poorly understood external influences. Domestic policy entrepreneurs often see homeland states and interstate organizations as holistic actors, but in reality they are not 'actors' in a substantive fashion. Instead, they represent interlinked 'political fields' that resolve to address joint challenges to their individual interests by pooling their individual legitimacy into collective action.[17] Brubaker's own studies focus explicitly on the 'nationality question' in post-communist Europe under circumstances whereby interstate decisions gained additional legitimacy not only by serving citizens of 'their' country but also by amending the wider regional interests that are shared with groups of other ethnic origins.[18]

The important caveat in Brubaker's argument is the need to treat actors' preferences in terms of 'real effects' while focussing on relational intent. If anything, Brubaker draws attention to the importance of subjective perceptions of relations between actors. This has an epistemic implication for case studies of relationships between any two actors of his triadic nexus that has been used as a metaphor in numerous studies of inter-state relations in post-communist Europe. Dual linkages in the nexus exemplify '(1) the close interdependence of relations within and between fields; (2) the responsive and interactive character of the triadic relational interplay between the fields; and (3) the mediated character of this responsive interplay'.[19] More important, multidimensionality does more than imply the never-ending engagement of minority groups, national and external states' political institutions—it also posits the nation-state building as a crucial rationale in the relationship between the three elements of the nexus, making the ethno-national state design the prerequisite for domestic institutions for engagement with minorities resident within a given state territory.

What we hold to be of particular importance in Brubaker's scholarship is that although dominant narratives of nation-state building and some form of redress for resident non-dominant groups have been extensively studied both comparatively and in case studies, such studies have not queried the long-term impact of designing political institutions in post-communist states in an explicitly ethno-national form.[20] As a result of designating one ethnic community, the rightful owner of the country, groups who have found themselves resident in a 'wrong' state were right to be worried about their prospective representation and equal participation in institutions of the post-communist state.

The institutionalisation of nation-states characterised by reference to a dominant ethnic group brought a distinct type of political legitimacy centre stage and privileged all claims of collectivities made vis-à-vis the state institutions. In fact, throughout the 1990s, studies of ethnic diversity management

in post-communist states have often been concerned with the possible outbreak of ethnic conflicts on the European continent because of the impact
nation-state building had on both the dominant and the non-dominant communities.[21] Most have assumed that unlike under the communist regimes
when the dictum 'national in form, socialist in content' was to give a perspective on the social world without specifying what the term *content* actually meant, or what was meant by *national*, the content of post-communist
states' minority policies is clearly apparent.

As we discuss in the following section, post-communist nation-state
building has solidified ethno-national claims to state ownership, privileged
access to economic resources available in that state, and ultimately engrained
ethnic hierarchies in social relations in a pattern similar to that of the communist past. As the danger of inter-ethnic violence has subsided across the
region and more stable mechanisms of governance have been put into place
designed to abate the inter-ethnic accommodation of minorities in post-communist Europe, it has maintained its 'national form', albeit with 'European
content'.

2. THE CENTRALITY OF ETHNIC IDENTITY
DURING TRANSITION

In most societies, markers of ethnic identity are widely used in interpersonal
interactions to invoke a sense of group solidarity through the socialisation of
members by strengthening social ties and in general preventing group fragmentation. Yet different cultural practices and means of communication do
not necessarily cause co-ethnics to show mutual solidarity at all times, and
ethnicity gains importance only as a referent through which sense can be
made of existing social cleavages. As such, everyday reference to ethnic
identities explains and/or legitimises differences in status, exposure to differential treatment and maps onto attitudes salient for social interactions. Different employment structures and ethnically distinct types of political representation all provide clear reference points in the mobilisation of minority
groups who perceive that they have been 'wronged' by particular social,
economic or most frequently, political projects.[22]

It is these subjective perceptions about 'ethnic' differences that are exploited by political entrepreneurs who reify ethnic identity. They establish
clear social and political boundaries that reflect characteristics ascribed to in-
group members, and which determine the criteria for access of individuals to
what are often perceived to be group assets.[23] In the context of ethno-national state-building, contestation concerning access to state institutions has
shifted from the streets into the domain increasingly regulated by laws and
policies of the nation-state. At this juncture we ought to emphasise that

throughout post-communist Europe, the institutional responsiveness of the nation-state to all citizens they serve has been indeed open to contestation, signalling the fundamentally democratic nature of newly (re-)established polities.

Yet the debate concerning the emphasis placed on ethnic identity by newly established political institutions has accompanied the process of nation-state building across the region. This debate has been accompanied by a growth in theoretical explanations of the reasons by which political actors of all colours have sought to collapse two distinct (post-communist) processes of state *and* nation building. Given the predominance of political elites of the majority among those who have been involved in post-communist state design and the structural advantages enjoyed by the member of the majority in 'their' states prior to transition, much of the scholarship has suggested that consolidating titular groups' claims to statehood was part and parcel of a *successful* democratisation process. [24] However, given our focus on political institutions' socialising effect upon political actors, we should also note that at the time maintaining and securing the pivotal role in (re-)designing the institutions of the state during the transition was but one of several options available.

All communist states were constituted as quasi nation-states of the dominant majority with political institutions, laws and constitutions serving primarily the members of the titular majority in those countries. Remarkably, despite the obvious diversity of domestic populations, post-communist institutions have not been redesigned to account for the diversity of domestic populations and to facilitate their political participation and, implicitly, foster democratisation of state-society relations. Instead, institutions in place under the previous regime were carried forward, replicating territorial approaches to ethnic diversity management in the (re-)instated states. As a result, previously diverse and competing political factions of distinct national, cultural and linguistic communities were able to qualify democratic transition in terms of building nation-states where interpretations of national sovereignty were from the start tightly knit with the ethno-national ascendancy.

What is more, political institutions privileging majorities' access to resources of the state across the post-communist area have additionally referred to resident minorities—national, ethnic, linguistic and religious alike—as potential nations sharing the geographic territory of de jure mono-ethnic states. [25] Minority communities are thereby framed as constituting a potential threat to the identity of the titular nation, as well as of the nation-state, and, as such, also the territorial integrity of the newly established polity. Political elites could further advocate 'nationalising' policies with which to rule over resident minority populations. This has had a double effect on minority-majority cooperation within national institutions. First, by enhancing opportunities for titular groups, the vast majority of society was co-opted behind the ethno-national state-building project, marginalising ethno-cultural claims of the minority from political arenas as illegitimate ethnic politicking.[26] Having secured greater representation of majorities' own interests in the political arena, decision making at the national level was then effectively about furthering majority interests and the consolidation of majoritarian-oriented governance mechanisms.[27] Though democratically elected, representatives of titular communities have been co-opted into ethno-national state building at the cost of excluding interests and misrepresenting issues relevant for ethnic diversity management.

Secondly, while political institutions and the content of policies became increasingly culture-blind, post-communist citizens viewed all things political as utterly cultural in their design. Minority participation in ethno-nationally defined institutions of the state became possible, but the members of national parliaments and governments were to become like those of the majority in all but their private interactions. To take part in the political process of newly established states, the political representatives of minority populations had to implicitly accept the growing collusion between the national and democratic form of governance.[28] As constitutions, such as the Croatian example, show, majority ownership often stipulated state ownership. Under such conditions, it is easy to delegitimise political activity undertaken by minority activists as being against the interests of both nation and state.

Such logic had a profound impact on state institutions' view of ethnic diversity at home and regional implications for the management of minority issues. Indeed, in some quarters all post-communist states have become viewed as homelands of territorially concentrated ethno-nations.[29] As a result, non-dominant communities, particularly where there was a history of ethno-territorial minority mobilisation, have on occasion rallied to carve out regions where these regionally dominant groups could become de facto majorities. While to a degree the territorial management of ethnic diversity can be seen as a tool for promoting—and protecting—minority cultures, language and rights, increasingly the territorialisation of ethnicity is being viewed as a convenient tool for the majority to protect 'their' state from minority claims and/or the renegotiation of statewide institutional arrangements.

More important is the fact that during the period of EU accession, effectively addressing the ethnic component of nation-state building across the post-communist area was widely accepted as the chief marker of successful state consolidation. In part, inter-state disputes over minority rights issues sometimes involving the kin-state of the domestic minority made the accommodation of minority rights, flexible regulation of language use and inter-ethnic relations vital for acknowledging success in post-communist nation-state building.[30] The process of negotiating accession to the EU allowed for all nation-states in the post-communist region to demonstrate that state consolidation is essentially one and the same as the representation of territorially concentrated ethno-nations and the democratic evolution of their political projects. As we noted above, this strategy allowed a degree of individual minority participation in and contribution to the process of political change, but nation-state building also highlighted the possibility of the internal contestation of post-communist regimes.

Strategies deployed aimed at mobilising the support base at the national scale with reference to the ethno-political grievances of the minority often relay the unique potential for regional patterns of mobilisation. Where a minority is territorially compact, it is said to be more likely to have been successful during the period of democratisation in achieving better representation at the state level.[31] Received wisdom alludes to the fact that political entrepreneurs can better maximise their actions in regions of concentrated minority settlement. This is because during the communist period all members of society were alert to institutional resources they could claim as a result of self-identifying with the titular ethnic group of the region in which they lived.[32] Indeed, the compact settlement of ethnic groups minimises the costs of collective action. It is therefore logical that little attention has been paid to ethno-national reasons for mobilisation and the later dismemberment of communist regimes.[33] This in turn prevents scholars from ascertaining the crucial importance of ethno-national state building in the transition from communist to liberal democratic rule.

The wider scholarship posits that rather than the subjective positioning in the ethno-national social framework, it is socio-economic inequalities that sponsor ethnic solidarity. Indeed, communist nationalities' policies placed a premium on individual identification with one or another ethnic group as a means of gaining access to (limited) resources available in the territory of the ethnically defined group.[34] With political and ethnic identities often mapping onto ethnic identification, institutionalised forms of ethnically based exclusion pushed individuals to associate with their ethnic group in order to advance territorial and adjacent political management of their identities. Notably, ethno-political mobilisation is easiest when a nascent class of political entrepreneurs are able to tap into political institutions that have already relied on ethnic identity for their effective delivery of service.[35] As the post-communist states formalised the criteria of political membership and put institutions in place aimed at guaranteeing privileged relations on behalf of the titular group with the state, political mobilisation along the lines of ethnic groups has remained an attractive option within the new political institutions.

Cultural bias in the institutional design of states has also imbued post-communist political elites with a ready-made reference point to design policies that favour ethnic majority communities.[36] As the post-communist region has embarked upon transition with the declared goal of installing democratic governance in what were previously communist political institutions, the reorganization of political space has barely touched upon the ethno-national form of the state.[37] Multinational and multilingual federations dissolved into more—yet not entirely—ethnically and linguistically homogenous polities, sometimes accompanied by the internal realignment of administrative regions in order to allow resident ethnic groups to become majorities in given administrative units.

This facilitated an orderly transition to democratic politics in states that experienced multiple reorganizations, in economic, social and not least the cultural sense.[38] Much more, the exchange of political elites happened within a context where citizens' interests in credible policies, the prospect of European integration, and the accountability of state institutions required pooling legitimacy behind contested politics. Within such a context, the existence of well-financed and administratively competent governments was key to ushering in democratic reform and installing (more) accountable institutions across the post-communist space. The route to achieving this goal lay in the alignment of statewide political processes with the overall interest of the nation.

3. THE IMPACT OF NATION-STATE BUILDING ON THE INSTITUTIONALISATION OF ETHNICITY

Undoubtedly, the prospect of EU accession facilitated an improvement in inter-ethnic relations in most post-communist societies. For the greater part, some form of constitutional guarantees for protection of minority interests and language rights made past ethno-political conflict appear less likely. However, the promulgation of minority-friendly legislation has not always translated into the effective application of policies on the ground. In regions where minority communities are in the majority, forms of protection and policies supporting cultural diversity have taken the shape of ethno-territorial separation with distinct sets of competencies for regional administrations. For individuals of minority background residing in mixed or state-majority-dominated administrative units, exposure to statewide ethno-national institutions has often meant that an outright zero-sum choice has to be made between cultural and linguistic marginalisation or assimilation.

As a result, nation-state building has effectively become the source of legitimacy of independent statehood for majority groups, but at the same time, it laid the groundwork for mobilisation that ensured that ethnic identity became the most salient form of identity over and above all others.[39] The situation was compounded by the limited functionality of democratic political structures that ensured key actors' privileged access and impacted on the strategic evolution of political institutions with the references to the interest of the 'nation' that 'owned' the state.[40] So while majorities across the post-communist area have further linked the perceptions of state futures with national self-determination, minority groups sought to make sense of their own experiences of exclusion with reference to the fact that consolidating nation-state institutions seemed to exclude minorities from the political process.

One crucial issue overlooked across the scholarship on post-communist state-building strategies is the conflation of nation-state building and democratic consolidation of post-communist states in advance of EU accession. Indeed, Juan Linz stated as long as twenty years ago that ethnic diversity is a challenge to democratisation in a post-communist area.[41] More to the point, as James Fearon and David Laitin point out, democracy does not constitute a 'magic bullet' for inter-ethnic peace and stability.[42] Although there has been considerable research on the 'democratic peace', it only concludes that democracies do not fight one another but makes no predictions whatsoever about the levels of democracy necessary for sustained inter-ethnic and/or social stability. Crucially, democracies do not quell conflicts ethnic or otherwise; rather, they 'relocate conflicts from battlefields to the political arena'.[43] More recently, Wolfgang Merkel and Brigitte Weiffen have demonstrated that the ethnic heterogeneity of a given population does not hinder democratic consolidation.[44]

In part, Don Horowitz argues that democracy evolves best in societies with the fewest ethnic cleavages and/or ethnic conflict, when majority or minority rule might even be detrimental to a truly representative nature of democracy.[45] Daniele Conversi also notes that majoritarian democracies create conditions in which ethno-national ideologies may thrive, a condition exacerbated by the adoption of neoliberal policies.[46] Others argue that how well democracies handle or prevent ethnic conflict depends to a large degree on specifically how democratic institutions are designed.[47] The 'tyranny of the majority' is said to leave minorities disempowered and plays into the hands of those who can make a good case for the use of violence.[48] As discussed above, on occasion, post-communist states did offer a space in which to express dissenting opinions about the initial state design to members of minorities if they resided in administrative units where their interests could be better served. Yet, with state institutional design relying upon the ethno-political mobilisation of the majority, minimising the risks of another group's mobilisation against these very same institutions became increasingly difficult once states became acknowledged as serving one ethnic community in the international arena.

Institutional adaptation is therefore democracy's core advantage in discouraging ethnic mobilisation, and should act as a powerful deterrent for ethnically framed conflict.[49] However, under conditions of simple majority rule in the ethnically defined setting of nation-state institutions, identity groups are unlikely to seek change, which would result in more limited space for the nonviolent pursuit of their goals.[50] Adopting measures for 'citizen-based peace-making' through 'middle-range actors [that] often have the trust of both top-level and grassroots actors' and who can build 'bridges to like-minded individuals across the lines of conflict'[51] is a sufficient measure of ascertaining a state's overall ascent towards ensuring parity-based coopera-tion. However, post-communist states in general, and specifically those that have joined the EU, have sometimes only further enhanced leverage for majority communities.

As we discussed above, nation-state institutions have effectively locked domestic political elites into a zero-sum game of extending minority rights provisions to domestic residents versus further consolidating state institu-tions' accountability to majorities. Indeed, as we can observe in Estonia and Latvia, eligibility to join the EU came about despite the unresolved status of many long-term Russophone residents who were—and remain—excluded from protection as domestic minorities.[52] In other countries, such as Roma-nia and Slovakia, participation in the political process and participation in decision making by members of minority communities has often played less of a role in national politics.[53] Although state institutions were designed to cater primarily to the majority, parties representing the Hungarian minority have actually been part of governing national coalitions. This to one side, majority representatives were seen as the driving force for state building, and that was deemed sufficiently democratic for post-communist states to accede to the EU. All of this underlines the notion that the post-communist transition has been geared towards enhancing sovereignty claims of the domestic ma-jority over decision-making processes in their states, allowing for only limit-ed progress in addressing comprehensively minority rights issues.

European integration for most post-communist states has been identified as a successful leverage in terms of nation-state building. However, studies often posit that the institutionalisation of collective—that is, ethnic identity in the context of EU integration—was inevitable given the normative back-ground of the European minority rights' regime designed to ensure the *invio-lability of state borders* and the *domestically* determined democratisation of state-society relations.[54] Once post-communist nation-state building was be-gun, representatives of titular groups could achieve best possible outcomes by tapping the sense of ethnic solidarity among their followers to press for amendments in political institutions and accommodate different, ethnically defined stakeholders in society—just as long as these were not to challenge majorities' decisive voice over political trajectory. In effect, both success and failure in accommodating ethnicity-based claims in political institutions re-flected the growing importance of titular ethnic identity *for* political institu-tions catering an ethnically diverse society.

This is precisely the core of institutionalist accounts of ethnic politicking that we are dealing with. Once social interactions are defined in terms of ethnicity, groups inevitably find it easier to frame issues, which are not necessarily ethnic, by tailoring their message to ethnically defined audiences.[55] This is the point at which 'the process by which a group goes from being a passive collection of individuals to an active participant in public life' is set into motion.[56] As members of the majority group self-identify and as the dominant community of the state is put into place, their choices of and policies for group protection become non-negotiable.

Much of the literature addresses post-communist state building and treats majority choices as an appeal to a set of identity markers (e.g., ethnicity, culture, language and such like) as a central reference point for the consolidating state institutions under conditions of uncertainty concerning state sovereignty. In this context, political actors have sought to improve their group's position with regard to a different set of markers (e.g., access to economic status, political office, etc.) and have consolidated political institutions in relation to set goals of nation-state building. In all cases, setting up institutions of the state for one specific, majority and titular nation has allowed the maximisation of political resources that disproportionately amplified that group's significance, attracted sympathetic partisan citizens and institutionalised access to state resources by making ethnicity not only socially but also politically salient.

This set of broader overlapping issues pertains to group cohesion, and resource allocation is found in scholarship on both social and ethno-political mobilisation.[57] A whole gamut of issues feature in the studies of ethnonational state building, such as rational ethnic behaviour, intraethnic cohesion, movements towards independence for a 'nation', conflict over access to scarce resources and ecological grievances over ancestral territory. All of these note the negative assessment of a mobilising group's position and attempts as the driver for change to revise the terms of cooperation between ethnic groups within the given structure of political institutions.

In this sense, therefore, nation-state building is but a particularly successful form of collective action against the background of changing institutional opportunities.[58] While ethno-national state building is frequently understood as the 'instrumental behaviour of political entrepreneurs' aimed at achieving tangible outcomes for their client ethnic groups, accounts of ethnicity-based mobilisation support the view that ethno-political leadership acts as arbitrators overseeing the access of co-ethnics to scarce resources of the state.[59] The success of nation-state building strategies therefore can be measured by increased returns for the mobilised core group. Ethnicity, therefore, albeit a resource during the period of mobilisation, becomes nothing short of a political institution in societies that have successfully tampered the definition of a 'nation' whilst establishing a criteria of access to political institutions of 'their' states.

4. THE SUSTAINABILITY OF STATE-SOCIETY RELATIONS
IN POST-COMMUNIST STATES

Where does this discussion bring us in terms of identifying the ultimate opportunities to enforce policies of ethnic diversity management in the post-communist area during and crucially post-accession? Earlier we argued that the process of EU accession was largely limited to confirming the remit of the sovereignty of existing post-communist nation-states, however ethnically diverse. As such, the EU accession phase did not posit any distinct correctives to nation-states' treatment of their resident minorities. Rather, state institutions were urged to take into greater account the fact that their own ethno-national design was sponsoring the ethno-national mobilisation of resident domestic minorities. It also implied that the territorially bound and culturally distinct 'nations' were to be managed by ethno-national institutions in whose name they would speak.[60] Coincidentally, the temporary nature of EU accession pressures has also allowed domestic political actors to fortify the discursive importance of the nation-state in domestic politics.[61] The premise employed is that the collective representation of national interest is best achieved when operating with reference to the cultural identity of the core ethnic community. It is our intention to investigate how the peculiar understandings of states as sovereign domains of titular nations have impacted on the overall potential for the democratisation of states' relations with their ethnically diverse citizenries. Some observers go as far as to suggest that EU accession has imported a non-negotiable and politically legitimised *ethno-nationalist* mode of organization into the gamut of European regimes. This point appears to be particularly salient since the onset of the Euro crisis in 2008, as a result of the evolving crisis in Ukraine and the EU's failure to elaborate a coherent response to the arrival of Syrian refugees. It appears that to complete our overview of the interface between the nation-state and international regime for minority protection, we ought to consider the relationship between the state and its citizens that has emerged in Europe over the past two decades.

As is widely acknowledged, much of the effort of European organizations during the period of accession was dedicated to supporting state-building and consolidating institutions in pre-accession countries. During this process, both the international organizations and nation-states maintained intense cooperation that kept envisaged benefits in mind. Whereas a stated goal of joining the EU because it is a strong economic actor has been often emphasised by Central and Eastern European political elites and populations alike, we focus here specifically on the aspect of external recognition of state sovereignty and the acknowledgement of joint interests by accession states of the benefits future interactions are likely to bring to their status as credible, independent EU member-states. EU accession, of course, did not promise to impact directly on the relationship between states and their citizens in post-communist areas. However, with a better understanding of post-communist nation-states as sets of political institutions doing more than merely regulating the established relations between their ethnically diverse residents, it should now be more apparent why EU accession was seen as a major hallmark of the post-communist transition to a nation-state model of governance.

In particular, those states that had considerable minority communities on their territories, with vocal kin-states of those groups invoking international standards whilst struggling to stabilise the political process, found themselves in a comparatively weak position in asserting their sovereignty. Given that most states in the post-communist region lacked the economic resources necessary to assert themselves as players with any leverage in the international arena, all of them pursued EU integration as a self-interested goal of ensuring their ability to effectively manage domestic populations. Whether doing so by means of engaging with the EU and committing to the integration project or by advocating for maintaining overlapping cleavages within their domestic constituencies, post-communist states have achieved positive outcomes for their domestic publics as well gaining credence in the eyes of international partners.

However, cooperation on the part of political elites in post-communist nation-states with both international organizations and their domestic citizens has at all times been mediated through the institutions of a state that favoured the ethnic optic on the 'nation'. Although political elites were dealing with the external observers' input on desired changes to domestic institutions, their behaviour was responsive to urging for change, and in the light of persistent ethno-national state design opportunities for greater accommodation of ethnic diversity, it remained limited. The first wave of Europeanisation literature rightly suggests that EU engagement in state consolidation in the post-communist region has only prolonged the period of indecision about the remit of these states' commitment to their non-core constituents' marginalised citizens.[62]

The very nature of European accession as a top-down imposition of rules and norms to be transposed into national legislation has entrenched 'fragile state sovereignty' and perpetuated the perceived security dilemmas of states that have sought to emancipate themselves from communist legacies.[63] The absence of cross-community acceptance of central state authority as in Latvia and Estonia, or of substantive regional self-government as in Slovakia and Romania, has further cut down on state capacity to implement inclusive policies. The under-resourced political institutions and officials often lacking expertise have more often than not toed the line of suggestions emanating from Brussels. As such, they have been able to keep the impact of European conditionality at its minimum. The significantly watered-down expectations of the EU accession process have been minimised not because of limited clarity about the EU's own expectations from accession states' relations with their citizens, but mainly due to the limited legitimacy of institutions engineered domestically and functionality accountable to only one, ethnic majority segment of society.[64] Overall, the EU accession process therefore ensured societal stability over sustained democratic transition thanks to its comprehensive reform package, which could hardly be implemented in good faith by candidate countries, still in the process of ascertaining claims of sovereignty over their domestic populations.

On the other hand, increasing state capacity across the post-communist Central and Eastern European states has met with the EU preference to focus upon institution, rather than capacity building.[65] Under the conditions of limited experience of independent governance across the region, it seems that preparation for accession did in fact result in institution-building processes necessary for states to provide benefits and services to resident populations in the long haul. Yet lacking financial support and crucially impartial institutions responsible for collecting and redistributing economic resources across the entire set of residents, states were more effective in redistribution through existing institutional channels than by creating new avenues for accountable governance.[66] Pouring additional resources into institution building only supported the perception of domestic political elites concerning their role in overseeing and not changing institutions and facilitated the further consolidation of nation-states with their pre-existing institutions guaranteeing minimal accountability to majority residents.

Unsurprisingly, therefore, different strategies were employed by political elites to either win support from external monitors or demonstrate tokenistic compliance with European norms of managing ethno-cultural diversity. Post-communist states seeking EU membership therefore deepened their reliance on external acknowledgement of their successful policymaking to date.[67] Dependent on external finances to ensure domestic acquiescence and being regularly criticised for failing to meet standards of membership, most post-communist countries achieved minimal levels of state capacity to deliver services to all their citizens only after they had joined the EU. Thus there is a great need for continued structural reforms and the creation of dynamic political institutions accountable to all citizens that can also calm fears about the erosion of (ethno-)national sovereignty.

Since the onset of the accession process in 2004, post-communist states have incorporated legal changes into domestic law, developed new policy instruments and sought to successfully meet targets for policy performance with the EU normative blueprint. Yet legislative changes have often been followed up by inconsistent reforms in terms of policymaking and implementation.[68] Policymakers and scholars of Europeanisation alike anticipate that there remains considerable scope for state institutional change. There is a general consensus that Europeanisation has been shallow across the board in post-communist Europe specifically due to the paucity of Europeanisation mechanisms, and because of contradictions between EU and nation-state-driven integration mechanisms. [69]

The focus of research on regime (and by extension regional) stability in the post-communist area shows that all such countries have to one extent or the other been on the pathway to democratisation during the European accession period. However, very few states in the region have implemented normative benchmarks that could have prevented states from backtracking post-accession on their accountability and control of governmental performance. Indeed, it appears that ensuring sustained levels of institutional performance across post-communist states has taken a backseat since accession in favour of ensuring domestic and regional stability.

This is why it is essential to return to the starting point of the investigation of the reasons for which we have only observed superficial Europeanisation in the post-communist area when it comes to ensuring sustainable relations between states and their citizens in general and minorities specifically. With states as sets of political institutions that hold sovereignty in a clearly demarcated territory that are able to enforce policies over populations' residents therein, the crucial issue at stake is that of a classic European integration theory's focus on state sovereignty as defined in its core political institutions. With a more permanent drive at the EU level to apply the principles of subsidiarity, there appears to be a dearth of mediating agents between and within new member-states that justifies the relocation of decision making from the national to either the international, local or regional levels.

Furthermore, it is hard to see the extensive experience of national political elites' tutelage by EU monitors as being in any way conducive to nurturing support and loyalty to (European) institutions. As long as integration is seen as the process whereby political actors in several distinct national settings are persuaded to shift their loyalties, expectations and political activities towards a new centre, whose institutions possess or demand jurisdiction over the pre-existing national states, national sovereignty across the post-communist area has remained defined via ethno-nationally designed institutions of the state. [70]

At the level of the EU, we observe decreasing institutional capacity to institutionalise norms and spillover effects in new member-states. Such effects have been minimal across the new member-states over the accession decade, but increasingly became the norm across the entire EU after the onset of the economic crisis of 2008. In fact, there have been few incentives for member-states to yield domestic sovereignty to the quasi-federal centre on matters that were at the heart of nation-state building projects. As the original post-communist states' political institutions were designed as liberal nation-states for their ethnic majorities, there are few domestic areas in which minority issues can be brought to the fore. Thus, as post-communist states' capacity to communicate the interests of their citizens to international organizations has been limited and confined mainly to those that could be framed as constituting the ethno-political interests of the majority, the onset of the economic crisis has further decreased national governments' interest in implementing those elements of the EU's normative blueprint that contradict their domestic concerns for national sovereignty.

As alluded to earlier, in many cases, popular resistance to political change in the international arena is evoked as a result of incremental, technocratic integration, ushering the way for spillover effects. It denotes a process whereby a member-state becomes less willing to support the European regulation of certain policy issues, particularly those that impugn popular rising national self-confidence. This tendency is particularly apparent in those new member-states that lack a consistent normative commitment to both international actors and their domestic residents outside the framework of national sovereignty. This problem is compounded by a wider pan-European anti-EU backlash whose supporters fear the erosion of both national identity and sovereignty.

CONCLUSION

In this chapter, we have briefly discussed the background of the communist approach to ethnic diversity management, how it has been put to use by the ethno-political entrepreneurs of titular majorities during the late communist period and effectively remained unchallenged during the first decade of transition from communist rule. The compound effect of institutionalising polities as nation-states of the dominant majority has had a direct impact on perceptions of state sovereignty through the lens of the 'nation'. This interpretation of the state as being the domain of the national sovereignty of the titular ethnic group gradually made political processes national in form and filled it with European content.

In terms of domestic political institution building across post-communist states, we have related how these reflected upon the legacies of communist management of ethnic diversity by territorialising ethnic groups in their separate administrative units in order to undercut challenges of central authority by minorities' identitarian claims. At the same time, this protected majority dominated political arenas from all claims to equal, proportionate and effective representation of groups that mobilised around perceptions of cultural, linguistic and overall ethnic difference. In so doing, we have underlined that the newly (re-)established states have failed to put into place mechanisms of diversity management. Instead, they have systematically asserted the national sovereignty of the state with reference to the 'national interest' despite the obvious ethno-cultural diversity on the ground. In this sense, post-communist nation-states have effectively accomplished the 'return to Europe', not only by joining the EU as independent and sovereign states but also, and much more, as nation-states of the ethnic majority.

As we have seen, different modalities of nation-state building in post-communist Europe have evolved as a result of institutions being designed in order to ensure ethno-national ascendancy in the political process. While we do not doubt that some form of protection was guaranteed for resident minorities in all post-communist states, we have also considered the rationale and modus operandi of these institutions when it comes to identifying and protecting ethnically defined groups. As we demonstrated in the third section of the chapter, these all reflect on the structures of governance in post-communist countries. Unsurprisingly, these superficially replicated the liberal approach to state-society relations embedded in the norms of domestic sovereignty. The decision-making and implementation institutions that the European Union requested to be put into place during the accession phase have therefore inevitably failed to promote the interests of those under-resourced, marginalised and generally minority groups. In the next chapters we map the overlap of the underlining rationales for the maintenance of state sovereignty while providing often-tokenistic support for non-dominant groups resident in territories of nation-states. Along the avenues previously established, rather than via new institutional avenues, post-communist nation-states have opted for anti-discrimination legislation as a baseline for diversity management, bringing their approach to minority issues in line with that of the older EU member-states.

NOTES

1. Daphne Halikiopoulou, Kyriaki Nanou, and Sofia Vasilopoulou, 'The Paradox of Nationalism: The Common Denominator of Radical Right and Radical Left Euroscepticism', *European Journal of Political Research* 51, no. 4 (2012): 504–39, doi:10.1111/j.1475-6765.2011.02050.x.

2. Núria Franco-Guillén, 'Selfishness of the Affluent? Stateless Nationalist and Regionalist Parties and Immigration', *Journal of Ethnic and Migration Studies* (21 September 2015): 1–13, doi:10.1080/1369183X.2015.1082287; Sanjay Jeram, Arno van der Zwet, and Verena Wisthaler, 'Friends or Foes? Migrants and Sub-State Nationalists in Europe', *Journal of Ethnic and Migration Studies* (15 September 2015): 1–13, doi:10.1080/1369183X.2015.1082286.

3. Valerie Bunce, 'Rethinking Recent Democratization: Lessons from the Postcommunist Experience', *World Politics* 55, no. 2 (2003): 167–92; Beverly Crawford and Arend Lijphart, eds., *Liberalization and Leninist Legacies: Comparative Perspectives on Democratic Transitions* (Berkeley: International and Area Studies, 1997).

4. Dovile Budryte, *Taming Nationalism? Political Community Building in the Post-Soviet Baltic States* (Aldershot: Ashgate, 2005); Dejan Djokic and James Ker-Lindsay, eds., *New Perspectives on Yugoslavia: Key Issues and Controversies* (London: Routledge, 2010); David S. Mason, *Revolution and Transition in East-Central Europe* (Boulder, CO: Westview Press, 1992).

5. Walker Connor, 'Nation-Building or Nation-Destroying?' *World Politics* 24, no. 3 (1972): 319–55; Juan J. Linz, 'State Building and Nation Building', *European Review* 1, no. 4 (1993): 355–69.

6. Walter A. Kemp, *Nationalism and Communism in Eastern Europe and the Soviet Union: A Basic Contradiction* (New York: St. Martin's Press, 1999).

7. Taras Kuzio, '"Nationalising" States or Nation-Building? A Critical Review of the Theoretical Literature and Empirical Evidence', *Nations and Nationalism* 7, no. 2 (2001): 135–54.

8. Beáta Huszka, 'Framing National Identity in Independence Campaigns: Secessionist Rhetoric and Ethnic Conflict', *Nationalism and Ethnic Politics* 20, no. 2 (2014): 153–73, doi:10.1080/13537113.2014.909153.

9. Mark R. Beissinger, *Nationalist Mobilization and the Collapse of the Soviet State* (Cambridge: Cambridge University Press, 2002).

10. Graeme Gill, 'Nationalism and the Transition to Democracy: The Post-Soviet Experience', *Demokratizatsiya: The Journal of Post-Soviet Democratization* 14, no. 4 (2006).

11. Juan J. Linz and Alfred Stepan, 'Toward Consolidated Democracies', *Journal of Democracy* 7, no. 2 (1996): 14–33.

12. Shari J. Cohen, *Politics without a Past: The Absence of History in Postcommunist Nationalism* (London: Duke University Press, 1999); Maple Razsa and Nicole Lindstrom, 'Balkan Is Beautiful: Balkanism in the Political Discourse of Tudman's Croatia', *East European Politics and Societies* 18, no. 4 (2004): 628–50.

13. Mihail Chiru and Sergiu Gherghina, 'Parliamentary Sovereignty and International Intervention: Elite Attitudes in the First Central European Legislatures', *East European Politics* 30, no. 1 (2014): 21–33, doi:10.1080/21599165.2013.858627.

14. Jan Buček, 'Responding to Diversity: Solutions at the Local Level in Slovakia', in *Diversity in Action: Local Public Management of Multi-Ethnic Communities in Central and Eastern Europe*, eds. Anna Mária Bíró and Petra Kovács (Budapest: Open Society Institute, 2002), 273–306; for comparison of the situation in Russia, see Alexander Osipov, 'Implementation Unwanted? Symbolic vs. Instrumental Policies in the Russian Management of Ethnic Diversity', *Perspectives on European Politics and Society* 13, no. 4 (1 December 2012): 425–42, doi:10.1080/15705854.2012.731933.

15. Erin K. Jenne, *Ethnic Bargaining. The Paradox of Minority Empowerment* (London: Cornell University Press, 2007); Zsuzsa Csergo, *Talk of the Nation: Language and Conflict in Romania and Slovakia* (London: Cornell University Press, 2007); Myra A. Waterbury, *Between State and Nation: Diaspora Politics and Kin-State Nationalism in Hungary* (Houndmills: Palgrave Macmillan, 2010).

16. Rogers Brubaker, *Nationalism Reframed: Nationhood and the National Question in the New Europe* (Cambridge: Cambridge University Press, 1996), 58–59.

17. Rogers Brubaker, 'Ethnicity without Groups', *European Journal of Sociology* 43, no. 2 (2003): 163–89; and an updated version of the same argument in Rogers Brubaker, 'Language, Religion and the Politics of Difference', *Nations and Nationalism* 19, no. 1 (2013): 1–20.

18. Rogers Brubaker, 'The "Diaspora" Diaspora', *Ethnic and Racial Studies* 28, no. 1 (2005): 1–19; Rogers Brubaker, 'Migration, Membership, and the Modern Nation-State: Internal and External Dimensions of the Politics of Belonging', *Journal of Interdisciplinary History* 41, no. 1 (2010): 61–78.

19. Brubaker, *Nationalism Reframed*, 69.

20. Andreas Wimmer, 'Does Ethnicity Matter? Everyday Group Formation in Three Swiss Immigrant Neighbourhoods', *Ethnic and Racial Studies* 27, no. 1 (2003): 1–36; Andreas Wimmer, 'Elementary Strategies of Ethnic Boundary Making', *Ethnic and Racial Studies* 31, no. 6 (2008): 1025–55, doi:10.1080/01419870801905612.

21. Pål Kolstø, 'Nation-Building in the Former USSR', *Journal of Democracy* 7, no. 1 (1996): 118–32; Harris Mylonas, Adria Lawrence, and Erica Chenoweth, 'Assimilation and Its Alternatives: Caveats in the Study of Nation-Building Policies', *Journal of Southern Europe and the Balkans* 2, no. 2 (2000): 141–48.

22. Stefan Wolff, *Ethnic Conflict: A Global Perspective* (Oxford: Oxford University Press, 2006).

23. Walker Connor, *Ethnonationalism: The Quest for Understanding* (Princeton, NJ: Princeton University Press, 1994).

24. Jonas Wolff, 'Democracy Promotion, Empowerment, and Self-Determination: Conflicting Objectives in US and German Policies towards Bolivia', *Democratization* 19, no. 3 (1 June 2012): 415–37, doi:10.1080/13510347.2012.674356; Nadya Nedelsky, 'Constitutional Nationalism's Implications for Minority Rights and Democratization: The Case of Slovakia', *Ethnic and Racial Studies* 26, no. 1 (2003): 102–28.

25. Paul Roe, 'Securitization and Minority Rights: Conditions of Desecuritization', *Security Dialogue* 35, no. 3 (2004): 279–94; Gwendolyn Sasse, 'Securitization or Securing Rights? Exploring the Conceptual Foundations of Policies towards Minorities and Migrants in Europe', *JCMS: Journal of Common Market Studies* 43, no. 4 (2005): 673–93.

26. John T. Ishiyama, 'Ethnopolitical Parties and Democratic Consolidation in Post-Communist Eastern Europe', *Nationalism and Ethnic Politics* 7, no. 3 (2001): 25–45.

27. David J. Galbreath, 'Securitizing Democracy and Democratic Security: A Reflection on Democratization Studies', *Democracy and Security* 8, no. 1 (2012): 28–42, doi:10.1080/17419166.2012.653737.

28. David D. Laitin, *Identity in Formation: The Russian-Speaking Populations in the Near Abroad* (Ithaca London: Cornell University Press, 1998).

29. Vera Tolz, 'Conflicting "Homeland Myths" and Nation-State Building in Postcommunist Russia', *Slavic Review* 57, no. 2 (1998): 267–94; Lowell W. Barrington, Erik S. Herron, and Brian D. Silver, 'The Motherland Is Calling: Views of Homeland among Russians in the Near Abroad', *World Politics* 55, no. 2 (2003): 290–313, doi:10.1353/wp.2003.0008.

30. Jeff Chinn and Robert J. Kaiser, *Russians as the New Minority: Ethnicity and Nationalism in the Soviet Successor States* (Boulder, CO: Westview Press, 1996).

31. Daniel Bochsler and Edina Szöcsik, 'Building Inter-Ethnic Bridges or Promoting Ethno-Territorial Demarcation Lines? Hungarian Minority Parties in Competition', *Nationalities Papers* 41, no. 5 (2013): 761–79, doi:10.1080/00905992.2013.801411.

32. Daniel Bochsler and Edina Szöcsik, 'The Forbidden Fruit of Federalism: Evidence from Romania and Slovakia', *West European Politics* 36, no. 2 (2013): 426–46.

33. Matteo Fumagalli, 'Framing Ethnic Minority Mobilisation in Central Asia: The Cases of Uzbeks in Kyrgyzstan and Tajikistan', *Europe-Asia Studies* 59, no. 4 (2007): 567–90; Eiki Berg, 'Ethnic Mobilisation in Flux: Revisiting Peripherality and Minority Discontent in Estonia', *Space and Polity* 5, no. 1 (2001): 5–26.

34. Andreas Wimmer, 'The Making and Unmaking of Ethnic Boundaries: A Multilevel Process Theory', *American Journal of Sociology* 113, no. 4 (2008): 970–1022.

35. Jacqueline Heinen, 'Public/Private: Gender—Social and Political Citizenship in Eastern Europe', *Theory and Society* 26, no. 4, Special Issue on Recasting Citizenship (1997): 577–97.

36. Terry Martin, 'Borders and Ethnic Conflict: The Soviet Experiment in Ethno-Territorial Proliferation', *Jahrbücher Für Geschichte Osteuropas* 47 (1999): 538–55.

37. Yuri Slezkine, 'The USSR as a Communal Appartment, or How a Socialist State Promoted Ethnic Particularism', *Slavic Review* 53, no. 2 (1994): 414–52.

38. Karl Cordell, 'The Ideology of Minority Protection during the Post-Communist Transition in Europe', in *Institutional Legacies of Communism, Change and Continuities in Minority Protection*, eds. Karl Cordell, Timofey Agarin, and Alexander Osipov (London: Routledge, 2013), 77–89.

39. Antje Wiener, 'Making Sense of the New Geography of Citizenship: Fragmented Citizenship in the European Union', *Theory and Society* 26, no. 4 (1997): 529–60.

40. Dora Kostakopoulou, 'Thick, Thin and Thinner Patriotisms: Is This All There Is?' *Oxford Journal of Legal Studies* 26, no. 1 (2006): 73–106.

41. Juan J. Linz and Alfred Stepan, *Problems of Democratic Transition and Consolidation: Southern Europe, South America, and Post-Communist Europe* (Baltimore: Johns Hopkins, 1996), chapter 12.

42. James Fearon and David D. Laitin, 'Ordinary Language and External Validity: Specifying Concepts in the Study of Ethnicity', Annual Meetings of the American Political Science Association, 2000.

43. John Paul Lederach, *Building Peace: Sustainable Reconciliation in Divided Societies* (Washington, DC: United States Institute of Peace Press, 1997).

44. Wolfgang Merkel and Brigitte Weiffen, 'Does Heterogeneity Hinder Democracy?' *Comparative Sociology* 11, no. 3 (2012): 387–421.

45. Donald L. Horowitz, 'Democracy in Divided Societies', in *Nationalism, Ethnic Conflict, and Democracy*, eds. Larry Diamond and Marc F. Plattner (London: Johns Hopkins University Press, 1994).

46. Daniele Conversi, 'Majoritarian Democracy and Globalization versus Ethnic Diversity?' *Democratization* 19, no. 4 (2011): 789–811, doi:10.1080/13510347.2011.626947.

47. Karl Cordell, ed., *Ethnicity and Democratisation in the New Europe* (London: Routledge, 1999); Montserrat Guibernau, *Catalan Nationalism: Francoism, Transition and Democracy* (London: Routledge, 2004).

48. Donald J. Maletz, 'Tocqueville's Tyranny of the Majority Reconsidered', *Journal of Politics* 64, no. 3 (2002): 741–63; Anthony J. McGann, 'The Tyranny of the Supermajority: How Majority Rule Protects Minorities', *Journal of Theoretical Politics* 16, no. 1 (2004): 53–77.

49. Lars-Erik Cederman, Andreas Wimmer, and Brian Min, 'Why Do Ethnic Groups Rebel? New Data and Analysis', *World Politics* 62, no. 1 (2010): 87–119.

50. Rogers Brubaker and David D. Laitin, 'Ethnic and Nationalist Violence', *American Review of Sociology* 24 (1998): 423–52.

51. Lederach, *Building Peace: Sustainable Reconciliation in Divided Societies*, 94.

52. Dmitry Kochenov, Vadim Poleshchuk, and Aleksejs Dimitrovs, 'Do Professional Linguistic Requirements Discriminate? A Legal Analysis: Estonia and Latvia in the Spotlight', in *European Yearbook of Minority Issues*, 10 (Nijhoff: Brill, 2013), 137–87.

53. Csergo, *Talk of the Nation: Language and Conflict in Romania and Slovakia*.

54. Philip Spencer and Howard Wollman, 'Nationalism and Democracy in the Transition from Communism in Eastern Europe', *Contemporary Politics* 3, no. 2 (1997): 171–88.

55. Davide Pero and John Solomos, 'Introduction: Migrant Politics and Mobilization: Exclusion, Engagements, Incorporation', *Ethnic and Racial Studies* 33, no. 1 (2010): 1–18; Jackie Smith, 'Exploring Connections between Global Integration and Political Mobilization', *Journal of World Systems Research* 10, no. 1 (2004): 255–85.

56. Charles Tilly, *From Mobilization to Revolution* (Reading, MA: Addison-Wesley, 1978), 69.

57. Stephen Shulman, 'Nationalist Sources of International Economic Integration', *International Studies Quarterly* 44, no. 3 (2000): 365–90; Mérove Gijberts, Louk Hagendoorn, and Peer Scheepers, eds., *Nationalism and Exclusion of Migrants: Cross-National Comparisons* (Aldershot: Ashgate, 2004).

58. Joane Nagel and Susan Olzak, 'Ethnic Mobilization in New and Old States: An Extension of the Competition Model', *Social Problems* 30, no. 2 (1982): 127–41; Philip G. Roeder, 'Secessionism, Institutions, and Change', *Ethnopolitics* 13, no. 1 (2014): 86–104, doi:10.1080/17449057.2013.844437; Susan Olzak, 'Ethnic Protest in Core and Periphery States', *Ethnic and Racial Studies* 21, no. 2 (1998): 187–217.

59. Bert Klandermans, 'New Social Movements and Resource Mobilization: The European and the American Approach Revisited', *International Journal of Mass Emergencies and Disasters* 4, no. 2 (1986): 13–37.

60. Roger Friedland and Robert R. Alford, 'Bringing Society Back in: Symbols, Practices and Institutional Contradictions', in *The New Institutionalism in Organizational Analysis*, ed. Walter W. Powell and Paul J. DiMaggio (Chicago: University of Chicago Press, 1991), 232–63.

61. Gergana Noutcheva, 'Fake, Partial and Imposed Compliance: The Limits of the EU's Normative Power in the Western Balkans', *Journal of European Public Policy* 16, no. 7 (2009): 1065–84; Aneta B. Spendzharova and Milada Anna Vachudova, 'Catching Up? Consolidating Liberal Democracy in Bulgaria and Romania after EU Accession', *West European Politics* 35, no. 1 (2012): 39–58.

62. Kevin Featherstone, '"Europeanization" and the Centre Periphery: The Case of Greece in the 1990s', *South European Society and Politics* 3, no. 1 (1998): 23–39; Maura Adshead, 'Europeanization and Changing Patterns of Governance in Ireland', *Public Administration* 83, no. 1 (2005): 159–78, doi:10.1111/j.0033-3298.2005.00442.x; Vivien A. Schmidt and Claudio

M. Radaelli, 'Policy Change and Discourse in Europe: Conceptual and Methodological Issues', *West European Politics* 27, no. 2 (2004): 183–210.

63. Triin Vihalemm, 'Crystallizing and Emancipating Identities in Post-Communist Estonia', *Nationalities Papers* 35, no. 3 (2007): 477–502; Margarita Zavadskaya and Christian Welzel, 'Subverting Autocracy: Emancipative Mass Values in Competitive Authoritarian Regimes', *Democratization* 22, no. 6 (19 September 2015): 1105–30, doi:10.1080/13510 347.2014.914500.

64. K. Henderson, 'Slovakia and the Democratic Criteria for EU Accession', *Back to Europe: Central and Eastern Europe and the European Union* (Abbington: Taylor and Francis, 1999), 221–40; Gergana Noutcheva and Dimitar Bechev, 'The Successful Laggards: Bulgaria and Romania's Accession to the EU', *East European Politics & Societies* 22, no. 1 (2008): 114–44.

65. Florian Bieber, 'Building Impossible States? State-Building Strategies and EU Membership in the Western Balkans', *Europe-Asia Studies* 63, no. 10 (2011): 1783–1802, doi:10.1080/ 09668136.2011.618679; Soeren Keil, 'Europeanization, State-Building and Democratization in the Western Balkans', *Nationalities Papers* 41, no. 3 (2013): 343–53.

66. Tapio Raunio, 'Holding Governments Accountable in European Affairs: Explaining Cross-National Variation', *The Journal of Legislative Studies* 11, no. 3–4 (2005): 319–42; Beate Kohler-Koch and Berthold Rittberger, 'The "Governance Turn" in EU Studies', *Journal of Common Market Studies* 44, no. 1 (2006): 27–49.

67. Jelena Džankić et al., 'The Governance of Citizenship Practices in the Post-Yugoslav States: The Impact of Europeanisation', *European Politics and Society* 16, no. 3 (2015): 337–46, doi:10.1080/23745118.2015.1061744.

68. M. Bell, 'The Implementation of European Anti-Discrimination Directives: Converging towards a Common Model?' *The Political Quarterly* 79, no. 1 (2008): 36–44; Malte Brosig, 'No Space for Constructivism? A Critical Appraisal of European Compliance Research', in *Trajectories of Minority Rights Issues in Europe: The Implementation Trap?* eds. Timofey Agarin and Malte Brosig (Oxon: Routledge, 2015), 6–23.

69. Ramona Coman, 'Strengthening the Rule of Law at the Supranational Level: The Rise and Consolidation of a European Network', *Journal of Contemporary European Studies* (24 July 2015): 1–18, doi:10.1080/14782804.2015.1057482.

70. Peter M. Haas, 'Introduction: Epistemic Communities and International Policy Coordination', *International Organization* 46, no. 1 (1992): 1–34.

Chapter Three

European Nation-States and Minority Representation

In the previous two chapters, we provided an institutionalist account of post-communist state building and interpretations of limited accommodation of ethno-national diversity in the area since the collapse of communist rule. We contend that the focus of political processes of post-communist nation-state building indirectly resulted from the emphasis communist political institutions placed on ethnic identities. As we have made clear in chapter 2, EU engagement with CEE candidate states during the period of enlargement has emphasised the importance of the political processes revolving around the ethnicity of the majority, state-bearing community. This confirmed the view dominant in post-communist societies about 'ethnicity' as a central resource for political mobilisation, participation and recognition of claims in the context of nation-states for both majority and minority groups in the region.

As we have also underlined, the gamut of contentious issues around access to and distribution of cultural, social and economic resources elevated 'ethnicity' to the status of a political institution in societies where it was previously habitually, though informally, deployed to make sense of political conflicts and to attain tangible ends. In multi-ethnic post-communist societies where over the past decades political decision making has been seen through the prism of 'nation', ethnicity offered a reliable resource for the mobilisation of ethnic kin to achieve perceptively shared interests. When eight post-communist states joined the EU in 2004, their political institutions were aligned to serve domestic residents, crudely limited to the state-bearing nations and practically establishing that the 'nation' mapped neatly onto the 'citizenry' of the nation-state.

Over the past decade and a half, theories have mushroomed that seek to explain the comparative success of European integration, democratisation and transition in post-communist EU member-states. Most interpretations gave prominence to the salience of ethnicity in post-communist politics as an effective mobilisation tool allowing lobbying for, ensuring and increasing the autonomy of a clearly marked, institutionalised group as a central political force in these states. However, studies of group-based mobilisation in Europe and across the world as a whole focus predominantly, possibly exclusively, on the representatives of *minority* groups: these studies identify a set of immediate causes, rather than fundamental reasons, for ethnic politicking, and in so doing neglect the origins of political instability, various accounts of political order and the role nation-state political institutions play as triggers for mobilisation in the first place.

As a result of the focus on minority groups rather than on nation-states, scholarship has remained limited to the examination of (a small number of) cases of ethno-political mobilisation that have challenged state institutional design. However, in our view, state institutions' 'ratchet effect' can account for a deeper preference for stability over political change, making post-communist states particularly interesting as examples of superficial change despite significant and sustained levels of pressure for substantive change. In the previous chapter, we identified two sources of pressure upon state institutions to change. The first was the European accession process where emphasis was placed on increasing institutional fit across the member-states. Secondly, we examined citizen mobilisation seeking to make nation-states more responsive to its core constituency, the majority nation. In this chapter, we trace these processes' interaction in several country cases across post-communist Europe in order to introduce the reader to the sets of issue cases to be discussed in following chapters.

To illustrate this theoretical discussion about the institutional origins—rather than actor driven origins—of superficial change in minority protection, the following sections of the chapter utilise three examples drawn from Central and Eastern European states. Most often, states' policies towards resident minorities are relayed to post-accession post-communist states changes that they would enjoy upon joining the EU. The perspective of accession most often invoked implies the existence of a one-off opportunity for domestic political institutions to be kept more or less stable by pushing through reforms that would otherwise face opposition from key actors in domestic politics. As we have discussed in the previous chapter, though many institutional reforms were put in place during the accession phase, they had only a peripheral impact on the design of domestic political institutions. In the process of accession, both the *acquis* and political conditionality were designed to strengthen, not revise, the existing political institutional design to serve dominant majorities, rather than account for ethnic diversity. This, in turn, maintained the 'national' optic on the 'political' process in states declared national homelands of the majority. As our following discussion shows, the focus on political institutions of post-communist nation-states allows us to explain the choices and behaviours of actors of the European minority rights regime, domestic elites and minority ethno-political entrepreneurs during and after EU accession.

1. ESTABLISHING STATES' CAPACITY
TO SERVE CITIZENS EFFECTIVELY

The scholarship on ethno-political mobilisation underlines that once ethnic mobilisation is set into motion, it can hardly be scaled down without credible external incentives to do so. In-group favouritism, ethnicity-based prejudice and discrimination are widely acknowledged to make sense of differences— real or projected—with regard to the access to limited social resources,[1] opportunities in the labour market[2] and ensuring provisions for the redistribution of political capital.[3] In newly established state structures, such factors are mentioned among those that enhance the ratchet effect in terms of political mobilisation particularly effectively.[4] The three countries we discuss throughout the rest of the chapter have all experienced ethno-political mobilisation of the majority community, resulting in the establishment of these groups' nation-states. As we have already indicated in the previous chapter, once the institutions of states were put into place, they have effectively channelled opportunities for policy development broadly favourable for the members of the titular majority in these countries, gradually consolidating state-bearing nations' broader influence in the state.[5]

The initial step in the nation-state building across the post-communist area was mostly expressed in the ethno-political mobilisation of the titular community of ethno-federal republics. As we have emphasised previously, where significant numbers of ethnic minorities were present in the territory of the new state, political entrepreneurs of the majority exploited the lack of ethnic homogeneity to mobilise their own putative constituency. In such instances, the ethnic diversity of the population has proven to be a crucial condition for the mobilisation of the minority after institutions of the state morphed to become benchmarking instruments for guaranteed access of majority representatives to scarce resources of the country. However, the ethno-political mobilisation of minorities becomes prescient only once majority groups have already successfully framed 'state politics' through the prism of the 'national interest'.

In all post-communist states, ethnic differences overshadowed social cleavages and other inter-group differences. Mobilising groups along ethnic lines was an easy rallying point for social, economic and political antagonism in the face of plummeting earnings and increased social insecurities. The literature on post-communist state building in particular focussed upon the variance in outcomes of ethnic politicking as an entry point for discussions on enhancing state capacity to create institutions accountable to their citizens.[6] Taking these points more seriously allows us to examine the avenues made available to the representatives of the majority to create structures for maintaining high levels of mobilisation, resources available and agendas focussed on ethnic core groups of the newly (re-)established states.

State building therefore coincided with competition between ethnic groups' residents in the post-communist states for access to a diminishing pool of national resources. Facing the increasingly ethnicity-focussed political rhetoric of the majority and gradually consolidating the institutional design of the states to serve the ethnic majority, political entrepreneurs of the minority were also in a good position to exploit similar tactics that have earlier yielded success for the state's majority.[7] In particular, the political entrepreneurs of compactly settled minorities availed themselves of ethno-political mobilisation strategies during the period of transition in appealing to their constituents in ways that resulted in the (re-)creation of independent sovereign countries of the 'new' titular nation.

Secession from multi-ethnic federal states offered an advantageous starting position for members of the national majority to successfully mould ethnic mobilisation into a regular political process.[8] Basic institutional avenues were already in place in socialist federations to place titular groups in republics at an advantage vis-à-vis local non-titular groups, and political mobilisation did not lose its momentum after sovereignty was reinstated. Once federal republics collapsed into their constituent newly independent parts, political opportunity structures previously implicitly favouring titular groups was reframed to explicitly connote statehood as sovereignty of given ethno-national groups in newly established states. Thus, it is correct to argue that ethnic mobilisation has accomplished its goals once a titular nation-state has been established de jure. Yet studies of transition politics dwell on domestic politics as if they do not require study of the ethnic mobilisation of the titular community that that state was established to serve over other resident groups.[9]

This is surprising given that ethnicity is almost always understood in studies of domestic politicking in post-communist societies as the utility maximising a *strategic* toolkit that allows us to make sense of an ethnically, culturally and linguistically diverse social reality that took place during the transition.[10] Studies of ethno-political processes across the post-communist accession states have underlined the importance of individual group members' interpretation of the social world in terms of ethnic insiders and outsiders to predict outcomes of ethnic groups' role in new polities.[11] Political institutions that were designed in a way favourable to one group of residents have also strongly featured in studies explaining the variance between desired and accessible resources for minority group representatives,[12] habitually noted as motors for mobilising in a collective manner, as well as assessing the legitimacy of central authorities' policy decisions during the period of EU accession.[13]

In societies where mutual mistrust, group grievances and ethno-cultural stereotypes are reflected in political institutions' treatment of ethno-cultural communities, state institutions were thus tasked with bringing higher returns when drawing attention to positive advantages state policies deliver for constituent ethnic groups. When devising constitutions in Lithuania, Macedonia and Slovakia, political entrepreneurs of the majority rallied around ethnic issues. This allowed political representatives sitting in constituent parliaments to hijack the ethnic vote by talking up grievances of their constituency and/or fanning concerns over resident minorities' allegiance to newly established state institutions.

The structural incentives for majority group mobilisation, however, have not disappeared at the stage of policymaking as all three countries wrangled about the most appropriate modalities with which to define the citizenry of their states in civic terms; yet at the same time they promulgated legislation on language use and education whilst ducking the issue of minority rights so as to ensure that the state and nation became coterminous.[14] Once the majority communities established 'their' nation-state institutions and created portfolios of laws and policies to further consolidate majority ethnic citizens behind the notion of a 'nation', challengers to the newly established domestic regime calling for the revision of political institutions to cater to the needs of the entire citizenry could be easily dismissed as a numeric minority, rather than viewed as an ethnically distinct segment of state populace.

The nationalising policies of post-communist states in general, and in our three cases in particular, emboldened other ethnic minorities to rally for greater accommodation vis-à-vis institutions of their host state. As the prospect of joining the EU loomed large, many groups across the post-communist region turned their attention to provisions of respect for minority rights as spelled out in the Copenhagen Criteria. In those cases, such as ours, where ethnic communities were regionally concentrated, some international and scholarly interest was indeed warranted. Yet many contributors discovered little more than the fact that minority ethnic groups have been agitating against the 'nationalising' state policies and little else.[15]

Some claim that relations between minorities and their states of residence depend largely on factors external to either nation-state majorities or minorities. In the first instance, it is often suggested that EU accession has resulted in short-term compliance on the part of domestic (majority) political elites with strategic concessions being made at the time when EU membership was still in question. Alternatively, other research indicates that norm transposition was taking place, with the accession countries effectively borrowing mechanisms to manage their ethnically diverse populations in a way 'old' member-states have been happy to advise based upon their own past experience. At the same time, scholars have looked at the minorities' kin-states to ascertain the potential for minority mobilisation,[16] at the rhetoric of minority political entrepreneurs to account for conflict intensity[17] and at the role of international organizations in taming nationalist attitudes of minority leadership.[18] Our theoretical framework, however, suggests a different interpretation of the partial success of majority political entrepreneurs' approach to steering minority contestations into a 'peaceful' direction. We suggest that the institutional opportunity structure that favoured majorities, while putting minority groups at a disadvantage, was in place in individual accession states, and it is precisely this mode of ethnic diversity management has been also at the core of the EU's approach to securing domestic peace and regional stability in the past.[19] In short, it mandated the nation-state with the ultimate say over the remit of support and protection allocated to groups that the nation-state itself was to designate a 'minority' on its territory and that formed the key to the emerging European minority rights regime. Additionally, accession countries were also to adhere to the principle of *national* sovereignty as defined in their own constitutions and spelled out in their laws to win (back) the trust of their ethnic majority nationals in the ability of the state to act as a sovereign over its territory, policies and peoples.

Thus, in order to maintain levels of trust from their core constituents, domestic actors in post-communist accession states had to follow the ethno-political agendas enshrined in the institutions of their nation-states. To do so effectively, they had to neutralise the impact of ethno-political mobilisation of minorities and reduce their impact on state institutional design, particularly in the light of pressures emanating from the EU during the accession phase. In so doing, they faced a twofold challenge.

First, political representatives of the majority had to play by the democratic rules *as spelled out in their constitutions and sets of policies already in place.* Post-communist accession states were de jure presented as states for their titular nations, albeit with some guarantees of recognition of non-dominant minority groups. Majority political entrepreneurs sought to foster inter-ethnic alliances in a bid to sideline co-ethnic competitors when issues of relevance to minority communities were at play.[20] Whilst providing for some tokenistic concessions to resident minorities, the overall tutelary role of majorities was maintained.

If we first turn to Macedonia, we find that prior to the redesign of the political institutional structure following the Ohrid Agreement of 2001, majority parties played a central role in creating policies and dominated the political process wholesale, resulting in an outbreak of inter-ethnic violence between Macedonian Slavs and ethnic Albanians early in 2001. In this context, parties representing minorities could only stand a chance of passing the electoral threshold when they mobilised effectively the available ethnic vote in their respective ethnic enclaves. Ethnic majority parties set out to out compete each other in ethno-political rhetoric, and allowed Albanian parties, the Democratic Prosperity of Albanians (PDPA) and the People's Democratic Party (NDP) to enter parliament with no agenda that allowed cooperation with the majority political entrepreneurs. This turn of events prompted a merger between the two Albanian parties, and after the 2001 conflict it propelled the Democratic Union for Integration (BDI) into parliament.[21] The BDI was visible during the electoral campaign immediately following the conflict and garnered around 70 percent of Macedonian Albanians' vote. In subsequent elections, it performed well but was not invited into a coalition with the ethnic Internal Macedonian Revolutionary Organization—Democratic Party for Macedonian National Unity (VMRO-DPMNE). In their stead, Albanian representatives were increasingly present on the lists of majority-led as well as other minority parties, collectively running as the Social Democratic Union (SDSM), the major opposition party which highlighted socio-economic, rather than ethnic-based, agendas in national and regional elections.[22]

In Slovakia, after 1998 the Party of the Hungarian Community (SMK-MKP) participated in a number of coalition governments, but, as it happens, its votes were regularly overruled when it came to issues of minority interest. More important, when ethno-national rhetoric became *en vogue* again with the arrival of a coalition that included the post-fascist Slovak National Party (SNP), some of the reforms implemented whilst the SMK-MKP was a coalition were reversed.[23] In Lithuania, the Electoral Action of Poles in Lithuania (LLRA) prior to entering into government in 2012 as part of a four-party coalition remained marginal and sidelined.

In both Slovakia and Lithuania, although the majorities' political entrepreneurs talked, little hard action followed. Majority political entrepreneurs could simply ignore the ethno-political rallying of minorities and succeeded in diminishing the popularity of ethnic minority politicians, even in minority-populated regions. As a result of these measures, across Macedonia's, Slovakia's and Lithuania's regions with significant minority settlement we testify to the precipitous growth in satisfaction with the de facto arrangements for regional decision making via decentralisation mechanisms.[24] This indicates that maintaining access to crucial resources for politicking and numeric majority representation granted majority political entrepreneurs opportunities to undercut the focus on minority ethno-political claims. The ethnic majority electorate, therefore, could rest assured that despite the high salience of ethnic issues for minority populations, the state's political resources remained firmly in the hands of the majority political elites who could—and have—dispensed some of these to minority-populated regions, thereby sanitising the national politics of ethnic factionalism.

Secondly, majority ethno-political entrepreneurs made it their priority to play the ethnic card when communicating on contentious issues to their electorates. This allowed their constituents to form a concerted electoral base against issues raised by political elites of the minority. The case with SMK-MKP is similarly illustrative in context. Although this party had ample opportunity to be visible in the political process with its overall 12 percent representation in successive parliaments, and its participation in government on several occasions between 2002 and 2006, it could only effectively engage in decision making on social, regional, legal and, importantly, EU-related issues where its constituents were in the majority.[25] At the national level, it remained marginal on nearly all issues that touched upon national politics. In the long run, this resulted in the SMK-MKP re-profiling itself (with little success) as a regional party, and as was seen during the 2010 parliamentary elections, when it yielded much of its electorate to the newly established Most-Híd (Bridge). As its name suggests, this party seeks to bridge the ethnic gap and in 2010 received the majority of the Hungarian vote.[26]

In Lithuania, the political elites of ethnically Russian and Polish voters were dependent on political entrepreneurs of the majority to take on the issues of minority concern. The very nature of the majoritarian politics, therefore, made it essential for the numeric minority in national politics to implicitly accept the decisive vote of the majority over issues of culture in the public domain. Here, Polish political entrepreneurs did not need to refurbish their electoral platforms during the 1990s, although they did so in later years, as their subsequent entry into government shows. The LLRA has a clearly defined geographical base, but its vote share is consistently lower than the Polish share of the population (6.6 percent).[27]

A much tougher competition for the electorate took place in Macedonia, where the ethnic Albanian vote was split along more radical fringe parties that contested local, but not national, elections.[28] Macedonia-wide parties, which expressed liberal and social democratic concerns, were catapulted into government in the predominantly Albanian-populated city of Tetovo and across Western Macedonia. The general shift from the ethnic platform to issue-based electoral competition in these cases is indicative of the ethnic framing of social, economic and political grievances losing momentum since majority ethno-political entrepreneurs did not put anti-minority policies into practice. Redrawing and reshuffling issues central to electoral competition largely resulted in minority political entrepreneurs being able to plug into mainstream political discourse. It also meant that the majority's representation under a single banner did not need to emerge as such, due to the ability of minority ethnic entrepreneurs to mobilise in enclaves where there was no effective inter-ethnic competition.[29] Issue-specific competition ensured minority entrepreneurs' and electorates' co-optation on the agendas of majority parties as the only possible avenue for minority representation in political decision making.

What were the issues of salience in Macedonia that prompted minority political entrepreneurs to roll out political campaigns and mobilise their electorates in the first place? In order to understand this phenomenon, we need to consider the central issues on the agendas of political parties, which allow us to identify the remit of their concerns with the limits of nation-states' institutions and their ability to serve their ethnically defined electorates. All parties seeking to represent minorities in Lithuania, Slovakia and Macedonia emerged to bring minorities into political institutions and lobby for interests germane to minorities in 'nationalising' states. Whereas the levels of the nationalisation of the political process in Lithuania, Slovakia and Macedonia were different, at the time of independence, all three states boasted political institutions that from the outset pulled majorities and minorities apart. In effect, all three countries inscribed the dominant role of their titular groups into their constitutions, passed legislation that required high language proficiency from all political elites in the titular language of the state and have seen electoral politics reshaped as a result of gerrymandering designed to reduce minority representation in national parliaments. These conditions made voting in favour of *minority* political entrepreneurs less effective under the circumstances where inter-ethnic competition institutionally weakened the representation of minority interests in national politics.

The institutional strain posed upon the effective representation of minority interest during the initial years of transition from communism resulted in the triumph of majority political agendas at the nation-state level. Minimal opportunities remained for the minority political entrepreneurs to communicate their policy suggestions to majority political entrepreneurs and their near-constant exclusion from government formation ushered in the emergence, and later success, of ethnic parties representing specifically minority-relevant interests. In the context of nationalising policies, the gradual exclusion of minority-specific interests from nationwide politics offered a useful rallying point for ethnic minority parties.[30] Yet the meagre opportunities for overall success despite gauging an ethnically defined support base impeded minority political participation at large, further reducing the chances for renovating the ethno-political agendas of majority parties.[31]

Overall, this left ethnic minority representatives with little option other than to compete in a formally democratic political arena with the representatives of the majority consolidating their nation-statehoods without contesting the overall legitimacy of the 'national optic' on the state. In this light, minority issues became only further compartmentalised and maintained prominence only in geographic and electoral districts where minority representatives could successfully outcompete majority political entrepreneurs. In our three cases, as almost universally across the post-communist area, minority groups mobilised on an ethnic platform demanding a greater say in the governance of regions where they happen to have a numeric majority. This fact in turn draws our attention to the importance of ethnicity as a resource in accessing political institutions of the state across the region.

Our three cases illustrate just one of the critical issues that have continued to play an important role in the transition from communist regimes, as it did during the period of further democratisation during the period of EU accession. All ethnic groups have viewed political institutions that serve them as citizens as tools to institutionalise their views on the political process, and as a means of exerting leverage for representation on a narrower basis of ethnically defined interest. The focus on political mobilisation of present-day minorities in the nationalising post-communist states therefore takes for granted the interactive nature and open-endedness of the process of the contested potential design of political institutions: while it is widely acknowledged that not all types of ethnic mobilisation are successful, there is no doubt that they all originate in wider structural contexts. As such, the creation of nation-states for a clearly defined majority population resulted in the institutionalisation of political processes that are framed in terms of relevance for ethnic identities' maintenance.

Political entrepreneurs of all stripes, therefore, have set the parameters for mobilisation that they have followed throughout, and reflecting this, ethnic politicking has been prominent since the transition from communism.[32] The very fact that the majorities' preference to mobilise the 'ethnic electorate' occasionally backfired only supports the view that it was the major driver in the political process and whose pursuit was central to maintaining the trust of the electorate in states' commitment to serve its majority. As can be observed in the Slovak case and Hungarian mobilisation during Mečiar's rule in Slovakia in the 1990s or after protracted neglect of claims for political accommodation of ethno-cultural diversity in Macedonia prior to armed conflict in 2001, politicking that did *not* involve nationalising rhetoric has been the exception rather than the rule for more than twenty-five years. Similar cases of the rise in ethno-political mobilisation in Lithuania relating to changes in native-language education of Poles in the early 2000s make clear that when majority political entrepreneurs toe *their* ethnic line, minority political elites responded in kind but rarely were able to bring in ethnic concerns into national politics, where no prior majority-led ethnic politicking was in place.

Consequentially, beyond the ethno-political rallying of the majority, which impacted upon the minority's interest and ability to develop its ethno-political agenda in response to the majority's mobilisation, it was the gradual institutionalisation of ethnicity as a critical referent in policymaking across the region that has been accepted by members of both the minority and the majority.[33] In line with our discussion in the preceding chapter, the lack of credible commitment of national political elites of the majority to manage ethnic diversity via guarantees of minority protection has been the cause of minority ethno-political mobilisation throughout the region. At the same time, the commitment of majority political elites to the principles of nation-state building and ensuring the dominant role of the titular nation therein has diminished minorities' support for state institutions and led them to look for external mediators/guarantors of their equality in the states formally designed to exclude them from equal participation.

In all three country cases, Albanians, Hungarians and Poles formulated their political claims in ethnic terms and in opposition to the majority's proclaimed goals, most successfully embracing the rhetoric of opposing ethnic 'discrimination'. It was precisely this focus on non-discrimination that was central to EU engagement in all three countries, but the overall intervention of the EU ahead of accession scarcely went beyond *acquis* conditionality to ensure effective legislation for the equality of all citizens of nation-states.[34] This specific form of engagement did not privilege focus on ethnicity as a reason for discrimination, on the one hand, while at the same time promoting state capacity to address issues with their citizens within the remit stated in national legislation, on the other.[35] Both of these types of EU engagement strengthened the ethnic perceptions of politics with the majorities while further disempowering the minorities from claiming that the origin of their experienced inequality lay with the design of the state as nation-states.

The institutions of the nation-state created in the early years of transition in multi-ethnic post-communist states were based on the view of ethnicity as an unalienable resource of the state and central to all political processes. As a result, while institutions of the state have invited state and non-state actors to seek amendments of political institutional structures in line with their group-based perceptions of whom the state should serve, all political actors in post-communist states needed to identify foremost as members of ethnic communities to achieve due representation in nationalising state structures. The central role attributed to ethnic identity in the design of political institutions allowed majorities, both elites and publics, to secure larger spoils in a process of resource redistribution while avoiding the revision of consensus on state ownership. Community-based claims for territorial autonomy at the end of socialism were seen as ushering in territorial separation in favour of creating contingent ethno-territorial nations, suggesting the persistent and thus institutionalised role of ethnicity in post-communist politics and politicking.

Overall, as we have shown in this section, though many scholars claim that ethic mobilisation was typical in the earlier years of communist demise it has subsided with the establishment of new regimes. However, as we have demonstrated, the new polities in Macedonia, Lithuania and Slovakia have inscribed ethnicity into their fundamental political institutions and created a useful reference point for politicking throughout. All political processes were essentially ethnic in nature. Studies of ethno-political mobilisation in the late communist years have significantly informed our understanding of the pre-requisites essential for successful ethnic politicking with the aim of establishing a nation-state for the dominant ethnicity and later facilitate the political mobilisation of the majority group behind the existing institutions of the nation-state. They put the comparative importance of class, ideological consistency and centre/periphery relations to the test, suggesting that nation-state building has been particularly successful where certain conditions were fulfilled.

Not only does this allow us to claim that ethno-political mobilisation maintained a critical role to increase the ethnic rallying of minorities in these nationalising states, but it also has facilitated the compartmentalisation of minority mobilisation to regions where they could attain any significant degree of success in amortising state institutions' impact on non-dominant ethnic groups. The three case studies have several implications for the larger context of understanding how nation-state building impacted perceptions of institutions as serving dominant groups across much of the CEE and required minority communities to rally for access to institutions at a regional level to serve the community that was in the majority.

2. STATES GAINING RECOGNITION IN THE CONTEXT OF INTER-STATE RELATIONS

As we have discussed in the preceding two sections of the chapter, different actors have sought to advance their specific interests in the context of post-communist state building: domestic political actors sought to consolidate their pivot position in policymaking but entrenched the ethno-national ascendancy principle in the national institutions, and nation-states were thus seen as trusted institutions by domestic citizens to deliver on their promise of preferential treatment of the ethnic majority domestically, and later in the regional context, especially with regard to the kin-minority in neighbouring states. At the same time, domestic political actors have been able to further consolidate institution building as an ethno-national project that allowed actors at the EU level to further perceptions of the link between the nation and the state, and minimise the challenge posed domestically by the presence of the minority to institutions of the state. Both domestic actors and European-level actors found them locked in a positive relationship with nation-state institutions, while at the same time neutralising contending claims of minority actors as well as external kin-states of minorities for revision of state-level institutions. Central to these processes was the institutionalisation of ethnicity as a politically crucial category for the functioning of nation-states domestically as institutions trusted by their citizens and esteemed by their neighbouring states as potent actors able to regulate domestic issues effectively. Where does the EU approach as an arbiter of domestic disputes over issues of minority rights and protection domestically, as well as inter-state organizations regulating the equal participation of all member-states, fit into this framework?

In this section, we illustrate how the engagement of the EU in and promotion of individual-focussed, non-discrimination rules has under-run the potential implementation of minority protection at large, while strengthening the group-based rationale of nation-state functionality in countries where ethnicity has remained the most salient identity of all politically relevant ones. It is our claim that the rule of individual equality rather than collective group rights has been effective in further privileging the resourceful citizens of states, while disadvantaging the under-resourced and politically irrelevant citizens—more often than not, members of minorities.

Our focus on the role the EU played in building states for the majority nations in three cases above indicates the overall preference of member-states for an individual country's political institutions to assume the responsibility for transposition and application of legislation agreed upon by members of the organization already in place before post-communist accession.[36] However, the 'light touch' approach to ensuring the criteria for EU accession were met as regards to minority issues in accession countries and can be explained best not by the limited capacity of both the organization and the states but as a result of common acknowledgement of sovereignty of nation-states over their territory, citizenry and policymaking capacities.

During the period of accession, Lithuania was exposed to a weaker form of political conditionality with the much broader aim of consolidating the leading role of the domestic majority over policymaking. This country's progress in the area of minority protection, therefore, was rarely identified as not having met its obligations vis-à-vis its minority groups and has rarely been studied as a non-compliant. The presence of three vocal minority communities in Lithuania (Russians, Poles and Roma) allowed the most effective way of ensuring control over political processes in the hands of Lithuanian political elites.

In the case of the Polish minority in Lithuania, its kin-state had also a rather limited space to call for increased protection and support of its ethnic groups in another EU accession country, because Poland itself had been dealing with minority rights issues in Upper Silesia. In this sense, to comply with directives on non-discrimination and minority protection during the EU accession, Lithuanian governments passed the law on equal treatment and instated effectively institutional benchmarks for the prevention of discrimination.[37] However, the implementation of the non-discrimination directive from 2005 came together with the ultimate dismantling of the comprehensive minority protection legislation in the country and the disbanding of the governmental office for national minorities in 2009.[38] The central institution in place to monitor implementation, the Ombudsman's Office of the Republic of Lithuania, functioned as an accredited national human rights office and ensured full compliance with the principles set out by the Council of Europe for minority groups as well as human rights protection. However, Lithuania's Ombudsman was established post-accession, indicating the alignment of domestic institutions with the norms of the minority rights lobby and observing that respect for individuals rather than group rights of minorities was driven by domestic considerations rather than as a result of the EU accession process.

Slovakia was the focus of much greater interest during the accession period for two reasons. First, domestic political elites failed continuously and repeatedly to heed concerns of international observers regarding *acquis* conditionality, particularly with regard to the rights of Roma.[39] Secondly, the Hungarian minority in Slovakia drew considerable interest from Hungary itself and hence made domestic minority issues a potential liability for the EU as a whole.[40] Creating a durable solution for minority groups in Slovakia therefore was a much more challenging case, especially as the ethnocentric rhetoric of Slovak political elites directly challenged both European observers' claims of institutional anti-Roma sentiment and Hungarian politicians' claims about discrimination against their ethnic kin. Neither stance presented Slovakia in a positive light.[41]

As in Lithuania, Slovak political elites were reluctant to entrench comprehensive minority rights and delayed the adaptation of comprehensive anti-discrimination legislation until May 2004, effectively until after EU accession. Similarly to Lithuania, the concentrated settlement of the minority in Slovakia facilitated its comparative success in electoral politics and later contestation of domestic majority policymakers to disengage from adapting institutions in order to accommodate the interests of minority groups. Although one could expect domestic policymakers to focus on adaptive strategies and negotiate the constraints of state institutions with those requests made by actors of the EU, we see here that the premium was placed on further entrenching the primacy of domestic policymaking within political institutions, foregoing their revision.[42] It was widely acknowledged that the Slovak state exists primarily to serve the majority interests. Coordinated policies on which to build long-term stable relations between ethnic groups post-accession were largely absent thanks to the vocal opposition of the SNP and Vladimir Mečiar.[43] It is on this basis that political actors continued to operate throughout the period of accession and as such sought to assess the best options for their ethnically defined core constituency.

However, the EU did not enter the stage primarily to act as an arbiter in domestic affairs and was reluctant to focus on issues of Hungarian minority protection and Roma non-discrimination.[44] Rather, principles of domestic sovereignty in decision making and the emphasis on external neutrality were emphasised in order to grant opportunities for domestic actors to consolidate the domestic rule of law. In so doing, the EU also indicated in no clear terms that with regards to the Hungarian minority in Slovakia, Hungary should not be involved in the dispute more than necessary in order not to destabilise domestic (Slovak) decision-making processes.

In this light, the Slovak constitutional court decided in 2005, in relation to positive discrimination legislation, to declare group-based support for minority rights as contradicting the equality principles of Slovakia's constitution. As such, all international organizations, the OSCE, Council of Europe and the EU as potential agents of domestic change have pushed for policy change to ensure non-group-based equality and have indirectly sided with the Slovak constitutional court on the principle of ethnic ascendancy in regulating domestic minority issues. The accountability of Slovak political institutions to members of sizable minority groups was thereby removed from the agenda of democratisation.[45] All in all, these dynamics only added to the perspective that both were operating following the principle of increasing state capacity to ensure that domestic policymaking stayed in line with the constitutional principles of nation-state sovereignty.

Slovakia's political entrepreneurs were talking up the issue of potential disloyalty on the part of the Hungarian minority and raised fears of Hungarian irredentism. In practical terms, conditions remained in place that allowed Hungarian political elites to function as before in the regions of compact Hungarian residence. Across Southern Slovakia, Hungarians continuously catapulted their own political entrepreneurs into regional administrations and cast near unanimous votes in favour of the SMK-MKP. Similarly, in Lithuania the regional concentration of Poles and their electoral loyalty to the LLRA allowed an in situ use of liberal legislation on ethnic minorities, passed before de facto independence of the country from the Soviet Union. Ultimately, in all three cases, the lack of coherence in the majorities' ethnopolitical entrepreneurs' action, as in Macedonia, or the lack of the majorities' opposition to de facto regional minority self-government, as in Lithuania and Slovakia, discouraged minority ethno-political mobilisation against the majorities' ethno-political agendas.

In Macedonia, ethnic Albanians were represented in national parliaments throughout the 1990s; yet only following the engagement of international actors in the aftermath of the 2001 conflict did proportional representation create ample opportunity for ethnic minorities to spill regional political dynamics into national policymaking (though again only to become marginalised in the majoritarian system). In post-Ohrid Macedonia, additional features of the political system were made available in order to facilitate minority ethnic-based mobilisation.[46] To get their foot in the door of national politics, political entrepreneurs of the Albanian minority had to frame their

claims in terms compatible with those of the Macedonian majority and col-
lect ethnic votes from their own electorate. Yet minority political entrepreneurs were unable to provide a distinct set of issues radically different from
those embraced by the political parties of the majority and thus had to rally
on an explicitly ethnic platform.[47] Ethnic politicking on minority platforms,
therefore, further established a clear majoritarian political culture that was
radically different from that of the majority in content, but highly similar in
form. Throughout the 2000s, Macedonian political parties drew on feelings
of resentment and geopolitical insecurity among the majority electorate to
legitimise a strict ethno-national perspective on state ownership, leaving
many minority members in the 'grey' zone of political participation, and
pushed for language regulations, including the outright prohibition of minority language use in public. Access to higher education in Albanian was cut
off with the erection of state borders to Kosovo, and, failing to produce
educated Albanian citizens, it foreclosed equal participation in the political,
social and economic life of all citizens of Macedonia.[48]

Given the diversity of post-communist societies and their shared aspiration to join the EU, European organizations were in a particularly strong
position to insist on a redefinition of states' relationship with their ethnically
diverse residents away from ethnic categories. This point was of particular
importance for countries that emerged out of former socialist federations,
including Lithuania, Slovakia and Macedonia. Revising ethno-centric political institutions so that they could account to all residents regardless of their
ethnic identities was an equally pressing issue for more homogeneous states
such as Poland, the Czech Republic, Hungary and Albania, all of which
hosted minority populations that represented fewer than 10 percent of the
overall population, as well as for comparatively large states such as Bulgaria
and Romania with regionally concentrated minority groups with a history of
antagonism with the titular majority.[49] However, rather than revising the
approach to nation-state building, EU integration only further allowed domestic elites to continue with their ambiguous relationship with resident non-
titular groups, while keeping their neighbouring states' rhetoric over competing narratives of nation building at bay.

Whereas Florian Bieber has consistently emphasised that the 'EU's approach has relied strongly on the effect of conditionality as a tool of state
building', and that the 'conditionality approach has been largely ineffective
in regard to state building',[50] there is indeed a point of concern about the
remit of policy delivery by post-communist states. Bieber identifies a lack of
national political elites' commitment to EU integration and issues relating to
the EU's failure to effectuate change in accession countries. Indeed, more
recently, Erin Jenne and Florian Bieber indicated in their study of Montene-
gro that 'the national institutions and nationalizing elites themselves may be
less important for the success of any given national project than the wider

environment in which they operate'.[51] That is, if national identities do not map on to identity cleavage across the geopolitical neighbourhood, nation-states will find it hard to consolidate political institutions and effectively deliver policies to manage an ethnically diverse society via institutions of a state servicing primarily the majority.

Across the board of Central Eastern European states, the EU accession played a pivotal role in confirming that the relationship between the originally nationalising state and its ethnically diverse populace is the domain of nation-state regulation. While in the first half of the 1990s post-communist states sought to consolidate their sovereign control over the population by foisting ethno-national ideology and culturalist political institutions on their populations, the prospect of EU accession led most to see their assertiveness as being rewarded by international organizations, most of which operated on the presumption that states are best left alone to determine their domestic policies.

Adherence to the Copenhagen Criteria not only made states that were to preferably serve majority populations only take greater consideration and pay lip service to the interests of all residents—majority and minority alike—but also signalled a new corrective for political claims of minority citizens versus the state: with the principle of anti-discrimination overriding that of minority group rights, institutions of the nation-states could now focus on the functionality of policies for the body of the citizenry. However, the original design of political institutions in place and practices on the ground lagged. This superficial restructuring of state-society interactions did not result in greater responsibility of the state towards the entire population. Different rates of commitment to equal access of majority and minority populations remained in place across the region, and state-bearing nations' privileged access to polity was rarely revised in full.[52]

These dynamics in minority participation, however have been the focus of research on minority protection primarily because the previous exclusion of individuals of certain groups remained omnipresent in the region despite *acquis* transposition. The increased visibility of individuals from non-dominant groups has been achieved at the expense, in our view, of greater attention to how domestic political institutions subverted change in the substantial betterment of minority situations. This has, in fact, liberalised access to the political process for those who were already showing sufficient ascendancy to national majority dominance in politics of polities serving the majority and policies hampering equal participation by minorities. Domestic political institutions in accession states, therefore, were tasked with the management of ethno-cultural diversity but maintained their design as institutions of nationalising states. Equally, international organizations were not entirely free to charge their member-states with abuse of jointly agreed norms and, as a result, watered down the requirements from and advice to political actors in accession states to enact principles of group protection.

This changing emphasis from minority to human rights in domestic and international arenas during and after the 2004 enlargement round serves as a useful point of illustration. In both time periods, the emphasis on minority rights has gained currency to ensure state capacity to entrench sovereignty over domestic populations as well as enhance social cohesion pressures on those who were likely to challenge the nation-state design. At the same time, the focus on empowering minority communities by offering guarantees through sets of minority-specific rights was undermined by the EU's preference for devolving to nation-states decisions on who was to be designated as a minority, factually allowing the exclusion of potentially problematic groups from the remit of minority protection.

By focussing on human rights via non-discrimination legislation, the EU encouraged nation-states to empower individuals rather than groups and engage positive policies to tap individual-focussed protection from discrimination. Many such accession states' policies therefore invoked minority protection but have done rather the opposite. They diffused the impact of positive measures that promoted group identities of majorities as the optimal benchmark for individual members of the minority to achieve in order not to face discrimination and, as a result, destabilised identity-based groups as actors able to challenge existing institutional set-ups.

This results in both international organizations and domestic political actors tasked with minority management operating within frameworks inscribed in domestic political institutions across EU member-states. Nation-state institutions' stability as structures despite their appearance as agents of change became even more paramount in the light of pressures experienced by domestic policymakers from international organizations during the accession phase. As most domestic political actors could facilitate only that domestic policy change that was possible and feasible in the context of institutions of nation-states already accepted as key to EU accessions, any innovation to challenges coming from either the EU or domestic actions was itself the result of political institutional pressures in other states. As structures central to all our understanding of interactions between international organizations, domestic political actors and sub-state, minority political elites, it is the capacity of domestic political institutions to frame actors' perceptions of possible and desirable actions that determined the likelihood of action, as well as on its dynamic and direction of policy changes domestically. The very stability of institutions of the state in the process of EU accession indicated that decision making at national levels will maintain centre stage regardless of the EU's common policy priorities.

One could legitimately expect that during the process of EU accession, some of the core institutions of the state in accession countries would experience some renovation in order to deliver better—that is, more liberal—political outcomes to citizens they affect. This is, after all, one of the benchmarks written in the Copenhagen Criteria for accession and relating to democratic decision making. However, given that different types of relations exist between actors at the level of international organizations and domestic policymakers, we are much more likely to see the façade of policy change without fundamental revisions of institutional designs of nation-states that determine policy developments in the area of ethnic diversity management.[53] In other words, we observe changes that do not necessarily translate into a more inclusive mode of political decision making. Rather, they indicate superficial adaptations to European directives within the context of the existing nation-state institutional framework.

Fundamentally, despite limited experience with democratic political institutions, post-communist policymakers were well experienced in ensuring the dominance of majoritarian principles: states' ethno-political agenda was coherent enough to render unanimous support from majority populations, but offered enough leeway for representatives of the minority to see opportunity in, for example, state policies of non-discrimination, so as to disengage from other minorities' concerns. Seeking integration into one, majority-defined ethno-national sociocultural and political opportunity structure, political elites of the minority across the region have changed allegiance so as to avail of perceived options for integration. This made it impossible for minority communities to envisage their own agendas as being coherent, without reference to the ethno-political agenda of the majority, disallowing consolidation of their political representation as anything but ethnic.

For example, when being monitored for EU accession, Estonian governments could not press too hard on resident Russian speakers (who were not even recognised as minorities but were relegated to the status of non-citizens) and offered a range of opportunities for minority individuals' integration into the political, economic and social life of the state. The Estonian state opted for a range of laws that guaranteed previously inaccessible opportunities for the country's minority groups. First came the relaxation in naturalisation procedures; then followed programmes supporting language acquisition, and ultimately a range of society integration programmes were put into place. These measures are largely believed to have helped dismantle Estonia's minority representation in parliament and caused the shift of the Russian vote from the 'Russian parties' to statewide—that is, majority-led—parties.[54]

The observers of nation-building strategies deployed across the post-communist world often conclude that political entrepreneurs of the majority have made a range of erroneous decisions that made their task of consolidating borders of the state with those of the nation more difficult. However, far from undermining the position of the majority, many crucial decisions in crafting political institutions of the state were rather effective in reducing opportunities for minority ethno-political entrepreneurs to mobilise their support base.

In the case of Romania, participation of the Democratic Union of Hungarians in Romania (UDMR) in governments between 1996 and 2012, especially during the period of EU accession, prevented more radical claims of the Hungarian minority from influencing the redesign of political institutions. Generous support brokered by the UDMR for regions where it garnered the Hungarian vote allowed resource redistribution according to majoritarian principles and benefitted regional majorities throughout the country. The compartmentalisation of minority representatives and the exclusion of more radical minority voices from participation in government coalitions mainstreamed concerns of non-core ethnics into Romanian politics.[55] Additional concessions granted access to higher education in Hungary and engagement with the kin-state of the minority through the institutions of the EU and further removed issues related to the institutionalisation of majority ethnicity in political institutions of the state from Romanian politicking.

Similarly, in two of the cases we discussed earlier, Slovakia and Lithuania, the effects of state institutions' integration into the EU framework on the one hand and the effects of domestic political actors' communication about their objectives as a part of EU accession confirmed that principle of national (read ethno-national) sovereignty would be principled. The two states are particularly interesting because they demonstrate two types of non-core resident communities: a national minority group with a 'state of its own' elsewhere, and the Roma community. It is often suggested that different groups have caused a differential impact of conditionality during the EU accession: *acquis* conditionality targeting the individual and softer political conditionality targeting group rights.[56] Eleven years on from accession, it is obvious that originally different institutional responses in Slovakia and Lithuania did not translate into long-term change in domestic actors' core beliefs about the utterly ethno-national character of the state. This comparison between Lithuania and Slovakia allows us to see that development in the non-discrimination and minority rights agendas did not preclude institutionalisation in majority favouritism in the public space. Indeed, domestic policymakers have often dismissed international actors' criticism of domestic policies as ultimately empty talk, because issues that needed transposition went against domestic institutional commitment to the majority nation.

Overall these case studies support the initial assumption made that only because majority political entrepreneurs have demonstrated the ability to shift their political preferences ahead of EU accession that ethnic issues have been taken off the political agenda entirely. Rather the opposite, for political elites have been more able to refer to issues germane to changes of political institutions in their favour as those serving the interest of the nation-state without referencing ethnic issues; when minority representatives made similar claims, these were easily dismissed as ethnic politicking.[57] Caught in the ethno-political crossfire of majority political entrepreneurs, minorities were unable to increase their appeal to accommodate ethnic, cultural, and linguistic rights for their groups in the situation in which the majorities were using minorities as scapegoats for a range of issues defined as non-ethnic on their own political agenda.

Where minority populations could not be marginalised by nation-states servicing the majority from the political process that found themselves under the scrutiny of international observers (either in the course of EU accession, as in Slovakia and Lithuania, or bound by the Ohrid agreement in Macedonia), they granted opportunities for self-administration, which in turn diminished calls for the ethno-political mobilisation of minorities at the national level. Yet again, majority political entrepreneurs have not withdrawn ethno-national rhetoric from politicking; rather, it became the *prerequisite* for participation in the political process, making it possible for minority political actors to engage in and challenge nation building and institutional consolidation of the states as ultimately national states of the majority.

CONCLUSION

What, if anything, can our approach offer by way of tools for analysing relations between states? This chapter argued that states' desire for recognition plays a significant role in politics at all levels, and this has implications for how states interact with one another, with their own citizens and with citizens of other states. The idea of recognition is, admittedly, primarily associated with 'identity politics', in our case states and groups of people by the desire for symbolic recognition on the part of marginalised groups. At this point we are in a much better position to validate our claims developed over the past three chapters—namely, that ethnic identity indeed has performed the function of the political institution in post-communist transition away from communism, a notion that later received tacit support from European security organizations supporting state building as a project of institution consolidation for and by the members of the titular groups.

First, ethno-political mobilisation of titular nations with the goal of redesigning political institutions of socialist states shows that the initial endowment with access to political institutions was differentiated on the basis of ethnicity. As such, ethno-political mobilisation was possible at the time, because perceptions of criteria for access to political participation and input into state building and institutional design of the state privileged titular political elites. Subsequently, the continued presence of political parties running on an ethnic ticket in all post-communist countries makes clear that although ethno-national mobilisation of the majority community might have abated following states' independence, these continue to fuel the ethno-political mobilisations of minorities.

Secondly, the involvement of international actors in the state-building processes across the post-communist region was closely aligned to direct links between monitoring implementation of non-discrimination legislation, either in connection to EU conditionality (Lithuania) or in securing good neighbourly relations of EU accession states (Slovakia) or regional stability in the EU neighbourhood (Macedonia). To this effect, monitoring was complemented with significant institutional, financial and technical support for state building and implicit acknowledgement of minority rights. The very fact of international involvement in and support for developing state institutions' accountability to resident minorities suggests that most, if not all, states in the region (and Macedonia, Slovakia and Lithuania specifically) were designed as nation-states of the national majority.

Finally, the political mobilisation of the populace in Lithuania, Slovakia and Macedonia has been severely limited; thus, its impact on changes of state institutions has been restricted. Yet, where mobilisation has taken place, ethnic communities that are not in the majority have almost exclusively been driven by it. It took place as a result of the limited responsiveness of state builders, almost exclusively majority representatives, to popular claims for greater accommodation of ethno-cultural diversity. This particularly, as our case studies illustrate, is indicative of the fact that ethnicity might have lost its role as a resource for the mobilisation of the majority, but this is because it became a distinct political institution in all three states.

NOTES

1. Enze Han, Joseph O'Mahoney, and Christopher Paik, 'External Kin, Economic Disparity and Minority Ethnic Group Mobilization', *Conflict Management and Peace Science* 31, no. 1 (1 February 2014): 49–69, doi:10.1177/0738894213501762.

2. Richard Wright, Mark Ellis, and Virginia Parks, 'Immigrant Niches and the Intrametropolitan Spatial Division of Labour', *Journal of Ethnic and Migration Studies* 36, no. 7 (2010): 1033–59.

3. Maria Berger, Christian Galonska, and Ruud Koopmans, 'Political Integration by a Detour? Ethnic Communities and Social Capital of Migrants in Berlin', *Journal of Ethnic and Migration Studies* 30, no. 3 (2004): 491–507.

4. Liora Norwich, 'Fighting by the Rules: A Comparative Framework for Exploring Ethnic Mobilization Patterns in Democratic Contexts', *Ethnopolitics* 14, no. 4 (2015): 354–81, doi:10.1080/17449057.2015.1015323.

5. Milada Anna Vachudova, *Europe Undivided: Democracy, Leverage, and Integration After Communism* (Oxford: Oxford University Press, 2005).

6. John T. Ishiyama, 'Ethnopolitical Parties and Democratic Consolidation in Post-Communist Eastern Europe', *Nationalism and Ethnic Politics* 7, no. 3 (2001): 25–45; Mária M. Kovács, 'Standards of Self-Determination and Standards of Minority-Rights in the Post-Communist Era: A Historical Perspective', *Nations and Nationalism* 9, no. 3 (1 July 2003): 433–50, doi:10.1111/1469-8219.00105.

7. Charles King, *Extreme Politics: Nationalism, Violence, and the End of Eastern Europe* (Oxford: Oxford University Press, 2009).

8. Timofey Agarin, 'Nation-State Building with the Bear in Mind: The Impact of the Russian Federation in Post-Soviet "Breakaway" Regions', in *Extraterritorial Citizenship in Postcommunist Europe*, eds. Timofey Agarin and Ireneusz Pawel Karolewski (Lanham, MD: Rowman & Littlefield, 2015), 109–34.

9. Sherrill Stroschein, *Ethnic Struggle, Coexistence, and Democratization in Eastern Europe* (Cambridge: Cambridge University Press, 2012).

10. Anna Drake and Allison McCulloch, 'Deliberating and Learning Contentious Issues: How Divided Societies Represent Conflict in History Textbooks', *Studies in Ethnicity and Nationalism* 13, no. 3 (2013): 277–94, doi:10.1111/sena.12045; Henry E. Hale, 'The Parade of Sovereignties: Testing Theories of Secession in the Soviet Setting', *British Journal of Political Science* 30 (2000): 31–56.

11. Susan Olzak, *The Global Dynamics of Racial and Ethnic Mobilization* (Stanford: Stanford University Press, 2006).

12. Maria Koinova, *Ethnonationalist Conflict in Postcommunist States. Varieties of Governance in Bulgaria, Macedonia, and Kosovo* (Philadelphia: University of Pennsylvania Press, 2013).

13. Sergiu Gherghina and George Jiglau, 'Explaining Ethnic Mobilisation in Post-Communist Countries', *Europe-Asia Studies* 63, no. 1 (2011): 49–76, doi:10.1080/09668136 .2011.534302.

14. For comparison, see Eiki Berg and Wim van Meurs, 'Borders and Orders in Europe: Limits of Nation and State-Building in Estonia, Macedonia and Moldova', *Journal of Communist Studies and Transition Politics* 18, no. 4 (2002): 51–74.

15. Pål Kolstø, *Political Construction Sites: Nation-Building in Russia and the Post-Soviet States* (Boulder, CO: Westview Press, 2000); Dmitry Gorenburg, *Minority Ethnic Mobilization in the Russian Federation* (Cambridge: Cambridge University Press, 2003).

16. Zsuzsa Csergo, *Talk of the Nation: Language and Conflict in Romania and Slovakia* (London: Cornell University Press, 2007).

17. Erin K. Jenne, *Ethnic Bargaining: The Paradox of Minority Empowerment* (London: Cornell University Press, 2007).

18. Judith G. Kelley, *Ethnic Politics in Europe: The Power of Norms and Incentives* (Oxford: Princeton University Press, 2004).

19. Chris J. Bickerton, Bastien Irondelle, and Anand Menon, 'Security Co-Operation beyond the Nation-State: The EU's Common Security and Defence Policy', *JCMS: Journal of Common Market Studies* 49, no. 1 (2011): 1–21.

20. David J. Galbreath and Jeremy W. Lamoreaux, 'The Baltic States as "Small States": Negotiating the "East" by Engaging the "West"', *Journal of Baltic States* 39, no. 1 (2008); Zhidas Daskalovski, 'Democratic Consolidation and the "Stateness" Problem: The Case of Macedonia', *Global Review of Ethnopolitics* 3, no. 2 (2004): 52–66, doi:10.1080/14718 800408405165; Stefan Wolff, '"Bilateral" Ethnopolitics after the Cold War: The Hungarian Minority in Slovakia, 1989–1999', *Perspectives on European Politics and Society* 2, no. 2 (2001): 159–95.

21. Eben Friedman, 'The Ethnopolitics of Territorial Division in the Republic of Macedonia', *Ethnopolitics* 8, no. 2 (2009): 209–21, doi:10.1080/17449050802243418.

22. Pavlos I. Koktsidis, 'Nipping an Insurgency in the Bud—Part I: Theory and Practice of Non-Military Coercion in FYR Macedonia', *Ethnopolitics* 12, no. 2 (2013): 183–200.

23. Kevin Deegan-Krause, 'Uniting the Enemy: Politics and the Convergence of Nationalisms in Slovakia', *East European Politics & Societies* 18, no. 4 (2004): 651–96.

24. Jurate Novagrockiene, 'The Development and Consolidation of the Lithuanian Political Party System', *Journal of Baltic Studies* 32, no. 2 (2001): 141–55.

25. Geoffrey Pridham, 'The Slovak Parliamentary Election of September 2002: Its Systemic Importance', *Government and Opposition* 38, no. 3 (2003): 333–56.

26. Tim Haughton, 'Exit, Choice and Legacy: Explaining the Patterns of Party Politics in Post-Communist Slovakia', *East European Politics* 30, no. 2 (2014): 1–20, doi:10.1080/ 21599165.2013.867255.

27. Richard C. M. Mole, *The Baltic States from the Soviet Union to the European Union: Identity, Discourse and Power in the Post-Communist Transition of Estonia, Latvia and Lithuania* (London: Routledge, 2012).

28. Maria Koinova, 'Why Do Ethnonational Conflicts Reach Different Degrees of Violence? Insights from Kosovo, Macedonia, and Bulgaria during the 1990s', *Nationalism and Ethnic Politics* 15, no. 1 (2009): 84–108.

29. Pavlos I. Koktsidis, 'How Conflict Spreads: Opportunity Structures and the Diffusion of Conflict in the Republic of Macedonia', *Civil Wars* 16, no. 2 (3 April 2014): 208–38, doi:10.1080/13698249.2014.927703.

30. See, for example, Christina Isabel Zuber and Edina Szöcsik, 'Ethnic Outbidding and Nested Competition: Explaining the Extremism of Ethnonational Minority Parties in Europe', *European Journal of Political Research*, 1 July 2015, doi:10.1111/1475-6765.12105.

31. Zsuzsa Csergo, 'Beyond Ethnic Division: Majority-Minority Debate About the Post-communist State in Romania and Slovakia', *East European Politics and Societies* 16, no. 1 (2002): 1–29.

32. Katie Attwell, 'Ethnocracy without Groups: Conceptualising Ethnocratiser States without Reifying Ethnic Categories', *Ethnopolitics* (22 April 2015): 1–16, doi:10.1080/17449057.2015.1035559; Elena Gadjanova, 'What Is an Ethnic Appeal? Policies as Metonymies for Ethnicity in the Political Rhetoric of Group Identity', *Ethnopolitics* 12, no. 3 (2013): 307–30, doi:10.1080/17449057.2012.730261.

33. Alexander Agadjanian, 'Revising Pandora's Gifts: Religious and National Identity in the Post-Soviet Societal Fabric', *Europe-Asia Studies* 53, no. 3 (2001): 473–88; Sean Carey, 'Undivided Loyalties: Is National Identity an Obstacle to European Integration?' *European Union Politics* 3, no. 4 (2002): 387–413.

34. Virginie Guiraudon, 'Equality in the Making: Implementing European Non-Discrimination Law', *Citizenship Studies* 13, no. 5 (1 October 2009): 527–49, doi:10.1080/136210 20903174696.

35. Jose-Maria Arraiza, 'Good Neighbourliness as a Limit to Extraterritorial Citizenship: The Case of Hungary and Slovakia', in *Good Neighbourliness in the European Legal Context*, eds. Dimitry Kochenov and Elena Basheska (Leiden: Brill Nijhoff, 2015).

36. Ece Ozlem Atikcan, 'European Union and Minorities: Different Paths of Europeanization?', *Journal of European Integration* 32, no. 4 (2010): 375–92.

37. Vesna Popovski, *National Minorities and Citizenship Rights in Lithuania, 1988–1993* (Houndmills: Palgrave, 2000); Thomas Lane, *Lithuania: Stepping Westward* (London: Routledge, 2002).

38. See chapter 9, in Timofey Agarin, *A Cat's Lick: Democratisation and Minority Communities in the Post-Soviet Baltic* (Amsterdam: Rodopi, 2010).

39. Peter Vermeersch, 'Ethnic Mobilisation and the Political Conditionality of European Union Accession: The Case of the Roma in Slovakia', *Journal of Ethnic and Migration Studies* 28, no. 1 (2002): 83–101.

40. Tanja Mayrgündter, 'The Implementation of the ECRML in Slovakia under Construction: Structural Preconditions, External Influence and Internal Obstacles', *Perspectives on European Politics and Society* 13, no. 4 (1 December 2012): 480–96, doi:10.1080/157058 54.2012.731936.

41. Frank Schimmelfennig, Stefan Engert, and Heiko Knobel, 'Costs, Commitment and Compliance: The Impact of EU Democratic Conditionality on Latvia, Slovakia and Turkey', *Journal of Common Market Studies* 41, no. 3 (2003): 495–518.

42. Monika Frėjutė-Rakauskienė, 'The Impact of the EU Membership on Ethnic Minority Participation. Parties of Lithuanian Ethnic Minorities in the European Parliament Elections', *Politikos Mokslų Almanachas* 10 (2011): 7–30.

43. Kevin Deegan-Krause and Tim Haughton, 'Toward a More Useful Conceptualization of Populism: Types and Degrees of Populist Appeals in the Case of Slovakia', *Politics & Policy* 37, no. 4 (2009): 821–41.

44. Karen Henderson, *Slovakia: The Escape from Invisibility* (London: Routledge, 2002).

45. Pieter Van Duin and Zuzana Polackova, 'Democratic Renewal and the Hungarian Minority Question in Slovakia', *European Societies* 2, no. 3 (2000): 335–60.

46. Jenny Engström, 'The Power of Perception: The Impact of the Macedonian Question on Inter-Ethnic Relations in the Republic of Macedonia', *Global Review of Ethnopolitics* 1, no. 3 (2002): 3–17, doi:10.1080/14718800208405102.

47. George Vasilev, 'EU Conditionality and Ethnic Coexistence in the Balkans: Macedonia and Bosnia in a Comparative Perspective', *Ethnopolitics* 10, no. 1 (2011): 51–76, doi:10.1080/17449057.2010.535701.

48. Cvete Koneska, 'Ethnic Power-Sharing in Bosnia and Macedonia: Institutional Legacies of Communism', in *Institutional Legacies of Communism, Change and Continuities in Minority Protection*, eds. Karl Cordell, Timofey Agarin, and Alexander Osipov (London: Routledge, 2013), 124–38.

49. Sandra Lavenex and Nicole Wichmann, 'The External Governance of EU Internal Security', *European Integration* 31, no. 1 (2009): 83–102; Sandra Lavenex and Frank Schimmelfennig, 'Relations with the Wider Europe', *Journal of Common Market Studies* 45, no. s1 (2007): 143–62.

50. Florian Bieber, 'Building Impossible States? State-Building Strategies and EU Membership in the Western Balkans', *Europe-Asia Studies* 63, no. 10 (2011): 1783–1802, doi:10.1080/09668136.2011.618679.

51. Erin K. Jenne and Florian Bieber, 'Situational Nationalism: Nation-Building in the Balkans, Subversive Institutions and the Montenegrin Paradox', *Ethnopolitics* 13, no. 5 (2014): 431–60, doi:10.1080/17449057.2014.912447.

52. Nevena Nancheva, 'Imagining Policies: European Integration and the European Minority Rights Regime', *Journal of Contemporary European Studies* (13 July 2015): 1–17, doi:10.1080/14782804.2015.1056725.

53. For an insightful study of most recent accession states, see David Phinnemore, 'And We'd Like to Thank . . . Romania's Integration into the European Union, 1989–2007', *Journal of European Integration* 32, no. 3 (2010): 291–308; Aneta B. Spendzharova and Milada Anna Vachudova, 'Catching Up? Consolidating Liberal Democracy in Bulgaria and Romania after EU Accession', *West European Politics* 35, no. 1 (2012): 39–58; Vassilis Petsinis, 'Ethnic Relations, the EU, and Geopolitical Implications: The Cases of Estonia and Croatia', *Ethnopolitics* (4 March 2015): 1–15, doi:10.1080/17449057.2015.1017317.

54. Jennie L. Schulze, 'Estonia Caught between East and West: EU Conditionality, Russia's Activism and Minority Integration', *Nationalities Papers* 38, no. 3 (2010): 361–92.

55. Melanie H. Ram, 'Romania: From Laggard to Leader?' in *Minority Rights in Central and Eastern Europe*, ed. Bernd Rechel (London: Routledge, 2009), 180–94.

56. Miroslav Beblavý and Emília Sičáková-Beblavá, 'The Changing Faces of Europeanisation: How Did the European Union Influence Corruption in Slovakia Before and After Accession?' *Europe-Asia Studies* 66, no. 4 (2014): 536–56, doi:10.1080/09668136.2014.899767; Dovile Budryte and Vilana Pilinkaite-Sotirovic, 'Lithuania: Progressive Legislation without Popular Support', in *Minority Rights in Central and Eastern Europe*, ed. Bernd Rechel (Oxon: Routledge, 2009), 151–65.

57. See the comparative discussion of mobilisation by stateless groups in Timofey Agarin, 'Flawed Premises and Unexpected Consequences: Support of Regional Languages in Europe', *Nationalism and Ethnic Politics* 20, no. 3 (2014): 349–69, doi:10.1080/13537113.2014.937629.

Chapter Four

Extoling Minority Rights and Implementing Policies

The collapse of communism and the establishment of democratic regimes in Central Eastern Europe went hand in hand with states' growing attention with regard to minority issues. A number of states that emerged from behind the Iron Curtain had a complicated and often violent history of state and nation building. The violent demise of Yugoslavia and the onset of ethnic conflict in the region led European organizations to focus increasingly on identifying resident minorities and ensuring their protection. During the process of European integration, the issue of minorities acquired high priority for the EU, OSCE and Council of Europe as the relationship between the states, their ethnically diverse populations and the nation-building process have been historically complex. 'Respect for and protection of minorities' in the candidate states has been as important for the purposes of accession monitoring as was the 'existence of a functioning market economy as well as the capacity to cope with competitive pressure and market forces within the Union' in order to be included in the so-called Copenhagen Criteria for accession.[1] As such, European organizations' interest in norm promotion was put squarely at the heart of post-communist nation-states' engagement with their commitment to eventually join the EU.

Though considerable attention was paid to the post–Cold War engagement of EU member-states with post-communist countries and significant norm entrepreneurship of political actors in both old and new Europe, the consistency of what has emerged as the European minority rights regime has remained open to criticism. Democratic transition in Central Eastern Europe made it possible for post-communist citizens to enhance political institutions' accountability, representation of diverse social interests and respect for human rights for these countries' majorities, but it also politicised domestic ethnic identities shaping residents' interests along the lines that many refer to as nationalist politics.

1. EUROPEAN INTEGRATION AND MINORITY ISSUES IN THE EU

Both enlargement of and integration within the European Union had been taking place for several decades before post-communist states finally emerged from behind the Iron Curtain and democratically elected political leaderships of post-communist states and quickly proclaimed that joining the EU and NATO were their foreign-policy priorities. Yet during the early 1990s, few instruments to ensure accession of such a different set of states were in place. Previously, EU enlargement proceeded in piecemeal fashion, incorporating several candidate countries at a time. Therefore, it is unsurprising that the EU is often seen not only as a promoter of democratic governance across the post-communist area but also as an external state-building entrepreneur engaged in a comprehensive review of government structures. The literature on EU-driven change, whether from the conditionality standpoint or from compliance-norm socialisation or internalisation perspectives, is abundant. However, as Tesser rightly points out, 'Norm adoption did not necessarily mean norm internalisation'.[2] This is particularly remarkable as the overall 'European' content of many transposed norms across the post-communist area was largely amiss in the old member-states themselves. The only standard agreed upon by the member-states at the time was clearly held in the domestic character of policymaking in member-states in general and particularly in relation to the management of ethnic minority issues.

Indeed, member-states were reluctant to determine the scope of minority protection. Allegedly one of the central concerns for regional security across the post-communist world is that no minimal definition was agreed upon as to what makes up a minority. Only the groundwork of HCNM OSCE Max van der Stoel allowed him to propose an indicative, but utterly experience-based, 'I know a minority when I see one' quip to describe the mandate of his activities. As we have discussed above, not only were minority issues perceived in old member-states as linked directly to the notion of state sovereignty, but, across the post-communist region, dynamics of nation-state building have additionally equated minority situations with those of state security.[3] This is broadly seen in the literature as reflected in the reluctance of member-states to anchor minority clauses in the EU primary law and deal with all minority groups across the continent in a comprehensive manner.

Despite the Union's legislative and political opportunity to address minority issues systematically, the EU—particularly during the period of post-communist states' accession—was unable to challenge the central position of the nation-state in the European minority governance architecture. Instead, the OSCE and CoE were able to monitor progress of candidate countries towards EU membership consolidating—rather than challenging—the primary role played by the nation-state in the process of integration and have ushered stability rather than change in the nation-state-dominated approach to minority issues management in the EU as a whole. The exclusive approach of nation-states has therefore evolved separately from the emerging supranational governance in matters related to other policies coordinated across the Union and dominated many of the studies about the transposition, as opposed to the implementation, of minority rights norms in the new states.[4]

This external Europeanisation perspective on the application of loosely defined European standards of minority and human rights protection has restricted more than merely the ways in which policies have been adopted and understood on the ground. In a much more fundamental manner, observers of policymaking have suggested that the central issue at stake during the EU accession of post-communist states was the protection of minorities from the nation-states in which they reside.[5] Indeed, so powerful is this narrative that the discourse on minority protection has taken root across the sub-discipline and has equally often led to the emergence of the literature on minorities' empowerment.[6] We, however, believe that far from protecting minorities, nation-states, especially those whose sovereignties were being systematically challenged either by domestic ethno-political entrepreneurs of the minorities or by minority kin-states, as well as a result of population circulation across Europe, have developed various means to protect *majorities* from minorities' claims.

This, after all, has been the dominant modus operandi of the European approach to minority issues since the early twentieth century, when national sovereignty was founded upon practical but fundamentally conflicting logics of nation-state building and erecting polities where the majority, rather than a myriad of minorities, would be protected from external meddling.[7] Alongside major boundary changes in Europe after World War I, the unabridged territorial sovereignty of states was unanimously seen as a central tenet for the lasting peace in Europe.[8] This was vividly witnessed by the inability of the League of Nations to act effectively on behalf of minorities, given that post 1919, the power of the nation-state easily over-ruled the implementation of minority rights. The states established for Balts, Poles, Czechoslovaks, Yugoslavs, Romanians and Bulgarians were all built around the notion of territorial majorities. This principle equally underlined the drawing of boundaries in other parts of Europe at the time, as can be witnessed today in the northern part of Ireland. The aftermath of WWII creating a stable Europe of nation-states only further entrenched the vision of territorially bound ethnic nations, which were propped up by the two competing ideological blocs.

When it fell to Soviet domination in 1944 to 1945, the eastern part of Europe saw an unprecedented wave of forced migration, carried out in concert by the victorious wartime allies. It above all affected ethnic Germans deported from former parts of Germany annexed by the Soviet Union and Poland as well as from their former areas of settlement in Eastern and Southeastern Europe. In addition, it affected millions of Poles, Lithuanians, Ukrainians, Belarusians, Hungarians, Slovaks, Romanians and Bulgarians, who were deported from their ancestral homes to within the borders of their kin-states. As for surviving Jews, they were not spared the further misery of further forced migration and, on occasion, pogroms. Rhetorically, if not in fact, such 'population exchanges' were designed to reduce once and for all inter-ethnic competition.

The emergence of the UN world system has only further supported the view that 'what the world needs now is not protection for minorities but protection from minorities'.[9] The League of Nations model of minority protection was discredited as a meaningful tool to ensure the stability of inter-*state*, not inter-*ethnic*, relations. At the same time, while boundaries of nation-states had been reshuffled and then frozen by the Cold War, minority issues were slowly demoted to the back burner of policymaking. The focus on individual human rights was much more palpable to the nascent nation-states, as these 'were considered compatible with domestic policies aimed at both the assimilation and the transfer of potentially disloyal minorities'.[10]

Rather than revving the League of Nations' obligation toward the minorities, the UN underlined its obligation to protect individual human rights, in itself an issue of contention for many a contemporary observer in the light of nation-states' reluctance to engage with the reality of ethnically diverse populations. The UN Charter (1945), Declaration of Human Rights (1948) and the Convention on the Prevention of the Crime of Genocide (1948) all define the rights of individuals in a negative form as those of the protection of individuals rather than groups. The European Convention on Human Rights (1950)—which crucially came into force only after the internationally sponsored policy of forced migration in Europe had been completed—has stipulated protection from discrimination on the basis of 'race, colour, language, religion, association with a national minority' but has not provided for tools of implementation. Additionally, the International Covenant on Civil and Political Rights (1966) confirmed the right of minorities to practice their own culture and language, whilst in the same year the International Covenant on Economic, Social and Cultural Rights also specifically mentioned their applicability regardless of race, language or religion. However, abandoning the notion of group rights and adopting a strong focus on individual rights, security in interstate relations was far from being achieved at this point. Overall, the granting of minority group rights and the delivery of policies ensuring minority protection beyond non-discrimination were at the discretion of the individual nation-states. As Galbreath and McEvoy note, international agreement at this stage implied 'a basis for protection against discrimination rather than the empowerment of minority rights' and often required bilateral treaties and kin-state involvement on behalf of the minority group. [11]

For all its pace-setting role in the evolution of inter-state cooperation at the height of the Cold War, the Helsinki Final Act (1975) has been often lauded as having introduced the human rights dimension into the European normative architecture. However, despite its binding conclusions, it also set out that nation-states rather than citizens or groups shape inter-ethnic relations in Europe. Although the Helsinki Final Act made respect for human rights an essential element for peace, the main implication of the agreement lay in its consolidator approach to state boundaries in Europe. Thus, later the then EC put human rights on the agenda to encourage the mobilisation of citizens outside the narrow confines of socialist public space. [12] In so doing, however, it also opened the door for minority groups to develop cross-ethnic networks, usually supported by sympathetic Western activists to mount pressure on socialist states that lacked legitimacy in delivering on their promise of national self-determination across the board of communist states. [13] However, despite scant attention being paid to minority issues by international organizations during the final decade of communism, there existed a general sympathy for freeing oppressed nations from communist rule and widespread support for the national self-determination of individual peoples from the 'communist yoke'. This only further points to the critical importance the view of a territorially bounded nation played throughout the period on both parts of Europe.

The sudden disintegration of what is now known as the 'last major empire' witnessed the emergence of minority issues in international forums. This happened not least because the emergent nation-states inherited ethnically diverse populations and had to find accommodating relations with these groups' kin-states for the sake of domestic and regional stability. Much more important, the lifting of the Iron Curtain brought the image of a united Europe to mind while reminding one of great transformations seen in Western Europe after World War I. References to the Paris Peace treaties abounded and caution about minority issues and group rights suddenly made their way into the international arenas where claims for protection were often mixed with assertions of nation-state sovereignty over the resident populations of post-communist states. [14] The outbreak of ethnic violence in the Western Balkans not only challenged the view of peaceful ethnic coexistence in the former communist bloc but also underlined the precarious balance nation-states needed to maintain within their boundaries when ascertaining the power of the domestic majority and its authoritative role in defining the guiding role of the nation-state in the phase of transition.

The eruption of inter-ethnic violence particularly allowed continuous framing of minority issues within the state security paradigm. As the EU alongside the Council of Europe and OSCE have become involved in conflict resolution arising mainly over the status and rights of ethnic minorities, efficient management of ethnic diversity became the means of conflict prevention in the European neighbourhood. These engagements were in part compounded by the rhetorical commitment to the 'respect for and protection of minorities' signposted in the Copenhagen Criteria, which placed a premium on nation-state-initiated policies and envisaged domestic resolution of contentious issues before they could be brought to the attention of international organizations.

Although the Copenhagen Criteria were later embedded in the *acquis*, protection of minorities remained confined to being a political prerequisite for nation-states to address outside the binding framework. In the absence of a comprehensive set of policies and a firm legal basis for implementing minority—that is, group rights—the EU relied on the Council of Europe's Framework Convention for the Protection of National Minorities (1995) as a benchmark against which to evaluate candidate commitment to minority protection. Along with reports from the OSCE's High Commissioner on National Minorities (HCNM), the FCNM presented the reference point for the evolving European minority rights regime in its external application: only countries that were keen on joining the EU were expected to fulfil the criteria settled therein; yet all those states that were already members could maintain the position of interested disengagement with the FCNM.

The nature and scope of change anticipated from European integration ahead of more effective management and indeed support for ethnic diversity has not materialised even when the most willing political elites in the region have campaigned to that effect. It is likely that the low-intensity engagement with the normative background of European integration in the post-communist region has delivered at best a series of suboptimal outcomes to account for the ethnic diversity of their populations. Yet EU integration established that independent political entities in the region are the primary protectors of ethno-national interests of their resident majorities with the support and acknowledgement of the European inter-state community. [15]

During the period of EU accession, considerable changes in the area of minority rights protection were adopted in the candidate states. As a result of European conditionality, minority groups across much of Central Europe can access and have the means to participate in traditional politics. However, (more) recent research shows that despite putting a range of minority protection standards into place, across many states implementation of these norms lacked depth and coherence and remains ambiguous. [16] The issue of minority policies therefore provides an interesting testing ground for assumptions about the dynamics of policy developments in the EU member-states after the external pressures to comply subside. Indeed, minority policy was but one of many public policy areas in which the EU played a decisive role in lobbying national political actors to consider implementation and enhance provisions for minority-interest representation during the accession phase.

The case of minority-related policy changes is extremely illustrative in this context, showing just how deeply the overlaying institutions impact on dynamics of choice with domestic policy actors as well as how the effectiveness of norms in the EU is hampered by an institutional ratchet from below. Galbreath and McEvoy maintain that 'the ability for IOs to put pressure on states to change their minority rights legislation and practice is minimal without the pressure of enlargement'.[17] This presents a significant discrepancy for EU member and candidate countries in terms of their motivation to address issues related to minority protection. The *acquis* is based on non-discrimination and individual rights from which it follows that the implementation of international protection norms is individual based. At the same time, both the Council of Europe and the OSCE have been operating their missions and delivering reports on the situation of minority groups, exerting considerable conditionality pressures on candidate countries.[18]

It is therefore unremarkable that during the period of post-communist countries' accession, member-states privileged individual rights and the non-discrimination approach, having later rooted these in the *acquis* rather than focussing on minority group rights.[19] The Lisbon Treaty of 2007 mentions 'the rule of law and respect for human rights, including the rights of persons belonging to minorities' as fundamental values of the Union right at the very beginning (Article 1a), but how this commitment was to be served for the purpose of installing minority rights remained and remains uncertain, given that the Treaty itself contains no binding descriptive clauses in the area of (group) minority rights. Overall, by setting out policies that were to be implemented in the candidate countries while demoting minority protection domestically to being a second-order issue, the EU effectively signalled that while state capacity and national sovereignty were high on its agenda, compliance with the agreed norms of minority group protection only mattered as long as candidate countries faced the realistic prospect of accession.

2. INTERNATIONAL NORMS AND DOMESTIC ADAPTATION

The alignment of domestic legislation with European norms in areas as diverse as minority protection, market liberalisation, foreign direct investment and environmental regulations has been widely perceived as reflecting choices of domestic elites in response to pressures (compliance) or internalisation of international rules of the game (socialisation). During this phase, a whole new approach to analyses of international influences on domestic politics emerged to deal with the crucial dimension of the integration process: promotion of policy priorities.[20] In so doing the focus of recent research has been on 'international socialisation', 'compliance' and 'implementation' on the part of states and actors in the modern state system as if these were anthropomorphic actors.

It is not surprising, therefore, that some states are presumed to be under-, while others are over-, socialised, with the difference explaining state behaviour regarding post-accession compliance.[21] There is little doubt of how choices made by states could have been improved, but these discussions frequently neglect the negative opportunities that one needed to take into account in order to determine the dynamics, as well as the types of behaviours, political scientists observe and interpret. Such perspectives homogenise attitudes of agents involved in negotiating change, the focus on outcomes and neglecting the process itself. Because of this, they also assume that some actors are under-socialised actors (i.e., states) vis-à-vis the international community (especially in discussions on conditionality as the socialisation process) and thoroughly over-socialised vis-à-vis domestic publics (especially in discussions of international rewards extended for states' compliant behaviour).

Much of the past research analyses choices of political actors in terms of their success/failures, but it rarely sets these choices against the background of institutional opportunity structures. As a result, the focus has been laid squarely onto the role played by the accession conditionality of the candidate countries. It is often noted that conditionality equipped the EU with a very strong tool for leveraging domestic policy change, which in most cases resulted in formal compliance and adoption of legal norms, but was rather deficient in terms of implementation. Thus, it appears remarkable that scholarship has systematically defined *conditionality* as 'the interaction between multi-level actors, perceptions, interests, differentiated rewards and sanctions, temporal factors and different degrees of institutional or policy compliance'.[22]

Furthermore, despite difference in approaches, foci of case studies and methodology and conceptual toolboxes deployed, all analyses explain state compliance as if states were homogeneous actors. States are often perceived as actors shaping the international community. Social and political actors operating at the level of national politics are mostly seen as homogeneous agents of change. Studies of political parties and elites and of minority activism often discuss these actors' actions by pointing out the competing logics these select competitors follow when assessing and addressing decisions made at an international level and transposed into nation-state-level politics.[23] In so doing, the scholarship has focussed domestic political decision making across the EU member and candidate states as objects of conditionality, on the one hand, and as an outcome of learning, on another.[24] With the 'respect for and protection of minorities' made a requirement for accession in the Copenhagen Criteria, EU monitoring of this protection made sense insofar as candidate countries had to pay at least lip service to the standards and submit to scrutiny by the CoE and OSCE. EU member-states, however, though exercising considerable leverage over the monitoring process, were not subject to the same level of attention, a point noted often by the candidate countries that drew parallel between their domestic situations and those in the 'old' member-states.[25]

The wealth of literature on conditionality and its impact on domestic policies in candidate countries, and the simultaneous success *and* failure of conditionality in candidate countries, has been our focus of attention.[26] While on the one hand, the successful outcomes of the installation of minority protection policies and anti-discrimination laws has been witnessed across the board of new member-states, the EU, Council of Europe and the OSCE could claim effectively having brought about norm compliance. At the same time, however, the results of these policies have been put into questions after new member-states have joined the EU, and as many experts note, progress remained superficial and mainly touched upon legal measures, neglecting their practical enforcement.[27] The time limitation of conditionality pressures, therefore, has often been seen as a credible threat to coherence of normative space across Europe with regards to both minimal minority protection and systematic application of non-discrimination. It is here that we can effectively see that the mechanics of European integration have been directed at developing state capacity and consolidating polities, rather than policies dealing with contentious issues of minorities.

Aside from considering the fact that political elites have systematically undercut opportunities for agenda setting and claims making for domestic minorities after post-communist states have re-established national sovereignty, the impact of European integration on the effective management of ethnic diversity remained in the doldrums. This is because Western European member-states relied on domestic civic actors to influence regional policies and thus substitute state-driven with actor-driven and closer-to-people means of accommodating minority issues.[28] The widely acknowledged absence of vibrant civil society in post-communist Europe has presented a window of opportunity for nation-states to further channel minority-related activities in the direction desired. Building upon the widely shared suspicion on state authority across the post-communist region, the existing domestic political structures allowed both governments and political parties to amplify the role of existing state institutions in policymaking and further limit the influence of societal actors in day-to-day politics.[29] With domestic publics' loyalties and expectations focussed on political entities serving ethnic majority interests, the limited ability of states to withstand global challenges in economic, political and security challenges makes the idea of national sovereignty particularly attractive for new member-states. As discussed in the previous chapters, individuals from minority communities were already considerably constrained from entering and contesting the domestic policies during the initial years of transition and the alignment of European organizations behind state institutions in place, and the explicit support for growing state capacity has placed minority participation in policymaking on a par with political elites of the titular majority and made it ever more difficult.

The high dependency of political actors on the fragile set of institutions ensuring reliance of the states on factors external to, yet crucial for, domestic stability in economic, political and security arrangements have allowed political elites to maintain lukewarm public support of their public for the integration project.[30] It is not surprising, therefore, that studies of the EU's impact on domestic policy change on minority issues have focussed on actors rather than on institutions as origins of change. Indeed, attempts to make sense of post-accession behaviour in states and in communities favour an agency-focussed explanation of trajectories, rather than those that centred on explanations of institutionally determined change.

The resonance of international norms has been seen as an important factor in the state adoption of policies aimed at minority protection. Yet how do we reconcile the international advocacy work in favour of minority groups with the role that the nation-state and implicitly its institutions use to deliver these? Indeed, as Jeffrey Checkel has noted, domestic preferences for 'pre-existing norms were key in affecting agent willingness to comply with the injunctions of emerging European understandings'[31] and respond to input from international organizations as well as minorities' kin-state.

In the context of domestic decision making, therefore, the degree of fit between the inter-state norm and need for cooperation on issues of mutual interest have generated joint understanding about and consideration of nation-state interests with regard to ensuring the exercise of domestic sovereignty over the entirety of resident populations. Heather Grabbe observes that interactions between candidates and EU member nation-states created the space for new political agendas that had a permanent effect on the policy-making process by 'absorbing EU imperatives, logic and norms into domestic policy . . . empowering modernisers to change specific policies and reform political institutions'.[32] Naturally, these mutual relations were not limited to the period of accession negotiations and to candidate countries but were also witnessed in the EU member-states, all of which can be easily traced back to the growing importance of joint decision making on the basis of mutual respect for state sovereignty as well as core domestic institutions of states involved in cooperative relations in the context of accession.

The very fact that the European integration as such did not resolve issues related to the minority position of the member-states should also be kept clearly in sight at this point: despite the fact that (Western) Europe has been widely perceived as a conflict-free zone where the salience of ethnic issues had not caused instability in nation-states, the accession of post-communist countries has helped halt inter-ethnic contestations in more than just the eastern part of Europe. Spain and the UK have had their domestic, ethnic conflicts for decades and were only able to negotiate resolution with Basque and Northern Irish insurgencies in the course of the late 1990s.[33] In both of these cases, international involvement has been crucial to conflict settlement; yet the emerging set of issues in relation to the metropolitan centre and the Basque Country and Northern Ireland provinces have been made possible to a large extent thanks to the reshaping of state institutional architectures, albeit without altering the boundaries of the state itself. Similarly, the situation of German speakers in South Tyrol has been in the focus of European policymakers' attention since Austria and Italy took their grievances to the UN General Assembly to seek mutual agreement on the status of the minority rather than negotiate via the institutions of the Council of Europe.[34] All of these cases demonstrate that in the absence of arrangements at the nation-state level, minority groups are likely to lobby for international involvement to resolve issues of their protection. Failure to reach a durable solution to minority claims in the framework of the nation-state therefore did not hamper interstate relations unless the kin-state of the minority was prepared to lobby international organizations outside the EU framework.

Since the onset of post-communist democratisation, the consolidation of post-communist publics around the liberal ideals and internalisation of democratic norms was often analysed with reference to Central and Eastern European states' treatment of their resident minority communities. Policies targeting minority communities are particularly instructive for analyses of states' commitment and the advancement of liberal democratic norms. The numeric dominance of a state's titular nation allows it to sideline minority interests when setting political agendas, thereby ensuring reasonable interest representation. Under these circumstances, members of minority communities frequently have either found their interests to be underrepresented or were faced with outright exclusion from participation in power politics. On the one hand, the commitment of domestic political elites to their own publics in terms of creating and implementing policies on state territory to the advantage of European integration is vague and unclear. On the other, norms underlying state sovereignty and governments' ability to sustainably adhere to them are in a precarious position as regards the EU's own view on the role nation-state-based politics play in joint projects. Thus, political structures facilitating public support for deeper European integration and normative convergence into a coherent regime for ethnic diversity management based on non-discrimination have largely failed to challenge the nation-based model of state consolidation, democratisation and European integration inside the EU.[35]

Though institutionalist literature has long been criticised for taking an overtly static view of institutions that excel in explaining political stability, it fails to account for situations in which institutions break down and become a dependent variable in a larger process of political and social change. However, as deeper Europeanisation requires state authorities to assume greater responsibility for steering policies and initiating and implementing reform, limited domestic capacity to maintain integrity over decision making and independence of political economy demonstrate that structural conditions in place are likely to be the major stumbling block on these countries' road to deeper and comprehensive cooperation within the EU.

However, the debate on liberal policies and tangent social integration issues inside the EU and including all member-states has gained momentum over the past decade, adding depth to our understanding of why cultural diversity in European societies should not be taken for granted. Although across the enlarged EU, nation-states envisaged policies as decision making on issues of relevance for all residents, many member-states continue to lag behind the coherent normative blueprint found in the Treaties that is essential for and supportive of cultural diversity and representative of diversity and different ethnic communities on territorially bound nation-states. Despite the fact that practically all EU member-states recognise that they govern multi-ethnic societies, they fail to match rhetoric with the promotion of positive relations between the dominant and non-dominant groups.

Following post-communist accession, the EU lost the political muscle to request minority protection on the part of new member-states. This is instructive for understanding the remit of EU engagement in empowering the majorities in these countries vis-à-vis the minority populations resident therein. So despite the regularly produced progress reports on new member-states, international organizations were left with a patchy policy-focussed approach. However, while the European minority rights regime was in large part driven by the Council of Europe and the OSCE as both monitors and advocates of minority protection and have been able to advise the EU on progress, after EU enlargement we see the regime being driven by entirely legal concerns as enshrined in the EU *acquis* and later building upon the decisions of the ECJ. As such, the purely political—and as such normative—pressures on candidate countries have become a formal legal procedure, referring to a set of much more powerful legal instruments at the hands of the European Commission.

The scope for the application of EU law establishes the principle of non-discrimination on the basis of citizenship, putting migrant EU citizens de facto at an advantage compared with third-country nationals and requiring states of residence to treat all EU citizens equally with their own nationals.[36] This is achieved, if by no other means, than by exempting EU citizens from established practices of the testing of the knowledge of the local 'culture', language and history, which is recognised as a norm across member-states when testing third-country nationals during the naturalisation process. Ultimately, the protection of EU citizens from the possible intervention into their lives by the authorities of their state of residence is directly connected with the obligation to respect the identities of citizens of other member-states. It clearly applies not only to the member-states as such but also to their nationals, who are entitled to live anywhere in the Union without being forced to relinquish their cultural, political and socio-economic ties with their country of birth/origin.[37]

The conflict between the commitment to grant special rights to minorities and the fundamental importance of the status as EU citizens should not be underestimated in the context of the union of nation-states. Not only are EU citizens the most, if not the only, privileged group in the view of EU law, but they also illustrate the tension inherent to minority rights' protection and special rights enshrined in the EU legal system. Despite the markedly innovative vision of the EU that is set in the law, our everyday experience that borders between EU member-states are losing their importance has direct implications for EU citizens who are not members of the majority nation-state community.[38]

Crucially, the formal equality of all EU citizens means that the member-states' policies aiming at the 'integration' of all migrants effectively are being undermined at least in part by discouraging assimilationist tendencies in the territory of the nation-state. There is no doubt that, should EU law not prohibit nationality discrimination, member-states would eagerly subject EU citizens to the same treatment.[39] Kristin Henrard, among others, maintains that EU citizens should remain privileged and only third-country nationals should be systematically tested for the purpose of societal integration. 'This again makes sense in the context of the European integration process, since [third-country nationals] come from outside the EU Member-states and hence pose a particular challenge in terms of integration'.[40] Such statements repeat the nation-state-focussed project at the heart of the EU, suggesting that cultures of insiders are superior to those of the outsiders. Moreover, EU law does not allow abrogation from the principle of equality of EU citizens, preventing the creation of national legislation to impede the exercise of free movement, extending the essence of European integration effectively to all citizens.

3. CHALLENGES OF MINORITY ISSUES IN A EUROPE OF NATION-STATES

The present-day policies of ethnic diversity management found in EU law underline the notion of ethno-national pluralism moderated by member-states and emphasise the internal diversity of European societies. In so doing, however, the EU has clearly signposted the relevance of the nation-state as the central institution with regard to the recognition of minority groups. Arguably, the liberal anti-discriminatory approach found in various parts of the EU's treaties cannot deliver adequate policy propositions to diversity regulation because it fails to account for the domino effect that providing recognition to non-dominant groups would have on the emergence of further group-based claims for recognition, redistribution and protection.[41] However, the EU's constituent members operate precisely on the premise that internal recognition of differences does produce finer distinctions about the uniting set of political institutions that ought to cater to the culturally diverse societies. Policymakers across individual member-states are said to have been particularly reluctant to agree on a definition of *minority* for the purpose of the EU-wide approach to rights of non-dominant groups in the context of Europe at large. Specifically, the focus on the migrants and residents, differential treatment of minorities with and without a kin-state abroad and the variegated geometry of integration policies found in member-states questions the foundation of the liberal democratic principles based on the existence of group-specific rights of titular citizens of EU member-states and the presumed ethno-national neutrality of the EU institutions. Claims for recognition of the special status of the marginal minority groups and multiple marginalised social groups, such as Romani, trans-border and migrant communities, bring issues of access to resources to the centre of debate on the EU's liberal individualist approach to dealing with minority issues.

Whilst absenting itself from the discussion on what qualities determine groups' status as a minority, the EU factually guarantees the sovereignty of the nation-state as regards decisions on whose claims are legitimate, and which groups are mimicking the dominant narratives to claim their piece of the nation-state. These claims often do seek access to crucial resources of the state and operate within the context of state institutions that place majority cultures, languages and individuals at an advantage. Liberal debates on social integration therefore tend to tacitly accept the internal disagreement on the signposted policy objective: accommodation of interests of diverse societies by pursuing policies of integration.[42]

In maintaining its external role as an arbiter of claims between citizens and the state, the EU legal foundations further underline the nation-state as a subject while minorities are acknowledged to be objects of legislation. In this case, resident aliens, migrants and marginalised groups do receive a share of their right to be protected under human rights and non-discrimination legislation but are systematically excluded from active participation in the decision-making process as groups are explicitly different from the majority of the states where they reside.[43] As multiple debates on liberal multiculturalism underline, there appears to be no non-discriminatory way of distinguishing between individual identities from however vaguely defined notions of group belonging in the absence of the institutional background against which to assess the 'minority' status of a person. Ultimately, since 'ethno-national identity' has yielded prominence in the legal and political discourse of nation-states to the notion of individual capacity for independent decision making, Europe's liberal democracies have placed personal liberty on the centre stage of interactions with the nation-state.

Whilst an increasing number of ethno-cultural minorities across the EU contest bona fide objectives of those representatives who speak in their name in legislatures, representative bodies and as civil society groups, the systemic inclusion of minority groups at the level of nation-states into EU political discussion is obvious. Equality between individuals of different cultural backgrounds can hardly be guaranteed as long as it is the group that forms the focus of non-discrimination and equality protections.[44] This is because individual freedom to choose cultural and linguistic loyalties is framed (and limited) by assumptions made about these groups and in anticipation of patterns of participation by the members of the majority. Beyond making individual autonomy central for implementing equality in political participation and representation of interest in practice, it would require the revision of the EU-wide role of the nation-state in decision making over minorities in their territories.[45] In the context of exchange between the resourceful members of the majority and those representing the marginalised minority, arguments of both sides on political preferences and their goals have considerable institutional backing at the level of the EU institutions, and not in the context of nation-states claimed by one ethnic group.

Across the board of EU member-states, where the integration of minorities, migrants and marginalised groups has witnessed success, members of these communities have gained visibility once they have obtained proficiency in the state language, and ultimately engage in politics on par with and akin to the constituent majority of their countries of residence.[46] The institutions of EU member-states therefore identify and focus non-dominant groups precisely on the basis of their difference from the dominant society. Regardless of states' provision for members of non-dominant groups to 'dispose' of their individual claims and inviting them to see individual-based protection as a part of their institutionally defined opportunities for inclusion, individuals of non-dominant groups are assimilated into the nation-state political community in more than just a political manner. Only once individual members of non-dominant groups mimic the actions of the majority can they enjoy a parity of opportunity with those of the nation-state-defining majority group. Most such cases are referred to in terms of individual willingness and personal abilities to grasp opportunity provided to citizens regardless of his/ her group membership.[47]

Perceptions of choice-based identity as a centrepiece of institutions underlying sovereignty legitimise access to political membership. Indeed, the European liberal democratic agenda on Roma inclusion fails to meet its objectives, because among other things, it empties institutions of their (most obvious) group-referential cultural content, thereby providing for group-blind opportunities to function in the capacity of a citizen of the Union, member-state or civil society group. As a result, public policy spaces are increasingly defined as culturally unspecific containers of individuals, cooperating on the basis of common needs and ideals—that is, as individuals unconstrained by the institutional opportunities provided. In the process, the individual choices are 'primordialised' and preferences, rather than national, ethnic and linguistic identities, gain salience, in which previously chosen identities, such as professions, skills and places of residence, were important. Such a rationale and explanations thereof fail to appreciate that the blueprint for individual choice and action successfully pursued by members of non-dominant groups has been designed for members of majority communities.

The two lessons learnt from the internal debate on liberal approaches to ethnic diversity management provide a point of departure from which to consider the effects of European integration policies upon groups marginalised in the context of nation-states.[48] Firstly, individual options to pursue and enjoy autonomy in the context of nationalising states are informed primarily by the perspective on and experience with nation-state institutions that serve the majority group in the territory of the state. Secondly, the egalitarian implications of the EU integration project are severely constrained by the group focus at each level of policymaking, pegging individual freedoms and opportunities for self-assertion to their identity within an ethno-national community served by institutions of the nation-state. Thus, as long as political institutions at the state level regulate societal interactions restrictively on the basis of ethno-national group difference, individual needs and capacities in the context of the EU will be seen as providing individuals with an opportunity to update their subjective positions in relation to identities projected upon them by the nation-state institutions.

This principle is at work in the cases of state interaction with their indigenous, non-dominant residents, such as the Sámi in Nordic states, *gens du voyage* in France or minorities with no kin-state across the post-communist area, such as Hutsuls, Ruthenes and Vlachs. The guarantee of an individual choice of identity—as is proposed by the EU's liberal pluralism—on the basis of which the person could opt for an 'ethnicised' treatment by state institutions, extends the options for greater formal equality between individuals affected. However, it does so only in addition to group-based individual choice. In this sense, individual choice of identity works to undermine the consistency of the group and limits the scope of group protection by political institutions of states as well as European organizations. In all cases, however, as long as members of the non-dominant community do not present themselves as the members of a group different from the dominant community in the domestic institutional setting, they are to gain greater acceptance with the dominant publics.

It is therefore unsurprising that we continue to observe that individual members of non-dominant groups perceive of individual liberty in choice and equality in terms of personal opportunity, whether real or potential. However defined, these are perceived, rather than being extant. Preference formation on the basis of individual, and not unquestionable group identities, allows liberal public policymakers to diffuse responsibility from political institutions to individual users of these institutional resources and thus also refocus the debate on social integration away from the group and place an onus on the individual. The notion that a society is integrated is thus effectively sidestepped because membership in any community is not perceived as being a matter of structural resources available to individuals but rather as a choice of any one person. Liberal policymakers thus posit that individuals make up collectivities only because they chose so, and as such communities already have cohesive ties that are co-founded in individual personalised choices of membership.

The above points out that the individual-focussed, non-discrimination approach to deal with minority issues across the EU challenges the ways in which we think about groups and conceive of cultural boundaries. Additionally, in emphasising the non-group basis of individual choice formation, rather than structural constraints that individual members of non-dominant communities face in their everyday interactions with the nation-state, it is assumed that any inherent inequality between majority and minority groups would be effectively addressed. Yet non-dominant groups do not participate in the political and social process on a par with members of the dominant group precisely because they face limits of individualist concepts embedded in the structural opportunities of the day.[49] Non-dominant representatives need to be more resourceful and more embedded in opportunity structures in order to compete with those individuals with prior access to extant resources.[50] The focus on the members of non-dominant groups therefore is often underpinned by their unwillingness to cooperate with the existing institutions of the dominant society, which also indicates that it is the dominant group that can be fully exempt from taking any note of non-dominant groups' specific expectations and requirements necessary for genuinely equal participation in the first place.

By design and operation, liberal democratic institutions suggest that policies should be thoroughly individual based to alleviate existing inequalities between individuals. Such approaches naturally produce perceptions of social integration as the individual-centred identification of persons with structural opportunities are used by more successful role models to gain access to resources already available to the dominant majority. Especially where non-dominant communities struggle to access scarce (and, at times, highly contested) resources, positions of influence and benefits are controlled by the dominant group, and minority members' motivation is driven by fear of becoming invisible in a society dominated by opportunities tailored to the needs of another community. Therefore, the process of adaptation to structural opportunities by individuals of non-dominant groups is determined by structural opportunities granted by and supplied by those individuals already able to alter the institutional opportunity structure, and as such having their own stakes in decision making over the members of all, dominant and non-dominant groups. To be effective, therefore, individuals from non-dominant groups must adapt to the rules set out by a dominant community, while the dominant group remains exempt from altering their patterns of behaviour.

The ubiquitous claims for special consideration of minority and migrant issues in the context of the EU therefore suggests that political institutions in place can account for ethno-cultural difference of societies they govern, but only in a limited way. Furthermore, with institutional design at the nation-state level preventing non-dominant communities and their individual members from making informed decisions outside the framework of the nation-state institution, group differences will be relayed to the existence of the national form even where they might share a European content.

CONCLUSION

As we have outlined in the previous three chapters, EU accession has seen candidate countries transposing a significant number of legislative documentation, the *acquis* into domestic legislation. As a result of this legal convergence across the EU, we have witnessed a period of increased and deeper integration. However, such integration has barely resulted in a Europe of the regions emerging on the horizon. Rather the opposite: while nation-states' legislation proliferated, the domestic sovereignty of these countries was solidly established in the overall understanding of the EU integration process being driven by nations that are indeed represented in the Union by their states.

We have also spelled out the focus of what emerged as the post-enlargement EU-wide approach to dealing with non-dominant groups' residents on the territory of the nation-states, as well as the tentative responses from social and political, domestic and European actors to the ethnic diversity of societies governed by de jure culture-blind nation-state institutions. Simultaneously, we have seen the renewed popularity of arguments positing a 'clash of civilizations' between Western and Eastern European societies, and a new legitimacy advanced for 'ethnic profiling' and 'racialisation' of minorities in the name of social integration domestically and political integration at the EU level. The rapidity with which these discussions unfolded is striking because of the Union's liberal-democratic tradition and (multicultural) make-up of its societies. However, as we made clear earlier, liberal individualist policies purporting to manage ethnic diversity has been complicit in shaping the worldviews of Europeans through the 'ethno-national' optic on the participation in politics.

Whereas 'old' member-states have experimented with liberal multiculturalism since the late 1980s, understandings of nationally defined citizenship in the new member-states were erected after the collapse of communism and further consolidated during the accession phase. The crucial feature of this ethno-national citizenship is less the lack of provision for ethnic minority inclusion and migrant incorporation and more about national majority tutelage over political institutions of the state they own. The accession of post-communist states therefore has challenged the commitment of the Union to minority issues as the basis of intergroup equity and equality *for* political participation. It also posited a hotly debated issue on the suitability of the nation-state centre to promote a concerted EU-wide solution to the limits of ethnic diversity management.

The major investment of majorities in shoring up the role of the nation-state in domestic policymaking and as a pinnacle of national sovereignty across the post-communist accession countries only further facilitated the use and abuse of cultural differences in the eyes of 'public opinion'. The implications of this for current policies of ethnic diversity management across the Union are yet to be seen. Yet over the next three chapters we argue that the bias in favour of dominant cultures has made claims against the equality to be granted to minority issues in the public space louder over the past decade. Our contention here is that while, rhetorically, liberal policymaking sought to avoid the trap of group-focussed decision making, in practice even liberal policies need collectivities to identify their objects, set targets and create benchmarks. Inevitably, policies opining for equality of opportunity for all have undermined individual choices outside the framework of the nationally defined state institutions serving the ethnically dominant, policymaking community, on the one hand, and supported as an effective tool of capacity building by the European organizations, on the other.

In short, we believe that the EU accession of post-communist states has effectively allowed the re-establishment of democratic governance in nation-states as serving primarily their majority in order to guarantee the stability of the overall intergovernmental system of the Union. At the very least, this perception of nationally defined sovereignty across the member-states de facto reinforces the differences in resources accessible to citizens of the EU member-states via structures granting them privileged access to institutions

of the state operating in their own language, promoting and protecting majority culture.

It is this context that makes up the core of our focus over the next three
chapters, where we address the specific role nation-states play as defining the
relations between the dominant majority and non-dominant minority groups.
Each of these chapters therefore challenges the point often made in discussions on the emergent minority rights regime in Europe, in that we primarily
focus on the role nation-states continue to play in the overall architecture of
granting resident citizens recognition as minorities, not explicitly recognising
their individual rights but in a subtle way projecting the majority into a
position of dominance in titular nation-states. In so doing, the relationship
between the minority and majority has indeed been de-securitised to a degree
that allows many to claim that ethnic conflict within nation-states is unlikely
at the present juncture. However, as we illustrate, the post-enlargement peace
across post-communist Europe has been possible precisely because there is
wide agreement across the post-communist region, and increasingly across
the EU as a whole, that the states belong to the titular majority group and as
such exists primarily to serve the needs of that group.

NOTES

1. Presidency Conclusions, Copenhagen European Council 1993, 7.A.iii, http://www.
europarl.europa.eu/enlargement/ec/pdf/cop_en.pdf.
2. Lynn M. Tesser, 'The Geopolitics of Tolerance: Minority Rights under EU Expansion in
East-Central Europe', *East European Politics and Societies* 17, no. 3 (2003): 503.
3. David J. Galbreath and Joanne McEvoy, *The European Minority Rights Regime: Towards a Theory of Regime Effectiveness* (Basingstoke: Palgrave, 2011).
4. Mark A. Jubulis, 'The External Dimension of Democratization in Latvia: The Impact of
European Institutions', *International Relations* 13, no. 3 (1996): 59–73; Edward Stoddard,
'Between a Rock and a Hard Place? Internal–External Legitimacy Tensions and EU Foreign
Policy in the European Periphery', *Journal of European Integration* 37, no. 5 (24 March 2015):
553–70, doi:10.1080/07036337.2015.1019487.
5. Gwendolyn Sasse, 'The Politics of EU Conditionality: The Norm of Minority Protection
during and beyond EU Accession', *Journal of European Public Policy* 15, no. 6 (2008):
842–60.
6. Geoffrey Pridham, 'Securing the Only Game in Town: The EU's Political Conditionality and Democratic Consolidation in Post-Soviet Latvia', *Europe-Asia Studies* 61, no. 1 (2009):
51–84; Frank Schimmelfennig and Arista Maria Cirtautas, 'Europeanisation Before and After
Accession: Conditionality, Legacies and Compliance', *Europe-Asia Studies* 62, no. 3 (2010):
421–41.
7. Jennifer Jackson-Preece, *National Minorities and the European Nation-States System*
(Oxford: Oxford University Press, 1998).
8. Tove H. Malloy, *National Minority Rights in Europe* (Oxford: Oxford University Press,
2005).
9. Quoted in Allan Rosas, Jan E. Helgesen, and Diane Goodman, *The Strength of Diversity: Human Rights and Pluralist Democracy* (Dordrecht: Martinus Nijhoff, 1992), 159.
10. Jennifer Jackson-Preece, 'National Minority Rights vs. State Sovereignty in Europe:
Changing Norms in International Relations?' *Nations and Nationalism* 3, no. 3 (1997): 85.
11. Galbreath and McEvoy, *The European Minority Rights Regime*, 62.

12. Richard Davy, 'Helsinki Myths: Setting the Record Straight on the Final Act of the CSCE, 1975', *Cold War History* 9, no. 1 (2009): 1–22; Hans-Joachim Heintze, 'Contradictory Principles in the Helsinki Final Act?' *OSCE Yearbook*, 2004, 289–99.

13. Daniel C. Thomas, 'The Helsinki Accords and Political Change in Eastern Europe', *Cambridge Studies in International Relations* 66 (1999): 205.

14. Samuel H. Barnes and Janos Simon, *Popular Conceptions of Democracy in Postcommunist Europe* (Budapest: Erasmus Foundation, 1998).

15. Sean Carey, 'Undivided Loyalties: Is National Identity an Obstacle to European Integration?' *European Union Politics* 3, no. 4 (2002): 387–413; Lars-Erik Cederman, 'Nationalism and Bounded Integration: What It Would Take to Construct a European Demos', *European Journal of International Relations* 7, no. 2 (2001): 139–74.

16. Melanie H. Ram, 'Legacies of EU Conditionality: Explaining Post-Accession Adherence to Pre-Accession Rules on Roma', *Europe-Asia Studies* 64, no. 7 (September 2012): 1191–1218, doi:10.1080/09668136.2012.696813; Ulrich Sedelmeier, 'After Conditionality: Post-Accession Compliance with EU Law in East Central Europe', *Journal of European Public Policy* 15, no. 6 (September 2008): 806–25, doi:10.1080/13501760802196549.

17. Galbreath and McEvoy, *The European Minority Rights Regime*, 80.

18. John O'Brennan, '"Bringing Geopolitics Back In": Exploring the Security Dimension of the 2004 Eastern Enlargement of the European Union', *Cambridge Review of International Affairs* 19, no. 1 (1 March 2006): 155–69, doi:10.1080/09557570500501911.

19. Will Kymlicka, 'Categorizing Groups, Categorizing States: Theorizing Minority Rights in a World of Deep Diversity', *Ethics & International Affairs* 23, no. 4 (2009): 371–88.

20. Antoaneta Dimitrova and Geoffrey Pridham, 'International Actors and Democracy Promotion in Central and Eastern Europe: The Integration Model and Its Limits', *Democratization* 11, no. 5 (2004): 91–112.

21. Gwendolyn Sasse, 'Tracing the Construction and Effects of EU Conditionality', in *Minority Rights in Central and Eastern Europe*, ed. Bernd Rechel (London, New York: Routledge, 2009), 17–31.

22. James Hughes, Gwendolyn Sasse, and Claire Gordon, 'Conditionality and Compliance in the EU's Eastward Enlargement: Regional Policy and the Reform of Sub-National Government', *Journal of Common Market Studies* 42, no. 3 (2004).

23. Michael Johns, 'Quiet Diplomacy, the European Union and Conflict Prevention: Learning from the HCNM on Issues of Social Cohesion', *International Journal on Minority and Group Rights* 19, no. 3 (2012): 243–65, doi:10.1163/15718115-01903006.

24. Thomas Risse, 'Neofunctionalism, European Identity, and the Puzzles of European Integration', *Journal of European Public Policy* 12, no. 2 (2005): 291–309.

25. Michael Johns, '"Do as I Say, Not as I Do": The European Union, Eastern Europe and Minority Rights', *East European Politics and Societies* 17, no. 4 (2003): 682–99.

26. Guido Schwellnus, 'Reasons for Constitutionalization: Non-Discrimination, Minority Rights and Social Rights in the Convention on the EU Charter of Fundamental Rights', *Journal of European Public Policy* 13, no. 8 (2006): 1265–83; Rachel A. Epstein and Ulrich Sedelmeier, 'Beyond Conditionality: International Institutions in Postcommunist Europe after Enlargement', *Journal of European Public Policy* 15, no. 6 (2008): 795–805.

27. Malte Brosig, 'The Challenge of Implementing Minority Rights in Central Eastern Europe', *Journal of European Integration* 32, no. 4 (1 July 2010): 393–411, doi:10.1080/07036331003797539; Tanja Börzel, Tobias Hofmann, and Diana Panke, 'Policy Matters But How? Explaining Non-Compliance Dynamics in the EU', KFG Working Paper 24, Free University Berlin, 2011.

28. Timofey Agarin, 'Civil Society versus Nationalizing State? Advocacy of Minority Rights in the Post-Socialist Baltic States', *Nationalities Papers* 39, no. 2 (2011): 181–203.

29. Frank Schimmelfennig, 'Strategic Calculation and International Socialization: Membership Incentives, Party Constellations, and Sustained Compliance in Central and Eastern Europe', *International Organization* 59, no. 4 (2005): 833.

30. Dimiter Toshkov and Elitsa Kortenska, 'Does Immigration Undermine Public Support for Integration in the European Union?' *JCMS: Journal of Common Market Studies* 53, no. 4 (1 July 2015): 910–25, doi:10.1111/jcms.12230.

31. Jeffrey T. Checkel, 'International Institutions and Socialization in Europe', *Arena Working Papers* WP 01/11 (2001): 581.

32. Heather Grabbe, *The EU's Transformative Power: Europeanization through Conditionality in Central and Eastern Europe* (Basingstoke: Palgrave Macmillan, 2006), 51–52.

33. Angela K. Bourne, 'European Integration and Conflict Resolution in the Basque Country, Northern Ireland and Cyprus', *Perspectives on European Politics and Society* 4, no. 3 (2003): 391–415.

34. Stefan Wolff, 'The Institutional Structure of Regional Consociations in Brussels, Northern Ireland, and South Tyrol', *Nationalism and Ethnic Politics* 10, no. 3 (2004): 387–414.

35. Chris J. Bickerton, *European Integration: From Nation-States to Member States* (Oxford: Oxford University Press, 2012); John K. Glenn, 'From Nation-States to Member-States: Accession Negotiations as an Instrument of Europeanization', *Comparative European Politics* 2 (2004): 3–28.

36. Triadafilos Triadafilopoulos, 'Illiberal Means to Liberal Ends? Understanding Recent Immigrant Integration Policies in Europe', *Journal of Ethnic and Migration Studies* 37, no. 6 (2011): 861–80.

37. Ines Michalowski, 'Required to Assimilate? The Content of Citizenship Tests in Five Countries', *Citizenship Studies* 15, no. 6–7 (2011): 749–68.

38. Dimitry Kochenov, 'The Internal Aspects of Good Neighbourliness in the EU: Loyalty and Values', in *Good Neighbourly Relations in the European Legal Context*, ed. Dimitry Kochenov and Elena Basheska (Nijhoff: Brill, 2015).

39. Ryszard Cholewinski, 'Migrants as Minorities: Integration and Inclusion in the Enlarged European Union', *JCMS: Journal of Common Market Studies* 43, no. 4 (2005): 695–716; Deborah Phillips, 'Minority Ethnic Segregation, Integration and Citizenship: A European Perspective', *Journal of Ethnic and Migration Studies* 36, no. 2 (2010): 209–25.

40. Kristin Henrard, 'An EU Perspective on New versus Traditional Minorities: On Semi-Inclusive Socio-Economic Integration and Expanding Visions of European Culture and Identity', *Columbia Journal of European Law* 17 (2010): 85.

41. Nancy Fraser and Axel Honneth, *Redistribution or Recognition? A Political-Philosophical Exchange* (London: Verso Books, 2003); Anne Phillips and Seyla Benhabib, 'From Inequality to Difference: A Severe Case of Displacement?' *New Left Review*, no. 224 (1997): 143–53.

42. Vassilis Petsinis, 'Croatia's Framework for Minority Rights: New Legal Prospects within the Context of European Integration', *Ethnopolitics* 12, no. 4 (2013): 352–67; Alexandru Grigorescu, 'Transfering Transparency: The Impact of European Institutions of East-Central Europe', in *Norms and Nannies, The Impact of International Organizations on the Central and East European States*, ed. Ronald H. Linden (Lanham, MD: Rowman & Littlefield, 2002), 59–90.

43. Ada-Charlotte Regelmann, *Minority Integration and State-Building: Post-Communist Transformations* (London: Routledge, 2016).

44. Anne Phillips, *Multiculturalism without Culture* (Princeton, NJ: Princeton University Press, 2007).

45. Axel Honneth, *The I in We: Studies in the Theory of Recognition* (Cambridge: Polity, 2012).

46. Timofey Agarin, 'Cooptation as Integration? National Programme "Integration of Society in Latvia" on Minority Participation', in *Minority Integration in Central Eastern Europe: Between Ethnic Diversity and Equality*, ed. Timofey Agarin and Malte Brosig (Amsterdam: Rodopi, 2009), 199–223.

47. Mary C. Waters et al., 'Segmented Assimilation Revisited: Types of Acculturation and Socioeconomic Mobility in Young Adulthood', *Ethnic and Racial Studies* 33, no. 7 (2010): 1168–93.

48. Will Kymlicka, *Multicultural Odysseys: Navigating the New International Politics of Diversity* (Oxford: Oxford University Press, 2007).

49. Cillian McBride, 'Democratic Participation, Engagement and Freedom', *British Journal of Politics & International Relations* 15, no. 4 (2013): 493–508, doi:10.1111/j.1467-856X.2012.00516.x.

50. For critical engagement, see Aidan McGarry and Timofey Agarin, 'Unpacking the Roma Participation Puzzle: Presence, Voice and Influence', *Journal of Ethnic and Migration Studies* 40, no. 12 (20 March 2014): 1972–90, doi:10.1080/1369183X.2014.897599.

Chapter Five

Excluding Roma from the Scope of Minority Policy

In the previous chapter, we discussed how the political mobilisation of state majorities during the period of transition (to EU membership) facilitated institutional consolidation and nation-state building as the paramount form of sovereign statehood in the post-communist region. European integration has further supported majority communities' claims to state ownership, and in more than one sense ensured the 'ethnic blindness' of political institutions to their inherent favouritism of the dominant ethnic groups. As we discussed above, once political institutions became consolidated and their content was no longer open to contestation by ethno-political entrepreneurs of the minority, post-communist states could rightly claim to have accomplished the 're-turn to Europe'. So, as the ethno-cultural claims of minority groups became secondary to national politics, majority political entrepreneurs came to dominate state institutions and promulgated policies that were favourable to individual members of the titular majority. Across the region, governments sought to favour and protect majorities, and provide a range of options for their resident minorities to pursue identitarian politics (see chapter 6). We need to ask, however, what effects have these nationalising institutions of the nascent nation-states had on groups with no external homeland. This is precisely the issue we address in this chapter by looking at the place allocated to Roma in European, nation-state and regional contexts.

It is widely acknowledged that Roma individuals and Romani communities as a whole are habitually excluded from political participation, have limited access to economic opportunities and are barred from participating in societal processes on a par with those of the majority as a result of a complex, yet overlapping, set of issues contingent upon their identities. Exclusion from the political process, limited access to education opportunities and marginalisation in the socio-economic sphere on the part of the Roma are acknowledged not to be the result of their individual or group choices.[1] They reflect their position of systematic marginalisation over past generations, the deep-seated prejudice of the majority and the concomitant need for additional support in the integration into societies of nation-states.

From the point of early transition from communism, Roma in all Central and East European countries have been badly affected by the changes in political, economic and social structure in the societies in which they live. Whilst communist regimes engaged in—at times brutal and degrading— practices of Roma assimilation, changes since the late 1980s have locked in and separated Roma from access of opportunities in post-communist societies.[2] Romanis' own perceptions and needs were conspicuous by their absence from the agendas of transition states and were only gradually brought back to the fore during the EU accession negotiations.

Numerous civil society and pressure groups, as well as European governmental bodies, promoted tolerance and acceptance of Roma as equal citizens in both post-communist and 'old' member-states. In all cases, as actual or potential EU citizens Roma individuals should have the potential to enjoy full protection under the EU law and come to enjoy their fundamental rights. However, across Europe Roma are perceived as putting pressure on the public purse, as challenging socially accepted norms, and are easily presented as incompatible with the societies in which they live. Further, because most Roma suffer from underemployment and social marginalisation in their home countries, the prospect of social exclusion and lack of integrative options in other member-states does not preclude them from moving from one state to another.

It is our claim that particularly as post-communist countries have sought to build titular nation-states, the case of Romani exclusion lends itself as an excellent example that illustrates the compound effect of nationalising policies on minority groups. The marginal status of Roma across the board of the European states made it easy for states primarily concerned with strengthening their sovereign capacity to enforce policies that favour the titular majority. In the process, Roma were cast in the light of unnecessarily burdensome citizens. With no state of their own, Roma therefore needs to rely on European institutions to promote their interests and speak for them in candidate and member-states.

1. THE EU AND THE ROMA

The general perspective on Roma across European societies is that they are treated in hostile, at times violent, ways by the local populace and are often targeted as a group due to racial prejudice deeply rooted in European societies' attitudes towards the Roma.[3] However, it seems that although prejudice against Roma appears in an ethno-racial or cultural guise, it is the role that Roma can perform in modern societies that galvanises the stereotypical representations of the group in public, and raises objections and rejection to their behaviour and way of life. Roma have the lowest levels of educational attainment throughout Europe, few can fulfil competitive requirements for accessing employment opportunities and the majority of group members lack financial means of support. All of these factors compel Romani communities to live in substandard accommodation, often illegally, especially in countries where they are not citizens. On reflection, the political reasoning for the migration of individuals of minority communities from the new EU member-states into more affluent societies in the 'old' EU member-states has much wider purchase than is usually acknowledged in many analyses. Ethnic and national minority populations from across the post-communist region have indeed the most reason to resettle in order to avoid the pressure from patronising states, destitute economies and lack of opportunity for upward social mobility, like migrants from majority communities.[4]

During the accession phase, the European Commission showed considerable interest in the situation of Roma, indicating on various occasions that improvement in the area constituted a priority before signing accession partnership agreements with a number of candidate countries, including Bulgaria, Romania and Slovakia. While some commentators claim that states seeking accession had no choice but to facilitate Roma inclusion policies as a result of European pressures, changes to domestic legislation are also said to have been spurious and their effects marginal when it comes to the protection of Romani interests.[5] Since the EU accession of 2004–2007 of states with large numbers of Roma citizens, the leverage of EU institutions in the policy field has been considerably reduced and improvements with regards to the Roma were no longer held to be a condition for a closer relationship between the EU and new member-states.

However, the inclusion of Roma in accession countries was not a one-off policy concern, but reflects the broader concern expressed by the Council of Europe and the European Commission about these groups' systematic exclusion from political, social and economic participation in all European states. Since the 1990s, European organizations have sought to address groups broadly collected under an umbrella term *Roma* as communities sharing similarly low social status and the experience of marginalization, as well as discrimination resulting from their belonging to that specific group.[6] Though member-states hosting different groups reproduced a range of self-designators or included diverse communities under the *Roma* label, Europeans' and national organizations' attention to these groups is best explained by their experience of political and social exclusion. Regardless of their overall numbers in the EU and across the European continent, Roma are seen universally as different in culture, language and ultimately ethnicity from the majority group in their states of residence.[7] Unsurprisingly, the Council of Europe and the OSCE have been particularly vocal in calling upon their member-states to recognise Romani communities as national minorities, in line with the FCNM. Such recognition was anticipated to provide Romani communities protection by the nation-states of which they are citizens, additionally allowing the EU to enforce and guarantee their protection under international law.[8]

The period since 2000 marked the evolution of the European approach to Romani inclusion. During that time, Romani exclusion was identified as an area of concern for public policy, systematic assessments of good domestic practice took place and Roma integration featured strongly in European framework documents, particularly those monitoring individual countries' progress towards *acquis* transposition. Even before the Central and Eastern European states had joined the queue for the EU membership, the Council of Europe was monitoring the adherence of these states to anti-discrimination legislation and practices intensely.[9] Since the 1997 Treaty of Amsterdam, member-states are also supposed to ensure equal opportunities and inclusion of all citizens into societal processes by adhering to adequate public policies. The *Acquis Communautaires*, including the Framework Directive on Equal Treatment in Employment and Occupation and the Directive on Equal Treatment between Persons Irrespective of Racial or Ethnic Origin and all EU member and candidate states, were designed to ensure the compliance of domestic legislation with these directives.[10]

This greater focus of European institutions on the situation of Roma has been more of a curse than a blessing for the successful addressing of Romani issues across candidate countries. First, the reiteration of the 'plight of European Roma' in diverse communications by the Council of Europe had made member-states reluctant to designate Roma as a domestic—that is, national—minority. The Europe-focussed rhetoric clearly evoked perceptions of Roma as a minority group deserving of a special set of rights, pitching groups' interests against those of post-communist accession nation-states and particularly those that were reluctant to admit additional responsibility in the light of pressures to be expected during the accession negotiations. At the same time, opening channels for multiple representations of Romani interests across European states has resulted in the refocussing of Romani advocates from issues of minority rights and protection to those of anti-discrimination.[11] Here again, anti-discrimination legislation was high on the agenda of the EU in the process of ensuring *acquis* transposition in candidate countries. The EU implicitly projected the situation of the Roma as a potential impediment for countries' accession to the Union, pitching the group against the majority of nation-states seeking the 'return to Europe'. So despite discussion of Romani issues in the regular monitoring reports of the EU, it appears that candidate countries' commitment to EU norms and not the de facto implementation of equality were seen as sufficient to conclude accession talks.

This limited success of addressing Romani exclusion in a systematic manner has been discussed widely in scholarship and generally has been explained by two factors. First, Romani exclusion was perceived as a 'problem' at the EU level and then handed down to candidate states to be resolved in the process of accession. However, seeing the root cause of Romani exclusion in discrimination by domestic societies effectively undermined the rationale of domestic sovereignty that was to ensure the privileged access of titular groups to state institutions and left little space for policies that would not revise the existing political institutions in favour of Roma in particular. [12] Secondly, the EU monitoring mechanisms relied on reports provided by Roma advocacy groups and international NGOs that often underline the limited resources available to states and called for EU funding to be diverted for Romani inclusion. This allowed candidate countries to strengthen their rhetorical commitment to and acknowledgement of criticisms from the Commission, resulting in the production of regular reports underlining the continued progress on minority accommodation. Candidate countries could not take this as anything but an indication of the fact that the EU would not formally sanction candidate states for their limited implementation of Roma-related policies. The failure of the Commission to include Romani exclusion on the agenda at high-level negotiations also pointed to the lack of the EU's own commitment to ensuring minority protection unless the point was made moot by member and candidate states, further demoting Romani issues to a low priority in the overall context of accession. [13]

In order to address the growing deficits of domestic inclusion policies, the then-EC showed resolve in 2003 and together with the Open Society Institute (OSI), governments of member-states and candidate countries with large numbers of Romani citizens, and intergovernmental organizations (UN, OSCE, CoE) launched 'The Decade of Roma Inclusion 2005–2015'. [14] The Decade indicated the commitment of stakeholders to facilitate individual equality in accessing services for all members of society, particularly in employment, education, health and housing. [15] Crucially, these priority areas relied on existing state institutions to deliver inclusive policies, rather than questioning the limited options for Roma to participate in the political, social and economic process on a par with the settled national majorities in their countries of residence. Documents relating to the activities of the Decade's assessment of Roma as requiring additional support in their country of residence do not reference Roma as a distinct ethnic community that is in any way different from the majority. In this sense, the Decade reflects the anti-discrimination commitment of the Racial Equality Directive to avoid reproducing negative stereotypes of members of their community and reflecting intertwined issues of socio-economic status and place of residence. [16] Individual participating countries did, however, explicitly endorse the group-based focus of policies developed from within the Decade: Bulgaria, the Czech Republic, Hungary, Romania and Slovakia all designed inclusion programmes explicitly for their Romani citizens, drafting policies for needs of the resident Roma as a group different from other minorities. [17]

Similar references to Roma as a minority group were later adopted in the European Parliament 'Resolution on the Situation of Roma in the European Union', defining Roma as a 'pan-European community' and as such entrenched the understanding that the European Roma were one and the same across the continent. [18] Although recognising Roma allowed addressing issues of discrimination to be addressed more efficiently, Romani inclusion into European societies was impossible to negotiate primarily due to Roma being citizens of member-states that stressed their specific nationalising institutions and policies in consolidating the majority's pivotal role in policymaking. Similar references to Roma as a minority group were later adopted in the 'Statement on Roma and Sinti' at the Working Sessions of the Annual Human Dimension. [19] This statement, prepared by the Informal Contact Group on Roma of the Intergovernmental Organizations, including the OSCE, CoE, the European Commission and the EU, refers to Roma as 'the most disadvantaged ethnic [*sic*] group in Europe'. If anything, the international organizations' engagement with the nation-states has indicated that European institutions will support member-states in dealing with issues of Romani exclusion, but 'the implementation of policies to improve the situation of Roma in terms of education, employment, health and housing' ultimately is the responsibility of the nation-state. [20]

The limitations of individual-focussed policies for Romani inclusion can be further evidenced in the Communication from the European Commission calling for an EU Framework for National Roma Integration Strategies (Roma Framework) to ensure that specific national, regional and local policies are in place with the focus on Romani needs. [21] The Communication maintained that the principle of equal treatment embedded in national legal systems as a result of the transposition of the Race Equality Directive should not prevent member-states from adopting and pursuing measures aimed at preventing and/or compensating for disadvantages linked to the racial and/or ethnic origins of European citizens. Though the Roma Framework was designed to complement and reinforce the EU's equality legislation and policies by addressing them at national, regional and local levels, the Council envisaged that the needs of Roma would be identified and addressed through explicit measures to prevent and compensate for the disadvantages they face, noting the lack of progress in Romani inclusion. [22]

If nothing else, the EC's Communication signposted the end of the group-based approach to resolving the puzzle of Romani inclusion in light of the growing resistance of nation-states to devise policies diverting resources to non-core communities on their territories.[23] Setting out a long-term perspective until 2020, it called on every EU member-state to develop policies specific to their Romani communities' situations. The EU noted that 'determined action, in active dialogue with the Roma, is needed at both national and EU level' to ensure accountability of political institutions on the ground tasked with social inclusion.[24] The established Roma Framework was the first document binding on all by EU member-states, regardless of their record with regard to Romani inclusion policies, numbers of Roma or participation in past Romani initiatives. Now, with all member-states required to report back their National Roma Integration Strategies (NRIS) within a year, nation-states were to identify dedicated institutions to undertake improvement in the situations of Roma on their territories.

In the past, some scholars have suggested that this shift in rhetoric pointed to acceptance of the fact that Roma exclusion is no longer perceived as a phenomenon affecting Romani communities in the same way at the European and at the national levels.[25] To the dismay of many Roma activists, others have argued that the Framework acknowledges that there is no European minority of Roma, and the NGOs focussing on the marginality as the community across the EU in the Framework ultimately gave up in this regard. However, in the context of the EU integration and equal parity of all states in their input into policymaking at the European level, the Commission's decision to return responsibility for Roma inclusion to nation-states implicitly acknowledged the central role domestic institutions play in recognising minority issues as well as carving out space for non-dominant groups in the framework of the existing institutions of the state serving the majority. Roma in Spain, Germany and Bulgaria might share a similar experience of political exclusion and social marginalisation, but they do so against the background of vastly different state institutions in their countries of residence. It is the acknowledgement of Roma as citizens of nation-states in the first place, and only secondly as citizens of member-states as EU citizens, that the Commission identified that Romani needs would need to be accounted for in a different manner across EU nation-states. Therefore, while the EU originally extended its protection and supported Romani groups in all member-states, it appears that the return to National Roma Integration initiatives also acknowledged the prevalence of domestic institutions at the point of delivering specific policies in responses to specific situations of Roma on the ground.[26]

National Roma Integration Strategies were assessed by the European Commission and summarised in the 'National Roma Integration Strategies: A First Step in the Implementation of the EU Framework', where the Commission reiterated the 'primary responsibility for Roma integration' of member-states.[27] While in the past the EU also recognised the importance of developing local, regional and national solutions to Roma exclusion, the distinguishing feature of the 'First Step' lay in the importance granted to

mainstreaming Romani issues. It was noted that 'regional and local authorities are indispensable for delivering change and need to be fully on board
when the strategies are reviewed and implemented'.[28] The commitment and
repeated emphasis on the 'adequate assessment of local needs' has been
reflected in the EU's sponsored European Roma Summits in 2008 and 2010;
yet these were organized to assert greater leverage of EU institutions over
national government policies.

In the past, similar initiatives have proven effective as a safety net for
communities that were not featured on the list of policy priory lists across the
EU member-states when their states of residence were unwilling while the
EU institutions were unable to push for greater inclusion on the basis of the
group rights approach. Since the narrative of EU engagement with Roma has
gone through the phase of internationalising—in fact Europeanising—the
discussion with but tenuous results, scaling policy focus back to the level of
nation-state indicates more than just an acknowledgement of the domestic
root of the Romani exclusion. Maintaining the language of Race Equality
Directive that Romani *individuals*, rather than *groups*, were excluded from
access to social, economic and political institutions that serve and speak to
the values, interests and resources of majority *communities*, the EU has de
facto acknowledged its own limits in addressing minority issues where member-states have proven reluctant to engage with a segment of their own citizenry.

Despite the fact that the Roma Framework speaks about the 'institutional
discrimination' the Roma face, the EU re-cast policies already in place in
individual member-states as best practice and implicitly acknowledged the
existing political institutions' 'national' optic on political and social inclusion processes of domestic residents. With reference to 'Roma participation',
EU has consistently favoured initiatives of domestic civil society and international nongovernmental organizations that do not challenge the political institutions' focus on explicitly non-ethnic issues as those worth pursuing.
Thus, in line with the overall aspiration of domestic policymakers in the new
member-states, the EU focus on Romani inclusion should be seen in the
context of the transformation favourable for domestic political actors who
sought to entrench the existing institutional design of states as serving majorities in their societies. While the EU made use of some relevant rhetoric
resources to increase acceptance of the inevitability of Roma inclusion policies during the period of accession and monitoring, at a later stage where no
sticks could be attached to ensure nation-states' compliance and implementation of more inclusive relationships with their Roma citizens, no other options remained in place other than returning responsibility for dealing with
exclusion issues to domestic political actors. As became increasingly obvious
over the monitoring cycles of National Romani Inclusion Strategies, nation-

states across the board of the EU are increasingly reluctant to prioritise Romani inclusion.

In assessing the reasons for the lack of progress in addressing Romani inclusion, it appears that both prior member-states and candidate countries have, first and foremost, de facto consolidated the view of sovereignty over policies in relation to the core group whom their states should serve. This perspective on the deficiencies of Romani integration across the EU today suggest several references to the overall context within which Roma as national and/or European minorities has been cast over the accession decade and since 2004–2007. First, the approach laid down in EU frameworks and assessed against during the accession phase was hardly specifically tailored to address Roma needs. Similar principles of non-discrimination and support for individuals rather than groups had been part of the OSCE and CoE dealings with minority groups across the post-communist region throughout the early 1990s, making for a reference point when candidate countries developed their programmes to tackle Romani exclusion. Domestic governments were reluctant to implement national Roma-inclusion policies because there was a stipulation not to redress exclusion by reference to group discrimination. Further, the integrated policy approach developed across the older member-states that candidate countries imported into their policymaking aimed at mainstreaming minority issues to indicate the ascendancy of the nation-state model of inclusion policies.

Secondly, mainstreaming allowed a wide range of issues to be glossed over in the process of development of national inclusion strategies for Roma, resulting in the production of formulaic and poor-quality policies that served as a box-ticking exercise, rather than acknowledging the systemic nature of Roma discrimination in restructuring debates about the ownership of the state to those of a 'return to Europe', and national governments only further obscured the national dimension of policymaking. This lack of priority given to resident minorities and marginal non-dominant groups such as the Roma was compensated by the growing relevance of countries' kin-minorities residing in neighbouring states.

Overall, while it was generally envisaged in the scholarship that following accession to the EU, post-communist nation-states would continue to improve their treatment of the resident minority groups, particularly Roma. Upon accession, former candidate countries sought rather to replicate initiatives deployed in neighbouring countries and demonstrated little policy innovation, and no considerable change in promoting institutions' greater accountability between state and society. As has been the case across the old twelve EU member-states, post-communist states have emulated inter-state agreements, domestic policies in the areas of education, employment, health and housing, and delegated effectiveness at the point of delivery to actors of civil society, further de-politicising issues that could have been interpreted in

an ethno-national key. As a result, European initiatives to facilitate and promote Romani inclusion have had only a limited impact domestically as it has
remained within the remit of the nation-state to change policies and states'
overall relationship with the Roma. The repercussions of the economic
downturn across the EU since 2008 and the re-channelling of structural funding previously incentivising the implementation of national Roma strategies
has witnessed growing neglect of Romani issues in domestic politics across
the new member-states.

2. ROMANI ISSUES AT THE NATION-STATE LEVEL

The discussion above has underlined not only that there is a clear perception
that the Roma face the threat of continuing exclusion across Europe but also
that the situation of Roma can only be remedied by nation-states by providing support for their citizens of Romani ethnicity. Overall, the discussion
above makes clear that the inclusion of Roma is an issue of importance
across the board of EU member-states, old and new, and that the EU alongside the OSCE has set an ambitious political target to facilitate the protection
of Romani interests domestically.[29] Yet exclusion remains the reality for
many Roma throughout Europe. As a result, 'many Roma still belong to the
poorest, most segregated, most discriminated against and least "integrated"
populations in Europe, and their chances for socio-economic mobility continue to be extremely low'.[30]

Over the past decade, not only Roma activists but also numerous academics have sought to institutionalise some form of shared ethnic identity for the
Roma community in order for them to be able to make stronger claims for
political, socio-economic and cultural protection of individuals at the level of
nation-states.[31] However, as we shall demonstrate in this section of the chapter, independent Romani and European initiatives as well as advocacy by
NGOs and academics alike have rather reinforced the view of Roma as
outsiders in the context of nation-states where they live. The political institutions of European nation-states therefore have provided additional avenues
for majority political elites to claim that Roma are not 'fit' for political and
social participation in the context of nation-states, which in turn resulted in
the continuous neglect of variegated problems the Romani community faces
when interacting with political institutions skewed in favour of nation-states'
ethnic majority.

In a somewhat sloppy, but nonetheless informative, distinction, Leonardo
Piasere has coined the notion of 'Gypsy Europes' to simplify the visible
Romani presence across the continent.[32] The core area of Romani presence in
Europe is the First Gypsy Europe, encompassing largely the states in the
wider Balkan area with the highest number of Romani population. Altogeth-

er, the region stretching from Macedonia to Slovakia holds around 10 percent of Europe's Roma populations. These states are clearly distinguishable from the Second Gypsy Europe, which Piasere locates in the Western part of the EU including Spain, Ireland, France and Portugal with an equal share of Roma in the overall European population, but having significantly lower representation in individual states. The central part of the European continent holds what Piasere refers to as the Third Gypsy Europe, whose countries' population has on average less than 1 percent of their local population.

These differences in the proportion of local Romani populations across the European continent do more than help in understanding the different approaches that individual nation-states have taken over the past two decades to remedying Romani exclusion. They also facilitate understanding states' overall preference to viewing issues of Romani exclusion in terms of ethnic stratification. With post-communist countries simultaneously facing greater numbers of Roma on their territories, pressures to accommodate their Romani citizens in the political process merits particular attention. Whereas communist regimes engage in intensive assimilatory policies targeting Romani communities, the demise of the centralised state and the simultaneous process of building post-communist national institutions offered an opportunity to Roma to elude control of the state apparatus. At the same time, many moved into urban areas as well as engaging in economic activities most suitable to their cultural preferences. Importantly, however, the historical marginalisation of Roma had affected their lifestyle and employable skills, which were badly suited for post-industrial post-communist societies, making the acquisition of necessary skills for participation in socio-economic processes during the period of EU accession extremely difficult.

Thus, as a result of Romani citizens having little access to institutional avenues through which to better their social and economic situation and articulate their interests in the framework of nation-state institutions, the post-communist transition has resulted in their (continued) marginalisation. Across post-communist Europe, Roma could not tap the political resources to access and ensure equal participation in social and economic processes on a par with the majority, seeing systematic historical rejection by members of the majority and, as a result, disengaging from the majority's ways of life.[33] Indeed, we observe consistent and raising antiziganist attitudes, and both the majority population and their political elites have showcased their reluctance to engage with and offer Roma opportunities to improve their standing in the affirmative-action style programmes.[34]

This reluctance of domestic political elites in post-communist states is not exemplary, as most Western European member-states similarly have largely tolerated Romani settlement as well as increasingly rare nomadism as long as these were not perceived as a drain on the public purse.[35] The historical development of political institutions across the Europe of Westphalian nation-states resulted in a tacit acceptance of a peculiar model of Romani inclusion across Western Europe: it focusses on protecting the rights of the majority from the incursion of Roma into the public domain and facilitated the co-existence of dominant and Romani groups while sponsoring the cultural assimilation of Roma into mainstream societies. The case of Spain in this context illustrates these dynamics: Over the past century or so, the country has applied several policy measures to deal with the situation of domestic Roma (referred to as *Gitanos*). When assimilation attempts resulted in the ghettoization of Romani communities, Romani collective gatherings were prohibited, as was the use of Romanes, wearing traditional Romani dress, performing in traditional dances and following a nomadic lifestyle, and other culture traits. Only the end of the Franco dictatorship in 1975 led to the revision of policies by the state and the lifting of the ban on Roma from settling in the 'Spanish districts' of towns and cities. While Spain has long since joined the EU and has subsequently operated an effective set of policies to facilitate Romani inclusion, Spain offers Gitanos a minimum set of rights, and their legal position depends to a large degree on the frameworks set in anti-discriminatory legislation. The country was particularly praised for delivering sets of supportive instruments that referred particularly to Romani collective cultural identity as a part of Spain's autonomous communities' framework, thereby allowing for Roma co-optation into nation-states, like political domains in independence-seeking Catalonia, among others.[36]

As in Spain, across post-communist Europe the legalistic approach to defining the beneficiary of state policies has reflected specific historical, social and political objectives of the consolidating nation-states. First and foremost, nation-states' approach to defining one or several, mobile or sedentary, linguistically and culturally distinct groups as Roma proceeded from the institutional context facilitating majority populations' perceptions of their own place in the structure of the nation-state. Roma are accorded legal recognition in twenty-one member-states of the EU; however, individual countries spelled out different sets of entitlements to enjoy group-specific rights in each context. Austria, Greece, Finland, Germany, Latvia, Lithuania, Romania, Slovakia and Sweden recognise Roma as a national minority, while Hungary, Netherlands, Poland and Portugal refer to Roma as an ethnic minority. Policy documents of the Czech Republic refer to Roma as both a 'national' and an 'ethnic' minority, while Slovenia recognises a 'Romani community', a policy rather than a legal category endowing Roma with sets of privileges that various 'national' and 'ethnic' minority groups enjoy in that country. We find a similar situation in Italy, where Roma are recognised as a 'minority' at the regional level only, with distinct implications for recognition of their cultural identity being reflected in the widespread reference to 'gypsies' (*zingari*) and 'nomads' (*nomadi*) in regional legislation. Somewhat differently, the Estonian government defines Roma as a distinct community within the ambit of its wider framework of National Cultural Autonomy and outsources the opportunities for recognition and pursuit of joint, ethnicity-relevant issues by the community.

The gamut of legal statuses on Roma across Europe is further complicated by the non-ethnic approach some countries take to their citizens, with the notable case of France. Here, the legal category of *gens de voyage* refers to Roma who are—or so it is assumed—nomadic; thus, they are different from other French citizens in their choice of a non-sedentary lifestyle. Somewhat similarly, the United Kingdom and the Republic of Ireland refer to *Travellers* as a category akin to indigenous people, with an implication that while Romani gypsies are perceived in ethnic terms (though with no territorial reference), *Travellers* encompasses a social group. These countries have recognised all Roma living within their national territories regardless of the citizenship criterion. This is especially the case in the UK and Ireland, which do not formally distinguish between citizens and non-citizens when applying the category of 'national minority' under the scope of the FCNM. So the UK has recognised Roma as a 'national minority' under the judicial interpretation of the Race Relations Act of 1976 and the Republic of Ireland accords rights attributed to 'national minorities' also to Romani individuals who are not Irish citizens. Although non-Irish citizens can benefit from a wide spectrum of rights, they are not entitled to political rights. Sweden offers another illustrative case, as it has not specified categories of minority groups protected under the FCNM. In all these cases, European nation-states spelled out the limits of institutions' responsibility for their Romani citizens, and as we have discussed in the preceding section of the chapter, they react to the EU-driven set of policies for Romani inclusion.

In short, the political institutions of nation-states that purport to promote inclusion of Romani communities and the empowerment of Romani individuals have been consistent in their operational working as institutions of the majority granting recognition of Romani issues only insofar as this allowed protecting the interests of the majority in the political sphere. State institutions' ethnic blindness to Romani issues, however, consistently referred the needs of these individuals and communities to their own resources when laying out the terms of cooperation that were hardly accessible to the marginalised Roma. The situation resulted largely from disagreement among myriad international and domestic political institutions, NGOs and individual activists concerning ways of averting further, and reversing past, effects of Romani exclusion in countries of the Council of Europe. As a result, the EU could only agree on what became a partial solution to Romani inclusion issues, and chose the only one that was institutionally possible within the existing framework: relay responsibility to nation-states. As we have discussed throughout preceding chapters, and in the light of the nationalising tendencies in all member-states, this process of empowering nation-states to deal with Romani issues resulted in further institutionalisation of ethnicity as a salient category and perpetuated further ethnicity-based exclusion.

The fact that nation-states maintain their decisive role in policymaking for Romani inclusion demonstrates that they remain the principal actors in outlining and guaranteeing the group-specific rights of members of these diverse groups. The decisive impact of institutions of the state in demonstrating neglect of Romani issues domestically was challenged by the EU during the period of accession negotiation with the prospective member-states and later also targeted the old member-states when passing the Roma Framework in 2009. However, none of these changes has substantially challenged the baseline for international cooperation on the principle of domestic sovereignty with regards to policymaking and implementation. Much of the rhetoric and policy measures put into place have been widely commented upon by Romani activists monitoring the implementation processes as constituting tokenistic concessions to European directives with little substantive change in the matter. Our brief discussion of the latest developments in Bulgaria illustrates these claims.

Case Study: Bulgaria

During the phase of EU accession, the Bulgarian government was faced not only with a lighter form of political conditionality that was to ensure the adaptation of procedures for effective governance but also with *acquis* conditionality that specifically targeted the legal background of its integration of Bulgaria's large Romani community. As such, the government could not take the asymmetry of power for granted and focussed, as requested by the EU, on anti-discrimination legislation with the focus on the Roma resulting in the adaptation of the 'Framework Program for Equal Integration of Roma in Bulgarian Society'.[37] The programme recognised unequal treatment as a pre-condition and driving force behind the problems faced by the Roma community, committed itself to combatting discrimination and inequality and updated and incorporated new proposals into national legislation.[38] However, this legislative adaptation was short-lived, particularly in light of the economic strain that the state experienced in pushing forward wider reforms in education, health and housing. Reports on internal discussions indicate that the Bulgarian approach to Roma exclusion prior to accession was little more than instrumental adaptation, while the authorities regularly questioned the unequal treatment of both Romani and Turkish Bulgarian citizens. Though legislation was in place as early as 2000, it was not until 2003 that any policy developments ensued, which was justified by the Bulgarian authorities by referring to the lack of administrative and financial resources for implementation.[39] Until 2006 the Bulgarian government focussed on developing strategies and action plans failing to allocate adequate funding for their effective implementation. By the time of Bulgaria's accession to the EU in 2007, only anti-discrimination legislation and bodies were in place to guarantee success-ful—albeit fragmentary—delivery of the objectives of the Framework Pro-gramme. Therefore, even after Bulgaria's accession to the EU, the main priorities outlined in the key fields of education, housing and employment remained in their embryonic form despite numerous policies in place, sug-gesting that citizens could avail themselves of equal opportunities.

In response to the European Commission's call to prepare National Roma Integration Strategies, the Bulgarian government outlined sets of action plans in the annex to the declaration in December 2011.[40] However, when the final decision on the content of the programme was made in January 2012, the annex containing the most specific changes and policy steps was removed from the document, resulting in protestations from Romani rights activists. Although the government indicated that this was only an administrative er-ror, specific proposals and the overall shape of Bulgaria's Roma integration strategy remained unclear for several months. Ultimately, the government action plan failed to address one of the central concerns flagged in previous monitoring reports on access to health care provisions and did not spell out mechanisms for monitoring the implementation. Furthermore, Bulgaria's Roma integration strategy was largely presented by domestic political elites as a one-off policy with no requirements indicated about the potential imple-mentation. It was also noted that insufficient funding was allocated to deliver on these projects, with only 49 out of 120 budgeted for, and of these funds scheduled, they were later reduced.[41] A grave administrative blunder also ensued after the publication of the Bulgarian Roma integration strategy on the official website of the Bulgarian president under the file name using a derogatory term for Roma, thereby further highlighting negative attitudes towards Roma with the officials tasked with tackling prejudice towards the Roma.[42]

The focus of EU conditionality on transposition and enforcement of anti-discrimination legislation has implicitly recognised that Roma minorities in accession states experience discrimination.[43] Implicitly committing to im-proving the status of Roma (alongside other minorities), programmes such as PHARE channelled considerable funds into the improvement of the situa-tions of Roma in accession states as a way of incentivising them to stay put in their countries of origin and seek integration into domestic societies and politics. Yet nation-states granting Roma special attention and developing inclusion programmes often had the opposite effect of what was intended, resulting in the stigmatisation of group members by the resentful majority populations who saw Roma as being a preferred policies' target group and as such a hindrance to EU integration.[44] Overall, these growing antiziganist attitudes on the part of domestic majorities further reinforced the perception that Roma ought to seek migration in order to avoid the stigmatisation in many of the new member-states, as they could now enjoy freedom of movement throughout the EU. However, as we will discuss in the next section, given that Roma were and remain largely unwanted co-citizens in most EU member-states, the treatment of Roma EU citizens offers an excellent testing ground for analyses of state strategies that demonstrate states' reluctance to assume responsibility and respond positively to citizens who are of a minority ethnicity residing in their territories.

3. ROMA AT THE LOCAL LEVEL

Whereas at the European and nation-state level we have traced the mutual recrimination about responsibility for Romani inclusion, the presence of Roma at the local and municipal levels across Europe make the identification of steps aimed at recognition of their rights more straightforward. There is plentiful evidence concerning the reluctance of the majority to engage with Roma based upon on the presumption of the latter's apparent criminal inclinations, their alleged nomadism despite generations-long sedentary lifestyles and questionable attitude to work. Stereotypes that 'gypsies lead a parasitic, opportunistic and transient life' are prevalent among all European societies and offer a handy reference point to legitimise antiziganist rhetoric, leading to the removal of Roma from localities where they are said to endanger common normative order. Thus, relegated to the margins of European societies overall, Roma find themselves at the fringe of public policy interest as we have discussed above and tend to be left to their own devices also in areas in which they live, occupying distinct socio-economic niche positions.

During the accession period, the EU sent a clear signal to post-communist states that discrimination against Roma as has been reported by monitoring organizations was impermissible because it happened exclusively on grounds of Romani ethnicity. At the same time, however, 'old' member-states sought to address the issue of Romani marginalisation in candidate countries by referring to these countries' obligation to pass anti-discrimination legislation and make them work.[45] Developing national strategies for Romani inclusion therefore has sought to attain different outcomes and performed different roles in individual countries that we can only summarise in this section. There is perhaps a general perception that policies of Romani inclusion may accord them a degree of acceptance and recognition as long as they simultaneously emphasise benefits of such policies for the majority. Secondly, domestic political actors were equally concerned over the degree of control they could exercise over other non-dominant groups on the territory of their nation-state. Finally, states are committed to and—as we will see in chapters 6 and 7—uphold the principles underlying international agreements in order to access recognition from international and regional organizations such as the EU and Council of Europe.

Being negotiated between nation-states and forming the backbone of the European minority rights regime, under pressure from the European Union, politicians in accession states therefore had to provide their domestic audiences with sufficiently persuasive rational programmes for addressing Romani issues in places where Roma live. The adoption of domestic policies addressing the issues of Romani inclusion in post-communist Europe implied that in the long run the Roma were granted, however tokenistic, incentives to stay put and avail themselves of economic opportunities in their localities of residence. At the same time, citizens of countries that have passed anti-discrimination legislation were precluded from claiming asylum when migrating across Europe with freedom of movement. This has only further circumscribed the effectiveness of domestically developed and locally implemented projects aimed at improving living conditions and access to education and opportunities for employment of Roma. On the surface, such policies appear to have been effective as across accession states Roma access to health care, housing and education and political participation in social, political and economic processes within the regions and nation-states has indeed increased. However, only in regions where Roma constitute a significant proportion of the population was the nation-state policymaking somewhat amortised at the local level.

Case Study: Slovakia and Poland

Let us now briefly turn to two further country cases: Slovakia and Poland. These are rather different in their overall numbers of Romani citizens, their territorial concentration and perceptions of the 'Roma problem' among their publics. Whereas in Slovakia it has been the issue of Romani poverty that resulted in policy steps and support for members of this marginal group, issues of cultural distinctness featured strongly on the agenda in Poland. Roma communities in both countries have been subject to repeated and forced resettlements by the communist authorities in the past. Discrimination against Roma during the communist years was open and state sanctioned, while in both countries communist rulers to a degree sought the assimilation of Roma into the majority population. All of this had a direct impact on the cultural fragmentation of communities and economic uprooting and resulted in deepening Romani poverty following the collapse of communism. The period of transition from communism has seen little improvement of Roma situations in either Poland or Slovakia, as they were often first to be excluded from economic opportunities in a competitive market-oriented environment.

Both countries, however, are comparatively homogeneous ethnically, though, as we have discussed above, Slovakia hosts a locally sizeable Hungarian minority in the south of the country. Romani poverty is equally viewed as a destabilising factor for the state capacity. Both Poland and Slovakia are, however, noted for rather limited availability of studies evaluating state engagement with Romani minorities at the local level of governance, while it is often noted that NGOs are being tasked with delivering relevant policymaking knowledge on Romani issues in both countries. Approximately 7.4 percent of the overall population of Slovakia identify themselves as Roma in the official census, and the majority of the community is concentrated in the east and southeast of the country.[46] Romani settlements form 'relatively autonomous social formations located in Slovak countryside inhabited primarily by the Roma population', which are also marked by great diversity of economic and social opportunities in this largely economically destitute region.[47] Despite great variation between different localities, the Slovak central government has not sought to develop policy approaches that reflect the variance on the ground; quite on the contrary, only policy solutions that were deemed urgent were implemented following prodding by the international actors such as OSCE and EU. As a result of the lack of perspective, such an ad hoc approach to policymaking has too often resulted in failure and has been accompanied by responsibility-displacement on the part of the national political leadership and local administrations. It is therefore reasonable to anticipate that local, probably even Romani, stakeholders would have engaged to a greater degree in developing and delivering local solutions to poverty-stricken regions and marginalised Romani communities.

Regrettably, this is only rarely the case in Slovakia. Stereotypical representations of the Roma within the Slovak majority have prevented the delegation of implementation capacity to the Roma. As Michal Vašečka has argued, government officials effectively blocked the involvement of Roma in the framework of governance, and have systematically referred issues back to Roma communities for resolution before highlighting the positive contribution made by the local political leadership.[48] As has been seen in the past, neglect and deferral of decisions in addressing poverty issues has deepened segregation, legitimised existing anti-Roma discrimination and reconfirmed that the existing state policies were sufficient, albeit tokenistic. At the same time, including Roma in decision making and especially in the oversight of policy implementation has been accompanied by an over-reliance on external funding to facilitate the comprehensive participation of community representatives in policy drafting, thereby limiting resources and scaling down priorities favoured by the local majority.

The perception of a cultural mismatch between the Polish majority and Romani groups in Poland worked in a similar way. This stereotypical view discouraged close cooperation between Romani and majority representatives in Poland during the 1990s and particularly during the period of Poland's EU accession, when once provision for Poland's German minority were fulfilled, few further questions were raised about the country's overall minority protection.[49] However, even before EU accession, the Polish government developed the 'Programme for the Benefit of the Roma Community in Poland (2004–2013)', indicating the preference for social inclusion as a tool—not as an objective—for minority's participation in national-state policymaking. Along the lines later found in Roma integration strategies across the board of post-communist states, the Polish government opted for streamlining Romani concerns and their integration with the interest of the wider public, despite indications that 'the Romani culture is vastly different from the majority'. As some observers of this policy's implementation have hinted, policymakers were pursuing two objectives with essentialising perceptions:[50] First, they played on stereotypes of Roma and 'eventually captivate[d] their imagination over positive features of the Roma culture' in order to seek alternative roots to leverage against commonly observed discrimination at the local level. Secondly, however, in focussing particularly on the cultural aspect of Romani difference, an effort was made to sneak in the multicultural project into the public domain where ethnic Polish perceptions played an increasing role with the evolving discussion about the cultural links with Polish communities in former eastern Poland, which today forms the westernmost parts of Belarus and Ukraine and the southernmost part of Lithuania.

The Polish state, however, asserted it to be 'indispensable' to smooth over the cultural differences in order to achieve effective implementation of the Programme. Assisting the Roma in maintaining their distinct cultural features therefore was in line with the conservation approach that has marred communist and post-communist states' approaches to management of ethnic diversity among their populations and maintained the public perception of an inherent heteronormative division between the majority and Romani citizens. In so doing, the Polish Roma integration strategy also reconstructed values and behavioural patterns of the majority as something of a non-negotiable standard for members of the Romani minority to assume their role as representatives and indeed advocates of their own group vis-à-vis the Polish majority. Despite the widely shared cultural explanations of Romani exceptionalism in Poland (as elsewhere), such references channelled attention to Roma via their participation in the labour market, further bolstering prejudice and the group's civilizational deferral and 'traditional' work shyness.

Overall, as both of these cases demonstrate, the failures to address Romani inclusion issues by the governments in Poland and Slovakia under the tutelage of the majority lay in too much focus on the impact Roma inclusion would have on dominant ethnic communities over the consequences of Romani exclusion.[51] Both cases resolving Romani issues through the prism of stereotypic representation of the Romani way of life have only further sponsored the tutelary style of policymaking to effect Roma inclusion. In the city of Wrocław, for example, Roma set up a residential complex and restaurant close to the city centre in the early 2000s, whereas local policymakers have regularly referred to vagrancy and work shyness of Roma in order to legitimise the lack of provision and engagement with the groups' lack of access to basic services in the area. In Slovakia, the lack of Roma involvement in drafting and delivering policies was often emphasised as the consequence of segregation of the Roma settlements and their largely rural residence. In one famous instance of Košice, the second largest urbanity in the country, Roma were removed from the town centre into what has effectively become the country's largest ghetto, Luník IX, with its own self-government institutions. Whilst in the past it was considered a 'no go area' for outsiders, it has gradually become a secluded zone, 'no outgo area', for its inhabitants.

CONCLUSION

Unsurprisingly, Romani activists have systematically advocated delegating greater legitimacy for decision making to the regional level and the institutionalization of Romani representations to decide over issues that concerned their community directly. Repeatedly, emphasis has been placed on the importance of local participation in the inclusion programs for Roma and has been articulated by reference to the Decade of Roma Inclusion, Roma Framework and later the 10 Common Basic Principles for Roma Inclusion. Particularly after a National Roma Integration Strategy (NRIS) was put into place across post-communist Europe, national governments began to argue that the local Roma were best informed about how exclusion works and what needs to be done to counteract its effects. The rescaling of policymaking to regions and municipalities with a high percentage of Roma inhabitants at the same time has seen increasing reluctance on the part of local governments to recognise Romani interests locally.

Operating within the context of national institutions and existing policies granting advantageous access to members of the majority, Roma citizens were allowed to sit as representatives in policymaking bodies, but they are known to have been marginalised in decision-making fora. Even in cases in which Roma were a part of the policymaking and decision-making process, their input into specific areas largely reflected the operational logic of serving the stability and supporting the existing institutions of the nation-state, so as to divert resources from state majority priorities. Policy initiatives implemented in Romani-inclusion projects have been tightly knit with the individualist, liberal European policy framework relying on the activation of existing skills and resources of the community as a whole. Thus, it has been often noted that despite the formal inclusion of Roma in political, economic and social processes in localities where they live, it is in fact the segregation between skilled/non-skilled labour combined with high levels of deprivation that makes it difficult for Roma to exit from their position of individual and collective marginalisation.

Thus, approaching Romani integration even at the sub-state level of policymaking and implementation was difficult in the context of political institutions presuming their cultural blindness toward the majority but implicitly framing all social issues in the language of ethnicity. All social integration initiatives targeting Roma presume freedom of the individual to avail themselves of integration opportunities and have been presented by policymakers as empowering the excluded *qua members of marginalised groups*. Yet this very core notion of freedom in choice is limited by the institutional backdrop that drives integration initiatives for Roma, and which in turn is a by-product of majority communities' reluctance to acknowledge the implicit bias and cultural stereotypes embedded in the institutional treatment of minority groups in nation-states and their majority societies.

NOTES

1. Timofey Agarin, 'The Root Cause of Romani Exclusion and the European National Roma Integration Strategies', in *When Stereotype Meets Stereotypes, Antiziganism in European Societies*, by Timofey Agarin (Hanover, Germany: Ibidem-Verlag, 2014), 223–43.

2. Zoltan Barany, 'Politics and the Roma in State-Socialist Eastern Europe', *Communist and Post-Communist Studies* 33, no. 4 (2000): 421–37.

3. T. Hammarberg, Commissioner for Human Rights, 'Human Rights of Roma and Travellers in Europe', Commissioner for Human Rights, Council of Europe, 2012; Jarmila Lajcakova, 'The Uneasy Road towards Remedying the Economic and Cultural Disadvantage of the Roma in Slovakia', *International Journal on Minority and Group Rights* 14, no. 1 (2007): 59–83.

4. Huub van Baar, *The European Roma: Minority Representation, Memory, and the Limits of Transnational Governmentality* (Amsterdam: Eigen Beheer, 2011).

5. Peter Vermeersch, *The Romani Movement: Minority Politics and Ethnic Mobilization in Contemporary Central Europe* (Oxford: Berghahn Books, 2006).

6. Helen O'Nions, *Minority Rights Protection in International Law: The Roma of Europe* (Aldershot: Ashgate, 2007).

7. Angus Bancroft, *Roma and Gypsy-Travellers in Europe: Modernity, Race, Space and Exclusion* (Aldershot: Ashgate Publishing, 2005); Gyorgy Csepeli and David Simon, 'Construction of Roma Identity in Eastern and Central Europe: Perception and Self-identification', *Journal of Ethnic and Migration Studies* 30, no. 1 (2004): 129–50.

8. Timofey Agarin, 'Travelling without Moving? Limits of European Governance for Romani Inclusion', *Ethnicities* 14, no. 6 (2014): 737–55, doi:10.1177/1468796814542184.

9. James Hughes, Gwendolyn Sasse, and Claire Gordon, 'Conditionality and Compliance in the EU's Eastward Enlargement: Regional Policy and the Reform of Sub-National Government', *Journal of Common Market Studies* 42, no. 3 (2004): 523–51.

10. Guido Schwellnuss, 'Anti-Discrimination Legislation', in *Minority Rights in Central and Eastern Europe*, ed. Bernd Rechel (Oxon: Routledge, 2009), 32–45; European Commission, 'Council Directive 2000/43/EC of 29 June 2000 Implementing the Principle of Equal Treatment between Persons Irrespective of Racial or Ethnic Origin', 2000, http://eur-lex.europa.eu/LexUriServ/LexUriServ.do?uri=CELEX:32000L0043:en:HTML; European Commission, 'Council Directive 2000/78/EC of 27 November 2000 Establishing a General Framework for Equal Treatment in Employment and Occupation', 2000, http://eur-lex.europa.eu/LexUriServ/LexUriServ.do?uri=CELEX:32000L0078:en:HTML.

11. Galina Kostadinova, 'Minority Rights as a Normative Framework for Addressing the Situation of Roma in Europe', *Oxford Development Studies* 39, no. 2 (2011): 163–83.

12. Peter Vermeersch, 'Reframing the Roma: EU Initiatives and the Politics of Reinterpretation', *Journal of Ethnic and Migration Studies* 38, no. 8 (2012): 1195–1212.

13. Aidan McGarry, 'The Dilemma of the European Union's Roma Policy', *Critical Social Policy* 32, no. 1 (2012): 126–36.

14. For general assessment, see Dena Ringold, Mitchell Alexander Orenstein, and Erika Wilkens, *Roma in an Expanding Europe: Breaking the Poverty Cycle* (Washington, DC: World Bank Publications, 2005).

15. 'Decade of Roma Inclusion 2005–2015: Terms of Reference', 2005, 5, http://www. romadecade.org/cms/upload/file/9292_file1_terms-of-reference.pdf.

16. European Commission, 'Council Directive 2000/43/EC' (Race Equality Directive).

17. Christina McDonald and Katy Negrin, *No Data—No Progress: Country Findings: Data Collection in Countries Participating in the Decade of Roma Inclusion 2005–2015* (Budapest: Open Society Foundations, 2010); 'Decade Watch: Roma Activists Assess the Progress of the Decade of Roma Inclusion, 2005–2006', 2007, http://siteresources.worldbank.org/PGLP/ Resources/NadirRedzepiDecadeWatchBackgroundPaper.pdf.

18. European Parliament, 'European Parliament Resolution on the Situation of the Roma in the European Union, P6_TA(2005)0151', 2005, point 27, http://www.europarl.europa.eu/sides/ getDoc.do?pubRef=-//EP//TEXT+TA+P6-TA-2005-0151+0+DOC+XML+V0//EN.

19. OSCE, 'Statement on Roma and Sinti at the Working Sessions 6 and 7 of the Annual Human Dimension Implementation Meeting of the OSCE-ODIHR, Warsaw, September 2007 HDIM IO/205/07', HDIM IO/205/07, 2007, http://www.osce.org/odihr/27315.

20. High Level Advisory Group, 'Report of the High Level Advisory Group of Experts on the Social Integration of Ethnic Minorities and Their Full Participation in the Labour Market', Brussels, 2007; Will Guy, 'EU Initiatives on Roma: Limitations and Ways Forward', in *Romani Politics in Contemporary Europe: Poverty, Ethnic Mobilization, and the Neo-Liberal Order*, eds. Nidhi Trehan and Nando Sigona (Basingstoke: Palgrave, 2010).

21. European Commission, 'An EU Framework for National Roma Integration Strategies up to 2020 (EC/COM/2011/173 Final)', 2011, 11, http://eur-lex.europa.eu/LexUriServ/LexUri-Serv.do?uri=COM:2011:0173:FIN:EN:PDF.

22. Ibid., 3. See also Iulius Rostas and Andrew Ryder, 'EU Framework for National Roma Integration Strategies: Insights into Empowerment and Inclusive Policy Development', in *Gypsies and Travellers: Empowerment and Inclusion in British Society*, eds. Andrew Ryder and Joanna Richardson (Bristol: Policy Press, 2012).

23. Aidan McGarry and Timofey Agarin, 'Unpacking the Roma Participation Puzzle: Presence, Voice and Influence', *Journal of Ethnic and Migration Studies* 40, no. 12 (20 March 2014): 1972–90, doi:10.1080/1369183X.2014.897599.

24. European Commission, 'An EU Framework for National Roma Integration Strategies up to 2020 (EC/COM/2011/173 Final)', 2.

25. Melanie H. Ram, 'Interests, Norms and Advocacy: Explaining the Emergence of the Roma onto the EU's Agenda', *Ethnopolitics* 9, no. 2 (2010): 197–217; Simon McMahon, 'Assessing the Impact of European Union Citizenship: The Status and Rights of Romanian Nationals in Italy', *Journal of Contemporary European Studies* 20, no. 2 (1 June 2012): 199–214, doi:10.1080/14782804.2012.685391.

26. Maja Miskovic, *Roma Education in Europe: Practices, Policies and Politics* (London: Routledge, 2013).

27. European Commission, 'National Roma Integration Strategies: A First Step in the Implementation of the EU Framework. COM/2012/133', 2012, 4, http://ec.europa.eu/justice/dis-crimination/files/com2012_226_en.pdf.

28. Ibid., 17.

29. Nidhi Trehan and Nando Sigona, eds., *Romani Politics in Contemporary Europe: Poverty, Ethnic Mobilization, and the Neo-Liberal Order* (Basingstoke: Palgrave, 2010).

30. Nando Sigona and Peter Vermeersch, 'The Roma in the New EU: Policies, Frames and Everyday Experiences', *Journal of Ethnic and Migration Studies* 38, no. 8 (2012): 1189.

31. For a critical overview, see Timofey Agarin, 'Angels with Dirty Faces? European Identity, Politics of Representation and Recognition of Romani Interests', *Ethnicities* 14, no. 6 (1 December 2014): 849–60, doi:10.1177/1468796814542186; Yaron Matras, 'Scholarship and the Politics of Romani Identity: Strategic and Conceptual Issues', *European Yearbook of Minority Issues* 10 (2013): 211–47.

32. Leonardo Piasere, *I Rom d'Europa: Una Storia Moderna* (Roma: Laterza, 2004).

33. FRA, 'The Situation of Roma in 11 EU Member States', May 2012, http://fra.europa.eu/en/publication/2012/situation-roma-11-eu-member-states-survey-results-glance.

34. European Commission, 'Roma Integration: First Findings of Roma Task Force and Report on Social Inclusion EC/MEMO/10/701', 2010, http://europa.eu/rapid/press-release_MEMO-10-701_en.htm.

35. Dualta Roughneen, *The Right to Roam: Travellers and Human Rights in the Modern Nation-State* (Newcastle: Cambridge Scholars Publishing, 2010); Julia von dem Knesebeck, *The Roma Struggle for Compensation in Post-War Germany* (Hatfield: University of Hertfordshire Press, 2011).

36. Oscar Prieto-Flores and Teresa Sordé-Martí, 'The Institutionalization of Panethnicity from the Grassroots Standpoint in a European Context: The Case of Gitanos and Roma Immigrants in Barcelona', *Ethnicities* 11, no. 2 (2011): 202–17.

37. Rumyan Russinov, 'The Bulgarian Framework Programme for Equal Integration of Roma: Participation in the Policy-Making Process', *Roma Rights, Journal of the European Roma Rights Centre* (2001), 2–3.

38. Ministerski Savet na Republika Balgarija, 'Ramkova Programa Za Ravnopravno Integrirane Na Romite v Balgarskoto Obshtestvo', April 1999, http://www.ncedi.government.bg/en/index.html.

39. Ibid., 39–41; Elena Marushiakova and Vesselin Popov, 'The Shades of Incomplete', in *Roma Education in Europe: Practices, Policies and Politics*, ed. Maja Miskovic (London: Routledge, 2013), 135–46.

40. Ministerski Savet na Republika Balgarija, 'Nacionalna Strategija Na Republika Balgarija Za Integrirane Na Romite (2012–2020)', 2012, http://www.nccedi.government.bg/page.php?category=125.

41. Center for Interethnic Dialog and Tolerance, AMALIPE, 'The Council of Ministers Adopted the National Strategy for Roma Integration', *News*, 22 December 2011, http://amalipe.com/index.php?nav=news&id=1010&lang=2.

42. The document has been later removed. For a picture, see http://econ.bg/Новини/В-президентството-интегрират-мангали-_l.a_i.387655_at.1.html.

43. Maria Spirova and Darlene Budd, 'The EU Accession Process and the Roma Minorities in New and Soon-to-Be Member States', *Comparative European Politics* 6, no. 1 (2008): 81–101, doi:10.1057/palgrave.cep.6110123.

44. Diana Elena Popescu, 'Moral Exclusion and Blaming the Victim: The Deligitimising Role of Antiziganism', in *When Stereotype Meets Prejudice: Antiziganism in European Societies*, ed. Timofey Agarin (Stuttgart: ibidem, 2014), 171–200.

45. Fundamental Rights Agency, 'The Situation of Roma EU Citizens Moving to and Settling in Other EU Member States', European Union Fundamental Rights Agency, 9 November 2009, http://fra.europa.eu/en/publication/2012/situation-roma-eu-citizens-moving-and-settling-other-eu-member-states.

46. Jarmila Lajcakova, 'Advancing Empowerment of the Roma in Slovakia through a Non-Territorial National Autonomy', *Ethnopolitics* 9, no. 2 (2010): 171–96.

47. Marek Jakoubek and Tomáš Hirt, *Romové: Kulturologické Etudy* (Plzeň: Aleš Čeněk, 2004).

48. Michal Vašečka, ed., *Čačipen Pal O Roma. Súhrnná Správa O Rómoch Na Slovensku* (Bratislava: IVO, 2002).

49. Katarzyna Celinska and Agnieszka Gutkowska, 'The Polish Roma: From a Persecuted to a Protected Minority', *International Journal of Comparative and Applied Criminal Justice* 38, no. 2 (2014): 157–71.

50. Slawomir Kapralski, 'Symbols and Rituals in the Mobilisation of the Romani National Ideal', *Studies in Ethnicity and Nationalism* 12, no. 1 (2012): 64–81, doi:10.1111/j.1754-9469.2012.01152.x.

51. A. Mušinka, et al. *Atlas of Roma Communities in Slovakia 2013* (Bratislava: UNDP Europe and the CIS, Bratislava Regional Centre, 2014), 652.

Chapter Six

Policies for Minority Settlement beyond State-Bounded Territories

For the time being, peace and stability in the wider post-communist region are not in question as a result of individuals taking up residence in a state other than their own. We anticipate, however, that in the coming decades the number of individuals holding multiple nationalities and residing outside 'their' state will grow exponentially across Europe as a whole. The issue will become salient for defining state relations with societies they govern unless we see a deeper and more comprehensive political integration of these countries into the EU. This development is predicated upon the enjoyment of the freedom of movement by citizens of all states, growing numbers of children born to parents with different citizenship and access to multiple nationalities as a result of changes to citizenship laws. While some scholarship has indicated appreciation of the impact domestic policymaking has on inter-state relations when it comes to resident non-citizens and non-resident citizens alike, we believe that the nature of nation-state building across post-communist Europe offers another reason for the exploration of the potential impact on the link between co-ethnics and the state is likely to have on inter-state relations across the post-communist region. Therefore, this chapter explores the effects of domestic politics of kin-states on countries of residence of their non-resident citizens as well as on whose residents that are affected by extra-territorial policies of their neighbours.

Certainly, the status of resident minorities has not specifically been put on the agenda of EU integration outside the framework of national sovereignty. However, with the expansion of the EU into post-communist Europe, conflict prevention between groups with states, as well as between states over groups they identified as being part of their nation, has become more feasible.[1] The accession of post-communist states to the EU offered a double opportunity for dampening conflict potential across the region and effected perceptions of ethno-national identity across the borders of nation-states. First and foremost, consolidation of state institutions has affirmed a dominant ethnic group's ownership and tutelage over the political dynamics in their states and has implied that minority communities would not be perceived in ethnic terms by the host state, while at the same time, they could freely affiliate—and were associated—with their kin-state in cross-border relationships.[2] Also, the granting of equality of opportunities, including in the economic sphere, for all EU citizens made contestation of domestic political institutions by those who perceived nation-states to be the preserve of the titular nation while patronising minorities to become an EU-wide issue of concern.[3]

Treading carefully between these at first sight contradictory achievements of the EU integration has been the priority for post-communist EU member and candidate countries. As we have discussed above, with all post-communist states designed as homelands of the majority, having significant numbers of minority groups on their territories and often facing close scrutiny by their neighbours about the treatment of co-ethnics offered a unique opportunity for reshaping state-society relations by further liberalising nation-state approaches to ethnic diversity management. This chapter will discuss how these processes played out in the new member-states. The focus of our chapter on trans-border communities brings forward the double-edged impact of European integration on inter-state relations in the post-communist region. Not only have regionally concentrated minority groups availed themselves of the resources at hand in their kin-states to access economic and social development opportunities, but many trans-border ethnic groups also increased their political mobilisation and have established political parties, all of which have been conducive to enhancing the responsiveness of domestic political institutions to resident minorities.

1. CITIZENSHIP ACROSS BORDERS

Despite a number of developments in public international law over the past decades, citizenship is still perceived as 'the last bastion in the citadel of sovereignty',[4] and states maintain significant freedoms when regulating who is to become their citizen. Regulations on access to citizenship remain the reserved domain of states' competence; yet these have the potential to cause a destabilising effect on bilateral inter-state relations. Access to citizenship for non-residents is not regulated by international law; each state determines under its own laws who are its nationals and how non-citizens can assert their right to national citizenship. However, states generally follow standards set by the international practice of ensuring good neighbourly relationship and non-interference in the internal affairs of their neighbours when outlining criteria for non-residents' access to domestic citizenship. As long as the stipulated requirements for naturalisation are met, and in particular a link between the individual and the state is proven, access to citizenship for non-residents is not regulated by international law.

With the rules of international law being rare in the context of citizenship, it is extremely difficult to define the limits imposed on states with regard to access to citizenship. 'It is for each State to determine under its own laws who are its nationals', and third parties have the possibility of refusing recognition of a person's citizenship if it should be established that access to citizenship has been granted in violation of international law.[5] Although the requirement of permanent residence is common for naturalization and is usually stipulated in the states' citizenship laws, states remain at liberty to waive requirements for their potential citizens as there are no *prescribed* norms in the international law on the issue.

In general, the conferral of citizenship upon non-residents has been treated cautiously. Recommendation No. 11 of the Bolzano Recommendations of the OSCE High Commissioner for National Minorities emphasizes that the 'states may take preferred linguistic competencies and cultural, historical or familial ties into account in their decision to grant citizenship to individuals abroad'.[6] The explanatory note to the Recommendations indicates, however, that 'the conferral of citizenship to persons residing abroad is clearly one of the most common cause of tensions and conflict. . . . The presence of a kin-state's citizens on the territory of another State must not be used as a justification for undermining the sovereignty and territorial integrity of that State'.[7]

Overall, the Bolzano Recommendations encourage countries to strike a fair balance when extending rights to, and protecting the interests of, their citizens on the territory of another sovereign state.[8] In each case, naturally, states have a wide margin of discretion, deciding on requirements for residency, language proficiency or ancestral lineage, but for resolution of interstate disputes over citizens, attention is usually drawn to the 'dominant and effective nationality' to determine which state ought to step in as a diplomatic protector of the individual in question. It is here that we see yet again the decisive role of political institutions designed to provide preferential treatment to one ethnic group among the many of those residing in post-communist states.

As we have discussed, resulting from the overwhelmingly national state building across post-communist Central and Eastern Europe, individual citizens of these states regard members of 'their' respective minority abroad as part of a bigger, 'trans-border' nation, for which they claim a certain responsibility.[9] Indeed, as early as 1996 Brubaker sounded the alarm about the ever-present role played by the nationalising state in the process of framing citizen perceptions of their rights in a certain state and processes of objectification of these rights in the context of nation-states for members of minorities. The role of kin-states as external guarantors, and at times protectors of their ethnic kin abroad, makes consolidation of democratic political institutions across post-communist Europe centre on their ethno-nationally defined core constituencies.[10] The sometimes belligerent rhetoric of kin-states drew attention to the status of ethnic minorities in accession states, attracting international attention and critically only further persuading ethno-political elites in the nationalising states that the local minorities should not be easily trusted.

Political discourse on national sovereignty in much of post-communist Eastern Europe irrespective of EU membership demonstrates vividly that statehood across the post-communist area is widely perceived in terms of national sovereignty over an ancestral territory populated by a community with shared ethno-linguistic identity.[11] The continued importance of the nation-state as the dominant model of popular sovereignty makes access to citizenship for resident and non-resident ethnics a particularly interesting yet remarkably underexplored field of study.[12] Eastern European post-communist states that have acceded to the EU are supposed to abide by provisions in support of the non-discrimination of minorities in their own countries as well as obliged to maintain and enhance good neighbourly relations with the host states of their kin minorities. Underlying case studies of EU member-states' policies vis-à-vis co-ethnics abroad is the implicit assumption that union membership makes positive opportunities available to non-residents in other kin-state EU members. Yet neither during the period of EU accession nor after have the very foundations of the ethno-national statehood of post-communist countries came into question. In the course of EU integration, nation-states had to ensure adherence to the principles of non-discrimination and respect for national minorities, providing minority rights complementary to the right for national self-determination of the majority.

Central to this is the dominant role attributed to one group in society over the design of political institutions as avenues—if not outright instruments—of ensuring equality between post-communist citizens, whether they be members of either dominant or non-dominant ethnicities. Dealing explicitly with challenges of nation-state building in the environment where ethnic diversity is prevalent and salience of ethno-national identity is reflected in political institutions, we see extraterritorial citizenship is much more than just a legal framework allowing non-residents access to membership of the political community of the nation-state where this group is in a majority.

One of the objectives of such kin-state policies observed across the CEE and illustrated in discussions of extraterritorial citizenship has been the practice of 'extraterritorial naturalisation, of granting of citizenship to persons living in another country which share certain characteristics (e.g., in ethnic, religious or linguistic terms) with the state offering them access to citizenship'. This practice has been particularly favoured by the states affected by territorial changes in the past and witnessed growing pressures from kin-minorities residing just across the border in the neighbouring state.[13] While there is no set of criteria to determine what constitutes the 'trans-border' nation, legal regulations with regards to extraterritorial naturalisations are vague, and nation-states across the post-communist area have applied the category flexibly. As long as good neighbourly relations between states of residence and states of citizenship have not suffered as a result, little attention has been granted to the phenomenon. Especially as the states across the world are increasingly committed to fostering and enhancing their relations with non-resident members of their political communities, it is the focus on the shared ethnic identity that distinguishes post-communist states' approaches to extraterritorial citizenship.[14]

In the past, concerns were raised with regards to extraterritorial citizenship generally perceived as being undesirable, but gradually evolving into an accepted practice in international law. Despite the fact that disproportionate numbers of residents across the post-communist area consider themselves to be a part of a larger nation, they are concentrated in their own nation-states, and this has had the potential to strain inter-state and good neighbourly relations within the EU as a whole.[15] We therefore need to ask whether the consolidation of post-communist state institutions as guarantors of ethno-national political projects has also eased the pressure on states of residents by outsourcing the responsibility for co-ethnics onto external kin-states of minorities. Should this be the case, we could certainly claim that European conditionality and late membership of post-communist nation-states has positively supported the view of majorities across the region that national state design is not only supportive of nationally defined self-determination but also a guarantee for inter-ethnic peace in the EU at large.

A competing line of research has addressed reasons for which states grant citizenship to non-residents in order to enlarge the body of citizens and project soft power of the state across its sovereign borders.[16] Scholars working within this paradigm tend to question the fit between the increasingly individually defined access of persons to citizenship in terms of the relationship with civic EU member-states and the largely ethno-national understandings embedded in regulations of access to citizenship for ethnic minorities across the post-communist area. Often found in this scholarship are questions about the very commitment of EU member-states to maintaining the connection between the national and political in state institutions. If nation-states can—and they do—include their kin-minorities abroad into the body of citizenry by referring to the right of citizenship as membership in an ethno-national community, have foundational principles of liberal democracy been really transposed into the domestic legislations of new member-states?

As the numbers of those individuals recognised as members of polity increases due to non-residents' inclusion, so does the policy outreach of the state beyond its geographic sphere of influence. With the principle of territorially defined sovereignty still being a legally binding guideline of inter-state relations, combined with the predominant focus of post-communist states on the consolidation of their ethno-national citizenry around institutions of the nation-state, new member-states present us with an interesting set of cases for study. As a result of largely ethno-national state building across the post-communist area, the merits of ethnic identity are high in currency, and civic nationalism is widely used to denote the same sets of phenomena.[17] State-building projects of the ethno-cultural majorities across the region have imported the views that following EU accession, states continue to belong to the ethnic majority in post-communist states. Therefore, we need to ask whether the consolidation of nation-state institutions impacted on state-society relations across the wider European region.

Regardless of the point of view adopted, it is clear that the EU has played an important role in ensuring the implementation of norms and international standards of minority protection across the post-communist region. Definitions of an ethnic, national or linguistic minority are ambiguous and reflect the authoritative decisions of numerically larger identity groups, usually sharing the same polity about the need for status recognition for distinct purposes.[18] Status recognition implies an additional measure of group-based protection by the state of residence and/or allows for access to preferential treatment in these groups' kin-state, thus privileging these individuals' access to opportunities granted by other states. A nation with its own territorial political unit is, therefore, a critical point of reference for the self-identification of groups that find themselves in non-dominant positions.[19] Cases from across the EU indicate that resident non-dominant groups are often framed as liabilities, rather than potential assets for a particular country's development and regional stability. The perceptions of minority groups' potential disloyalty are matched only by the dominant national community's eagerness to claim the nation-state for themselves.

Therefore, when we refer to members of minorities residing outside of the nation-state, we ought to think of citizenship identities outside the narrow box of the political membership of individuals. Resident and non-resident non-citizens challenge the ordered views about the overlapping identity of territory, citizenry and political institutions essential for consolidating nation-state institutions and democratic governance within the EU. This allows departure from the narrow political view of citizenship and closer scrutiny of what nation-states 'do' when they engage with other nation-states on behalf of their co-ethnics. We can additionally distinguish between the meanings majority and minority communities ascribe to their nationality/citizenship, which are frequently portrayed in public debates as the cause for ethnic politicking over access, ownership and treatment by state institutions in post-communist nation-states.

2. KIN VERSUS NATIONALISING STATES AND GOOD NEIGHBOURLY RELATIONS

Now that we have established that post-communist nation-states have relied heavily on the emphasis of the ethnic component in political institutions of their states to ensure resident populations' acquiescence during the period of transition, we can to turn to the impact regional domestic institutions have had on inter-state relations. This is a particularly salient issue in post-communist Europe for most minorities, Roma being the most prominent exception. Not only does the presence of the kin-state allow nation-states in the process of consolidating their rule over citizens to tap the rhetoric of displacing responsibility for ethnic minority groups onto other polities, but it also requires nation-states to engage with their kin-minority in other states.

It is worth turning to the mediating effects of kin-states in the context of affirming, if not outright securing, the primacy of domestic decision making over issues relevant to minority rights in the context of European integration. Interestingly, where the minorities' 'kin-states' have sought to often galvanise ethnic politics, they have had a greater impact of ethno-political mobilisation of nationalising the majority than on that of their own kin.[20] In most cases, the socio-economical vulnerability of the minority-populated regions allowed kin-states to promote themselves as protectors of their titular nations abroad, verbally attacking other nation-states' institution-building projects, especially at the end of electoral cycles. Ethno-political entrepreneurs of the majority seldom interpreted these as anything but an 'attack on sovereignty' or putting minority residents at an advantage in terms of labour market access, travel, and education, and more, versus limiting the majority's opportunities with the territory of a nation-state.[21]

The effect the kin-states' populations mingling with their kin abroad really did have was most certainly the consolidation of the majority's tutelage over minority issues in these states, allowing the ethno-political agendas of the majority to silence potential issues for inter-group dialogue. European organizations' engagement also undermined mobilisation options for minority groups on an ethnic basis, contributing to regional stability.[22] In the longer run, it demonstrated that the minorities' kin-states would be unable to co-opt disgruntled groups for internal and foreign policy purposes, unless they demonstrated a clear commitment to grant political resources for mobilisation outside their own borders.[23] This objective in part was achieved where agenda setting in kin-states favoured the ethnic dimension of interactions between states, especially indicating the economic support for kin minorities without overall challenges to domestic politics or political institutions.

For minority communities, the prospect of EU accession offered some opportunity to escape the nationalising logic of their states of residence. In addition, it guaranteed access to a range of crucially needed resources in their kin-states and suggested that all parts of the citizenry would be able to engage in policymaking domestically as long as they did not challenge the primacy of titular groups' in decision making. Yet in all cases in which minority communities were equally exposed to 'the nationalising state', their presence across the border of their kin-state further entrenched perceptions in that state as not only serving but also privileging titular residents by means other than sheer institutional dominance.[24] As such, it is of course impossible to represent domestic actors' rationales and calculation comprehensibly as seeking not only to establish a rapport with domestic constituencies of the majority but also to cater to regional perceptions of neighbouring kin-states of resident minorities about the general compliance with and respect for norms of minority non-discrimination.

However, the effects of rhetorical adherence to European norms in this area are easily identifiable in interactions that stem from states' adherence to the principle of respect for domestic sovereignty over the entirety of their neighbours' populations, including one's own kin. Furthermore, while the disenchanted domestic minorities lobbied actors in the EU and in their kin-states to put additional pressures on domestic majority policymakers, the institutional setting of the EU put a premium on domestic management of inter-ethnic relations between EU member-states. In demonstrating their ability to keep minority claims at bay, domestic policymakers have effective-ly demonstrated to both the policymakers in neighbouring states and their European monitors their ability to assert sovereignty not only vis-à-vis the ethnic core but also vis-à-vis the entire resident population.

Overall, minority individuals across the accession states have as a rule been granted the right to identify with and assert their preferences as a part of culturally distinct communities in their countries of residence. Having achieved this, their input into statewide political decision making was mini-mised. With governments focussing on delivering their promises to national majorities, all but tokenistic concessions to ensure minority visibility was confined to areas of minority territorial concentration.[25] Where minority resi-dents were present in high numbers, accession states were compelled to tolerate a number of measures. These included minority languages becoming the de facto working language in municipalities, enhanced visibility on bilin-gual street signs and the right to receive a mother-tongue education. In most other areas where the minority was present yet did not constitute in any way a significant political group, their cultural concerns have been brushed aside by reference to the duty of the state to deliver services to citizens regardless of their ethnic identities.

The rationale for greater protection of minority group rights was con-strained by the domestic design of state institutions setting out first and foremost to serve the majority community. This rationale of state institutions was accepted in the context of EU accession as the best possible means for domestic policymakers to further consolidate state institutional performance for the sake of regional and inter-state cooperation.[26] Insofar as the notion of state sovereignty overlapped with that of the state capacity to implement sets of European directives, titular groups' tutelage over the political process during the accession could be effectively translated into mutual esteem between states as able to manage domestic challenges to their sovereignty effectively.

While EU involvement helped set the agenda and was suggestive of the resources to be used by the nation-state to undermine the structural opportunities for the minority to mobilise, kin-states granted minorities' additional sponsorship for identity-based claims. As we have seen, throughout the period of international involvement, majorities in these states have effectively prevented minority mobilisations by redefining their political ends, redrafting political agendas and redrawing the borders between the groups within minority communities with the objective of facilitating the consolidation of nation-state institutions. This has prevented minorities' access to the institutional opportunity structures of the new polities, emphasising the ethno-cultural basis of the states and the special status the majority enjoyed in the political process of state building and institutional consolidation.

The current configuration of post-communist EU membership has only further confirmed that political institutions across the region are and can remain ethno-national in their outlook, despite provisions having been put in place for the rights of ethnic groups to be observed by their states of residence. Galbreath and McEvoy argue that nation-state building across the post-communist area has been particularly successful because all countries have engaged in the process to an equal degree, resulting in the securitisation of resident minorities across the whole region.[27] At the same time, however, as scholarship on the citizenship of non-residents suggests, nation-states providing access to political membership to their kin residing abroad further reaffirms the commitment of nation-states to protect its core, majority ethnic group interests from encroaching claims of resident citizens with a different ethnicity.[28] While ethnic minorities resident outside their kin-state have attested to using European organizations' forums and transnational nongovernmental organizations alike to seek leverage against policy preferences of their state of residence, it seems that state institutions, state territories and its citizenry are widely perceived as one and the same across the region.

While member-states have historically granted special attention to their co-ethnics abroad, with Danes in South Schleswig, German speakers in South Tyrol and Irish citizens in the UK all benefitting from inter-state cooperation within the EU, new member-states have equally emulated policies to appease their ethnic kin across the borders. However, under conditions when nation-state building projects across the region are contesting more than the legitimacy of accessing state institutions for local minorities, the communist legacies of ethno-territorial diversity management have ushered a set of unique dynamics into these relationships.[29] We observe two distinct rationales across the post-communist region: on the one hand, reconstituted nation-states have extended their right of citizenship to co-ethnics who have fled communist regimes, whilst, on the other hand, states that have experienced border changes over the past century have projected their cultural policies across the now established boundaries.

The Baltic States constitute an example of the first type when privileged access to Baltic citizenship drew attention to the purely legalistic treatment of extraterritorial citizenship that citizens of the inter-war Baltic States could claim regardless of their current place of residence and citizenship status. Discussion about granting citizenship to non-residents of Hungary has focussed upon residents of regions where a significant proportion of the inhabitants have been aggrieved by the nationalising policies of Slovakia, Romania and Ukraine. During the 1990s, all of these countries struggled to negotiate their own state and nation-building projects and (naturally) saw their efforts at nation-state building being undermined during the passage of the Hungarian Status Law of 2001.[30] The rhetorical engagement of successive Hungarian governments with the so-called Hungarian diaspora could easily lead to the supposition that extraterritorial naturalisation is a means of projecting Hungary's influence across the area lost with the Treaty of Trianon in 1920. While the matter of preferential naturalisation of Hungarians living in the neighbouring states constituted an area of mutual interest for Romania, Slovakia and Ukraine, the issues should have been resolved in mutual agreement rather than by unilateral action on the part of the kin-state. Instead, the introduction of preferential naturalisation for ethnic Hungarians living outside Hungary's borders resulted in prolonged tensions with Hungary's neighbours, whose own perceptions of successful nation-state building on their territory were challenged.

This example shows that the design of post-communist states as polities serving primarily, if not exclusively, the ethnic majority population is the key explanatory factor for comparative difficulty in dealing with ethnically diverse domestic populations while also applying similar sets of policies to co-ethnics abroad. Especially, as the consolidation of national statehoods has ushered the stewardship of state-bearing majorities over the political institutions 'their' state has applied across the region, the link between the ethnic and political identity of post-communist citizens has become more prominent and the role played by the kin-state salient in domestic political debates. In the mid-1990s, Will Kymlicka observed that many post-communist Eastern Europeans do not distinguish ethnic from civic nationalism because 'their' states are designed to serve the dominant ethnic community, making it particularly hard for domestic minorities to identify with constitutions and policies and in general be 'good citizens' of states that treat them as 'less equal' than members of the majority.[31] It is therefore obvious that despite the EU accession negotiations and membership of post-communist states, this link between the nation-state and its ethnic kin abroad has not only remained unrevised but also gained additional weight over the past two decades.

On the one hand, this was achieved by states passing laws and policies equating national sovereignty with the ethno-national ownership over political institutions. As observed in the cases of Estonia, Lithuania and Slovakia, among others, state constitutions implicitly identify the state majority as the rightful owner of the polity, legally ensuring the tutelage by the majority group over the post-communist transition. The imperative of state titularisation has further found support during the period of accession and input the consolidated European approach to the management of ethnic diversity by privileging co-ethnics and allowing co-ethnic non-resident-facilitated access to citizenship of their kin-states, as in Latvia, Poland, Serbia, Croatia and Slovenia. On the other hand, the securitisation of minorities has prompted many post-communist states to turn increasingly to their kin minorities abroad and allow access to domestic citizenship to non-resident co-ethnics, as in Hungary, Romania, Bulgaria and the Russian Federation.

3. THE IMPACT ON THE DYNAMICS
OF INTER-STATE RELATIONS

The post-communist-region Europe presents us with sets of cases in which ethnic groups that were previously in a minority position have been successful in altering institutional settings and establishing titular nation-states in the wake of the collapse of communism. Yet transition from communist to liberal democratic regimes has witnessed parallel processes of restructuring of political, economic and social institutions in all countries of the region.[32] Not only have those 'nations' previously part of the socialist federations of Yugoslavia, Czechoslovakia and, indeed, the Soviet Union attained sovereignty over their states, but all other nations of the region also asserted themselves as equal and respected partners of European institutions in the process of Eastern enlargement.

We should note here that past research has conceptualised normative standards projected onto aspiring member-states by analysing the response of domestic political actors to external pressures.[33] Yet it has barely discerned the same scale effects from the EU level in 'old' member-states.[34] It is necessary therefore to turn our attention first and foremost to the legal environment in which states seeking EU membership operated throughout the 1990s. This was constituted by the principle of good neighbourly relations, which all potential candidates had to abide by and needed to respect in order to become a constituent part of the EU.[35] All post-communist states had to fulfil the Copenhagen Criteria, which included political, economic and social benchmarks to assess the capacity of applicant states to perform as viable and reliable members of the international community of European countries that valued solidarity and cooperation.

Candidate states' commitments, either explicit or implicit, had to follow a variety of norms guiding their behaviours vis-à-vis other member-states, covering every aspect of policy formation and action. Though often questioned in the literature on European conditionality, the principle of nation-states' equality has been central to the process of European integration.[36] Although candidate countries have to implement reforms and transpose the bulk of European legislation, it is assumed that membership will result in equal access to and say in joint law and policymaking. The resulting sets of obligations candidate nation-states bore during the accession period would naturally lead to these states gaining in sets of rights once they achieve membership and should be seen as reflecting the mutual recognition of member-states as equal partners in decision making in a variegated universe of EU-related norms.[37]

From this point of view, inter-state recognition as actors able and willing to commit to mutual cooperation should be regarded primarily as the feedback mechanism for agents conceived as essentially norm guided in their interactions with one another. In particular, a switch to a more 'interactionist' account of reciprocal relations has considerable explanatory value in our case of relations between candidate and member-states: the guiding principle in such interactions is the idea that identities of nation-states as agents are produced through a process of negotiation of their obligations and rights.[38] We should therefore see states as group agents in the forum of international organizations who commit to multiparty decisions with other nation-states, as group agents. These issues of joint interest include matters as variegated as standards of food safety, the regulation of central bank independence, freedom of movement for EU citizens, as well as standards of accepting other nation-states' sovereignty over decisions implemented on their territory.[39]

At the same time, states interact with one another in smaller groups, elaborating the best possible strategies to achieve optimal outcomes for individual states. These narrower sets of interests include regional clusters of optimal policy decisions, such as cross-border cooperation, security of external borders or management and the movement of goods. In both cases, the underlying strategy seems to be that framing outcomes in terms of an individual agents' recognition as an esteemed and respected partner in any given forum places a premium not only on an international organization that features as a forum for negotiating—and, at times, arbitrating—divergent interests but also on nation-states as agents setting the criteria for mutual recognition as able and strategic actors.

It has been noted often that where two agents endowed with unequal resources face each other in order to seek mutually beneficial outcomes, less resourceful actors actually experience a struggle for recognition for equal status. In the context of EU enlargement, this is precisely the point often made regarding the limited opportunities for candidate countries to challenge or revise standards that the EU required them to implement prior to accession.[40] As some observers of the EU accession process remark with regard to the rationality of the accession process, the very decision of candidate states to continue with transposition and implementation of legislation and policies ahead of admission into the EU indicates one-sided recognition of EU's normative standards by the candidate countries in terms of guarantees for future benefits for their nation-state after the accession.

In inter-state relations, achieving esteem enables states to garner support from others, on the one hand, and to legitimise their own policies vis-à-vis their constituents and thereby enjoy parity of status with other sovereign polities, on the other hand. This brings out the interactive approach to recognition: the connection between the recognition of a state's authority over its citizens by these citizens and authoritative relations states come to enjoy in relations with other states as able agents of policy implementation. In this more interactive view, recognition on the part of other states is only of value to polities to the extent that these already recognise other members of the regime as, in some sense, competent judges of one's own performance.

This explains why the mutual recognition of states in their capacity to maintain sovereignty over their policy decision does not directly determine these states' relationship to their own citizens. It is because the authority of the international community as a whole, as well as individual other states, over the state seeking recognition is dependent, in the first instance, on that state's recognition of other states and the international community as relevant for its own identity as sovereign. Likewise, for states, judgements of those states that are not recognised as authorities can simply be discounted or dismissed, as this will in no way prevent a state from having its authority recognised domestically. Similarly, if the authority of the state is recognised by significant others (for example, international organizations such as the EU or pivot external states), state actors can safely refuse to acknowledge domestic challenges to their authority.[41]

States as agents seeking to maintain good neighbourly relations with one another must secure recognition from relevant others that they are entitled to for their chosen identity. As such, states undertake sovereign decisions over the populace in their territory, just as they are expected to accept acts of sovereignty performed by other states in their own territory. As agents, states engage in international forums to first avoid the misrecognition of their identities, and only second by conforming to the normative backdrop of interactions with other agents (i.e., states). They gain attention and, indeed, recognition as agents that are willing and able to abide by the rules established, agreed upon and followed by other states within the given framework of the inter-state relations as is established by the EU.[42] The reciprocity in and of inter-state exchanges in international forums therefore has little effectiveness of its own. International forums do not have the capacity to engage with its constituent agents (i.e., states) beyond the ability to appeal to interests shared and rationale accepted by all its participating agents.[43]

In the EU, member-states promote policies on their territories and project them onto other EU member-states in reflecting expectations that emerge in interactions with other states. In so doing, member-states adjust policies and practices according to the reactions of other states, rationally calculating the effects of their individual policy choices on other states, participants in the same forum where they seek recognition as reliable partners in the context of European institutional settings.[44] If one state deliberately treats another state's citizens differently from one's own citizens, on the condition that the differential treatment is prohibited, we have reason to anticipate a negative reaction from the state whose citizens are being treated disadvantageously. In the specific example in which the Hungarian state sought to extend its right for citizenship to nationals of other states who do not reside on the territory of Hungary proper by means of the Status Law, it has indeed elicited reactions of protest on the part of Slovakia and Romania, states whose ethnic Hungarian citizens were the primary target of the law.[45] Similarly, the community of European nation-states saw the Hungarian Status Law as a precedent for granting citizenship rights on the basis of ethnicity and thus potentially discriminating against some of the citizens of Hungary's neighbours and harming Hungary's relations with them, particularly Romania and Slovakia, both of which host substantial ethnic Hungarian minorities.

However, as agents, states also emulate one another's behaviour and anticipate that others will acknowledge the (mal-)application of norms: underlying this is a focus on the international legal order as one characterised by the separation of the legal tenets, encompassing modern ideals of the rule of law and equal rights of agents, as distinct from the status order of the past when one state's entitlement to esteem was tied to its (however defined) contribution to the common good. Conversely, recognition of state capacity to make policies and implement decisions is akin to social recognition because it creates the conditions under which the state can develop, establish and receive acknowledgement of their basic agency in context, when interacting with other states, as well as with their own citizens. By extending this line of argument into the domain of inter-state relations with regard to their citizens, the recognition states may seek for their particular actions, a particularised form of recognition that attends to the value and achievements of that state, is a form of particular esteem, rather than of universal respect.

This particular form of esteem is directly related to the principle of good neighbourliness signposted as a requirement for states seeking EU accession—inasmuch as the state ought to manage the populace resident on the territory under its jurisdiction, the state's ability to effectively implement policies on its territory should be seen as the source of esteem in inter-state relations.[46] Importantly, the level of esteem states receive can be determined by their commitment to the principle of good neighbourliness as a specific form of interaction reflecting on mutual respect as sovereign polities.[47] Thus, inter-state interactions in the enlarged EU reflect on both the ability of individual states to make decisions without unnecessarily antagonising states, whose interests might be affected by specific policies, and accepting the sovereign decisions of other states to implement policies effective on their territories and potentially affecting non-dominant groups of residents on their territory.

The distinction drawn here between states as actors in the context of international relations such as within the EU, and as institutions that determine the basis upon which these relationships can be built, is crucial. On the one hand, we see citizens of states finding themselves directly affected by sovereign decisions of their states of residence. On the other hand, these very citizens are also affected as a result of their states' decisions to cooperate with other countries in the context of a joint regime. In both cases, it is states that determine different sets of rules to be followed at two distinct levels of interaction—that between the states in the international forum and that between different individuals and/or groups of individuals in comparably similar circumstances in the context of the nation-state.

This leads us to differentiate two analytical levels when assessing origins of change and stability in the context of EU enlargement that have affected distinct policy areas. First, when observing political processes as a sequence of however long stable conditions, we ought to focus on institutions of the state that socialise actors operating therein into perceiving structural stability as necessary. Secondly, our observation of the structural conditions as underlying the competing rationales, specific to different actors at each period in time and at each level of analyses, must be cognisant of states' seeking to establish relations. Thus, we will be better able to identify the choice of (in-)action by individual states as a result of their assessment of challenges resulting from either change or the stability of the relationship they have experienced to date and that might result in them opting for institutional change or otherwise seeking to maintain institutional stability. Overall, identifying the structural options for states to change the existing parameters of inter-state cooperation allows us to separate the domains of the state's relation with the EU, other member-states and their own citizens.

So, the original signatories to the Treaty of Rome in 1957 sought to strengthen the unity of their economies and their harmonious development to ensure economic and social progress, as well as to confirm the solidarity and the development of their prosperity. Not only has the Treaty helped to institutionalise the foundation for the 'ever closer union among the peoples of Europe', but it also established a reciprocal framework for relationships of states as partners that are respected by the EU, esteemed by neighbouring states and trusted to safeguard citizens' interests on their territory.[48] The text below illustrates how nation-states interact with their citizens, other states and the EU when it comes to guarantees of and management of ethnic diversity.

All EU member-states have to confirm to a set of formal rules agreed upon in the process of membership negotiation. As part and parcel of this process, EU law has become increasingly relevant insofar as applicants aimed to become member-states and use this, and no other, international arena in pursuit of their individual interests. The *acquis*, EU legislation and policy blueprints, provide a reference point for these individual states to determine how and by what means they should gain respect from the EU as an institutionalised collective actor, esteem from other states as sovereigns over their policymaking and implementation, and trust from their core citizens to deliver services in line with and according to nation-state policies already in place. Yet the laws by which states are to abide are but a product of prior agreement and depend on compliance only as a set of rules acceptable to its constituent principle agents. Thus, member-states are actors operating in an institutional environment of the EU structured by law. They can do so only because they are guided by shared normative assumptions about the importance of institutional structures in place, registering mutually agreed-upon claims over the sovereign territory of the state while also acknowledging the innate interest of other nation-states in the status of their kin-minorities residing across the border in another country.

Tension related to building nation-state institutions designed to serve ethnically diverse societies across post-communist Europe highlighted the special attention states grant their ethnic kin abroad while showing limited commitment to domestic minority groups had led many to conclude that domestic policies were being driven by nationalist aspirations. Nation-states are indeed most often the homelands of one ethnic group, having a clear cultural and ethnic makeup. Perhaps unsurprisingly, national communities are more often than not thought of in terms of clearly defined territories, from which they 'hail', they 'own' and increasingly, 'govern'. The perception of the nation-state as serving domestic majorities, rather than all citizens regardless of their ethnic, cultural, religious and language identity, is largely taken for granted, as is the view that the ethno-political mobilisation of minorities is driven by their anti-state, rather than anti-policy, agendas.

Two parallel processes of nation-state building, on the one hand, and European integration, on another, have contributed to the evolution of what is presently considered the European minority rights regime: it reaffirms the majorities' central role in guiding the processes of inter-ethnic cooperation in their states while allowing both the minority and the majority groups to preserve their ethnic, cultural and linguistic identities. Herein lies the puzzling effect of the European approach to minority issues at large that allows us to return to the original institutional design of post-communist states. Based on the notion of nation-states' guiding role in determining the scope of domestic policies targeting minority issues, populations resident on the territory of post-communist accession states were able to consolidate their national sovereignty in order to serve their core ethno-national identity group, determining that the political processes would be of ethno-national form. Democratic consolidation across the post-communist region has activated similar institutional preferences across the board of states and infused interstate relations with mutual recrimination over the status of co-ethnics' targeting by the nationalising institutions of states in which they lived.

First and foremost, the shortcomings of such an approach rely on institutions of the state defined in ethno-cultural terms and therefore attributing one group a decisive say when dealing with individuals of other cultural backgrounds. Thus, non-dominant groups are not only re-created in their cultural features by the policies in place but also propelled into agitating for greater recognition of their difference and thus also their need for group-specific support as a result of negative treatment they experience in their interactions with political institutions. Precisely, this salience of cultural identities makes the perception of one's options as a member of a particular group extremely important for states to acknowledge their ethnic kin abroad as being placed into an uneven playing field with the titular majority of the nation-state where they reside. After the demise of communism, nation-state building confirmed the privileged relationship between states and their titular majorities, building upon the communist dictum that the nation-state is the bedrock of sovereignty over titular nations' ancestral territory. However, where limits of citizenry do not correspond to those of nations' dominant ethnicities, polities became 'nationalising states' not only at home but also abroad, enticing kin minorities' linguistic, cultural and later political affiliation with their homeland state.

On a more theoretical level, what we see across post-communist states are sets of state institutions that provide the best service to the members of particular groups—that is, titular nationals. An immediate effect of the national institutional design is the policy implication that *groups and not individuals* are subjects of change and objects of policies throughout. Along these lines, all European states promote minority protection policies with the help of institutions, nominally accountable to all individuals of the diverse society.[49] However, it has been frequently suggested that states do promote 'multicultural' ideologies at the expense of the pluralist view of group identities and undermining the liberal core of governing diverse citizenries by enforcing regimes devised by and for the resident majorities.[50]

Following this, we can note that current debates on multiculturalism observe that its distinguishing feature is the implicit or explicit attempt to honour liberal egalitarianism to reconcile the growing acceptance of cultural heterogeneity of the citizenry with the (neutral) institutions of the state. However, in many countries, political structures' functions are not culturally blind because the dominant groups use them all too frequently to support nation building. Although multiculturalism has grown out of the original idea of defending and promoting ethnic cultures of national communities, local minorities, or migratory communities, its area of application is limited to a context in which one culture prevails and can thus be taken to investigate state-society relations of post-communist states extending the right of citizenship to their co-ethnic residents abroad.

Research on possible reasons for halting the process of democratisation in such ethnically diverse societies shows consistent interest in states that either 'fail' or are 'fragile' because institution building and policymakers' decisions follow from 'identity building projects' of dominant ethnicities at the expense of resident minorities. A subsection in this field focussing explicitly on post-communist states identifies domestic political actors as principle causes for 'fits and starts' in democratic consolidation.[51] Remarkably, this literature rarely concludes that political actors of the minority cause disruption but points out that it is decisions of ethno-political entrepreneurs of the majority that alienate minorities from participation in state democratisation.

In reflecting on the domestic institutional dynamics of limited support for cultural and language rights of minority citizens, the instruments of the European minority rights regime have been supportive of a state institutional approach aimed at enhancing domestic policymakers' capacity to increase costs for minorities to claim external support, whether from the EU or their kin-states. This has taken place throughout the post-communist accession states where an individual-focussed, non-discrimination approach rather than group-centred, minority rights legislation was scheduled to be implemented into domestic law pre-accession. In such instances, law making, implementation and compliance all point to the gradually reduced ability of minority groups to input into domestic institutions with reference to group-related grievances.

CONCLUSION

Post-communist states are said to have been 'captured' by dominant identity groups that project a specific set of interests and priorities to both internal and external publics, thus combining the short- as well as the long-term interests of state-building projects. Kin-states' declared responsibility for ethnic kin abroad is much more than a simple reflection of the unique post-communist democratisation trajectories in the region. Here, state building has been attuned to the respect and protection of the rights of minorities. Yet titular, name-giving and state-bearing nations interpret the criteria for participation in the political process, define the criteria for the political inclusion of residents into the citizenry and, ultimately, grant the status of minorities to members of non-dominant ethnic groups.

Yet the fluidity of the nation-building project's goals and limited instrumental value of policymaking for the synchronisation of state- and nation-building agendas is ever more surprising as the constructed nature of national communities is a widely accepted view across post-communist Central and Eastern Europe. However, a detailed reading of policies on extraterritorial citizenship allows us to conclude that domestic majorities happily concede the artificiality of others' nations while defending the perennial character of their own. It is this belief that one's ethnic, cultural and linguistic communities are not to be questioned, which explains the lasting success in generating domestic solidarity and/or legitimising geopolitical weightlifting by states over their kin-minorities abroad. The link fostered between the nation-state's majority population and non-dominant co-ethnics residing in another state de facto 'naturalises' the perception of state ownership by and for a single ethnic community at home. At the same time, it projects similarly wrought concepts of homogeneity outwards onto non-resident co-ethnics, the nation-states where kin-minority resides, and across the region.

NOTES

1. Karl Cordell and Stefan Wolff, *Ethnic Conflict: Causes, Consequences, and Responses* (Cambridge: Polity, 2009).

2. Jeffrey Harlig, 'National Consolidation vs. European Integration: The Language Issue in Slovakia', *Security Dialogue* 28, no. 4 (1997): 479–91, doi:10.1177/0967010697028004008; Myra A. Waterbury, 'Uncertain Norms, Unintended Consequences: The Effects of European Union Integration on Kin-State Politics in Eastern Europe', *Ethnopolitics* 7, no. 2–3 (2008): 217–38.

3. Karl Cordell and Stefan Wolff, 'Germany as a Kin-State: The Development and Implementation of a Norm-Consistent External Minority Policy towards Central and Eastern Europe', *Nationalities Papers* 35, no. 2 (2007): 289–315; Conor O'Dwyer, *Runaway State-Building: Patronage Politics and Democratic Development* (Baltimore: Johns Hopkins University Press, 2006).

4. Peter J. Spiro, 'A New International Law of Citizenship', *American Journal of International Law* 105, no. 4 (October 2011): 694–746, doi:10.5305/amerjintelaw.105.4.0694.

5. Article, 1 *Hague Convention on Certain Questions relating to the Conflict of Nationality*, LNTS, Vol. 179, 89. See also, Article 3 of the European Convention on Nationality 1997 (ETS No. 166), stating that each state shall determine under its own law who are its nationals. States shall accept this law insofar as it is consistent with applicable international conventions, customary international law and the principles of law generally recognised with regard to nationality.

6. Knut Vollebaek, 'The Bolzano/Bozen Recommendations on National Minorities in Inter-State Relations & Explanatory Note' (OSCE HCNM, June 2008).

7. Knut Vollebaek, 'The International Politics of Minority Issues: Could the Early 1990s Return?' London School of Economics and Political Science, 7 May 2009, http://www.lse.ac.uk/publicEvents/events/2009/20090312t0911z001.aspx.

8. Elena Basheska, 'The Good Neighbourliness Condition in EU Enlargement', *Contemporary Southeastern Europe* 1, no. 1 (2014): 92–111.

9. Francesco Palermo and Natalie Sabanadze, eds., *National Minorities in Inter-State Relations* (Leiden: Martinus Nijhoff Publishers, 2011).

10. Rogers Brubaker, *Nationalism Reframed: Nationhood and the National Question in the New Europe* (Cambridge: Cambridge University Press, 1996).

11. Timofey Agarin, 'Nation-State Building with the Bear in Mind: The Impact of the Russian Federation in Post-Soviet "Breakaway" Regions', in *Extraterritorial Citizenship in Postcommunist Europe*, ed. Timofey Agarin and Ireneusz Pawel Karolewski (Lanham, MD: Rowman & Littlefield, 2015), 109–34.

12. Nadya Nedelsky, 'Constitutional Nationalism's Implications for Minority Rights and Democratization: The Case of Slovakia', *Ethnic and Racial Studies* 26, no. 1 (2003): 102–28; Tamara J. Resler, 'Dilemmas of Democratisation: Safeguarding Minorities in Russia, Ukraine and Lithuania', *Europe-Asia Studies* 49, no. 1 (1997): 89–106.

13. Iván Halász, 'Models of Kin Minority Protection in Central and Eastern Europe', in *Beyond Sovereignty: From Status Law to Transnational Citizenship?* ed. Osamu Ieda (Sapporo: Slavic Research Center, Hokkaido University, 2006), 255–79.

14. Andreea Udrea, 'A Kin-State's Responsibility: Cultural Identity, Recognition, and the Hungarian Status Law', *Ethnicities* 14, no. 2 (1 April 2014): 324–46, doi:10.1177/146 8796812472145.

15. Dimitry Kochenov, 'The Internal Aspects of Good Neighbourliness in the EU: Loyalty and Values', in *Good Neighbourly Relations in the European Legal Context*, ed. Dmitry Kochenov and Elena Basheska (Nijhoff: Brill, 2015).

16. See Ireneusz Pawel Karolewski, 'The Polish Charter: Extraterritorial Semi-Citizenship and Soft Power', in *Extraterritorial Citizenship in Postcommunist Europe*, ed. Timofey Agarin and Ireneusz Pawel Karolewski (Lanham, MD: Rowman & Littlefield, 2015), 65–88.

17. Nevena Nancheva, *Between Nationalism and Europeanisation: Narratives of National Identity in Bulgaria and Macedonia* (Colchester: ECPR Press, 2015).

18. Bernd Rechel, *Minority Rights in Central and Eastern Europe* (London: Routledge, 2009); Joseph Marko, 'The Concept of "Nation"', *European Yearbook of Minority Issues Online* 5, no. 1 (2005): 141–46.

19. Eric P. Kaufmann, *Rethinking Ethnicity: Majority Groups and Dominant Minorities* (London: Routledge, 2004).

20. Agarin, 'Nation-State Building with the Bear in Mind'.

21. Charles King and Neil J. Melvin, *Nations Abroad: Diaspora Politics and International Relations in the Former Soviet Union* (Boulder, CO: Westview Press, 1998).

22. Ada-Charlotte Regelmann, *Minority Integration and State-Building: Post-Communist Transformations* (London: Routledge, 2016).

23. David C. Earnest, 'The Enfranchisement of Resident Aliens: Variations and Explanations', *Democratization* 22, no. 5 (29 July 2015): 861–83, doi:10.1080/13510347.2014.979162; Anca Turcu and R. Urbatsch, 'Diffusion of Diaspora Enfranchisement Norms: A Multinational Study', *Comparative Political Studies* 48, no. 4 (1 March 2015): 407–37, doi:10.1177/0010 414014546331.

24. For a critical engagement, see Ephraim Nimni, 'National–Cultural Autonomy as an Alternative to Minority Territorial Nationalism', *Ethnopolitics* 6, no. 3 (2007): 345–64.

25. Susan A. Banducci, Todd Donovan, and Jeffrey A. Karp, 'Minority Representation, Empowerment, and Participation', *Journal of Politics* 66, no. 2 (2004): 534–56.

26. Timofey Agarin and Ada-Charlotte Regelmann, 'Which Is the Only Game in Town? Minority Rights Issues in Estonia and Slovakia during and after EU Accession', *Perspectives on European Politics and Society* 13, no. 4 (2012): 443–61, doi:10.1080/15705854 .2012.731934.

27. David J. Galbreath and Joanne McEvoy, 'European Integration and the Geopolitics of National Minorities', *Ethnopolitics* 9, no. 3–4 (2010): 357–77.

28. Rainer Bauböck, 'Morphing the Demos into the Right Shape: Normative Principles for Enfranchising Resident Aliens and Expatriate Citizens', *Democratization* 22, no. 5 (2015): 820–39, doi:10.1080/13510347.2014.988146.

29. Karl Cordell, Timofey Agarin, and Alexander Osipov, eds., *Institutional Legacies of Communism: Change and Continuities in Minority Protection* (London: Routledge, 2013).

30. Osamu Ieda, ed., *Beyond Sovereignty: From Status Law to Transnational Citizenship?* (Sapporo: Slavic Research Center, Hokkaido University, 2006).

31. Will Kymlicka, *Multicultural Citizenship: A Liberal Theory of Minority Rights* (Oxford: Clarendon Press, 1995).

32. Ireneusz Pawel Karolewski, 'Constitutionalization of the European Union as a Response to the Eastern Enlargement: Functions versus Power', *Journal of Communist Studies and Transition Politics* 23, no. 4 (2007): 501–24.

33. Mark A. Jubulis, 'The External Dimension of Democratization in Latvia: The Impact of European Institutions', *International Relations* 13, no. 3 (1996): 59–73.

34. Markus Haverland, 'Does the EU *Cause* Domestic Developments? Improving Case Selection in Europeanisation Research', *West European Politics* 29, no. 1 (2006): 134–46; Douglas R. Imig and Sydney Tarrow, 'Political Contention in a Europeanising Polity', *West European Politics* 23, no. 4 (2000): 73–93.

35. Basheska, 'The Good Neighbourliness Condition in EU Enlargement'.

36. Ole Waever, 'Identity, Integration and Security: Solving the Sovereignty Puzzle in EU Studies', *Journal of International Affairs* 48, no. 2 (1995).

37. Kristina Mikulova and Michal Simecka, 'Norm Entrepreneurs and Atlanticist Foreign Policy in Central and Eastern Europe: The Missionary Zeal of Recent Converts', *Europe-Asia Studies* 65, no. 6 (12 July 2013): 1192–1216, doi:10.1080/09668136.2013.813681.

38. Christophe Hillion, 'Enlargement of the European Union—The Discrepancy between Membership Obligations and Accession Conditions as Regards the Protection of Minorities', *Fordham International Law Journal* 27 (2003): 715–40.

39. Sigrun Skogly, *Beyond National Borders: States' Human Rights Obligations in International Cooperation* (Cambridge: Cambridge University Press, 2006); Beate Kohler-Koch, 'The Strength of Weakness: The Transformation of Governance in the EU', *The Future of the Nation-State. Essays on Cultural Pluralism and Political Integration*, 1996, 169–210.

40. Tanja E. Aalberts, 'The Future of Sovereignty in Multilevel Governance Europe: A Constructivist Reading', *JCMS: Journal of Common Market Studies* 42, no. 1 (2004): 23–46.

41. Yaniv Voller, 'Contested Sovereignty as an Opportunity: Understanding Democratic Transitions in Unrecognized States', *Democratization* 22, no. 4 (7 June 2015): 610–30, doi:10.1080/13510347.2013.856418; Thomas Gehring, Sebastian Oberthür, and Marc Mühleck, 'European Union Actorness in International Institutions: Why the EU Is Recognized as an Actor in Some International Institutions, but Not in Others', *JCMS: Journal of Common Market Studies* 51, no. 5 (2013): 849–65, doi:10.1111/jcms.12030.

42. Philippe Cullet, 'Differential Treatment in International Law: Towards a New Paradigm of Inter-State Relations', *European Journal of International Law* 10, no. 3 (1999): 549–82; Andrew Hurrell and Anand Menon, 'Politics Like Any Other? Comparative Politics, International Relations and the Study of the EU', *West European Politics* 19, no. 2 (1996): 386–402.

43. Alex Warleigh, 'Learning from Europe? EU Studies and the Re-Thinking of "International Relations"', *European Journal of International Relations* 12, no. 1 (2006): 31–51.

44. Fredrik Söderbaum and Luk Van Langenhove, 'Introduction: The EU as a Global Actor and the Role of Interregionalism', *European Integration* 27, no. 3 (2005): 249–62.

45. Stephen Deets and Sherrill Stroschein, 'Dilemmas of Autonomy and Liberal Pluralism: Examples Involving Hungarians in Central Europe', *Nations and Nationalism* 11, no. 2 (2005): 285–305.

46. Philip Levitz and Grigore Pop-Eleches, 'Why No Backsliding? The European Union's Impact on Democracy and Governance Before and After Accession', *Comparative Political Studies* 43, no. 4 (2010): 457–85.

47. Peter Van Elsuwege, 'Good Neighbourliness as a Condition for Accession to the European Union: Finding the Balance between Law and Politics', in *Good Neighbourliness in the European Legal Context*, ed. Dimitry Kochenov and Elena Basheska (Leiden: Nijhoff, 2015), 217–34.

48. For comparative discussion, see Jennifer Mitzen, 'Ontological Security in World Politics: State Identity and the Security Dilemma', *European Journal of International Relations* 12, no. 3 (2006): 341–70; Andrew Moravcsik, 'The Origins of Human Rights Regimes: Democratic Delegation in Postwar Europe', *International Organization* 52, no. 2 (2000): 729–52; Andrew Moravcsik and Milada A Vachudova, 'National Interests, State Power, and EU Enlargement', *East European Politics and Societies* 17, no. 1 (2003): 42–58.

49. Timofey Agarin and Ada-Charlotte Regelmann, 'Status Quo Multiculturalism: The Crux of Minority Policies in Central Eastern Europe's EU Member-States', *Journal of Minority Studies* 5, no. 3 (2011): 69–98; Nevena Nancheva, 'Imagining Policies: European Integration and the European Minority Rights Regime', *Journal of Contemporary European Studies* (13 July 2015): 1–17, doi:10.1080/14782804.2015.1056725.

50. Annamari Vitikainen, 'Liberal Multiculturalism Group Membership and Distribution of Cultural Policies', *Ethnicities* 9, no. 1 (2009): 53–74; Alexius Pereira, 'Does Multiculturalism Recognise or "Minoritise" Minorities?' *Studies in Ethnicity and Nationalism* 8, no. 2 (2008): 349–56.

51. Valerie Bunce, 'Rethinking Recent Democratization: Lessons from the Postcommunist Experience', *World Politics* 55, no. 2 (2003): 167–92.

Chapter Seven

Minority Rights for Migrant Communities

The integration of post-communist states into the EU and the opportunity for their citizens to benefit from free movement across the territory of the EU has been discussed widely in scholarship and increasingly so in the media. In the latter forum, concerns have been raised about the diffusion of popular sovereignty domestically once EU citizens arrive and gain access to scarce— and dwindling—resources of the state. However, the so-called EU migrants are legally simply enjoying their right for free movement in the context of the quasi-federal union of member-states and pursuing their choice of the place of residence and work among others.

This chapter will examine the specific origins of and underling concerns in perceptions of domestic residents with regard to migrants from other EU member-states. These concerns, as we understand them, reflect the larger framework within which we have situated the current volume, and that is the concern by the resident majorities about their privileged access to services and institutions of the state which they 'own', including their right to veto decisions, taking away their advantageous, if not outright privileged, position in the domestic decision-making process. These considerations are central to our concern about the impact that EU accession has had on domestic percep- tions of citizenship domestically and external views on the origins of national sovereignty across Europe. If anything, the EU integration project has from the onset aimed at revising states' relations with their societies as part and parcel of the wider project to create a notion of EU citizenship and as such to foster peace and stability across the continent.

As we discussed in the previous chapter, one of the central aspects per- taining to the European minority rights regime as a joint venture of EU member-states related to membership in the citizenry for participation in the political process. We have also illustrated that with the relation to Romani communities across the EU, being endowed with citizenship does not necessarily mean automatic right of access to services. More fundamentally, the freedom of movement across the EU also queries the homogeneity of 'homeland communities'. Whereas we have discussed the policies post-communist member-states put into place to incorporate non-resident co-ethnics into institutions of the kin-state, and have identified how the shifting domestic dynamics have failed to include Romani minorities across the EU, the focus on sending and receiving states of intra-European migrations will help us underline the growing consensus about the primacy of nationally focussed state-driven solutions to granting minority rights to residents of ethnicity different from that of the state majority.

Our initial focus lies with the European legal and policy frameworks concerned with people's movement across the EU. Next, we discuss how individual free movement has eased the pressure on many post-communist nationalising states to become more accountable to their domestic minorities. In the third step we focus on the responses of nation-states that have been at the receiving end of EU citizens involved in free movement, and finally we conclude with several observations about the implications of the nation-states' and the EU's increasingly critical stance that the intra-EU movement of people has on nation-states' dealing with migrants from outside the EU already in the territory of member-states as long-term *Gastarbeiter*, or Soviet-era migrants, as well as those who have reached the EU in recent years in the wake of civil war and state collapse in the Middle East and North Africa.

1. INSTITUTIONAL FRAMEWORK FOR INTRA-EU MOBILITY

With the collapse of communist rule, thousands of migrants sought to move from economically strained Eastern European states into a more liberal, and thus more prosperous, Western Europe.[1] Since the beginning of the 1990s, the westward movement of Eastern Europeans has been a contentious issue. Diverse as they were, migrant groups have been a challenge to relationships between the sending and host states. With the gradual lifting of visa requirements from 2004 for citizens of acceding states, member-states became open for all those with a valid passport or ID and a minimal sum of money. Thereby, internal migration gained further prominence in public debates across Europe.

The EU had taken an interest in the matter during the period of Central Eastern European states' accession, given that the principle of freedom of movement is an established element of the overall European project. Although some concerns were raised at the time when hampering free movement of citizens from the first round of post-communist enlargement was perceived as a violation of EU rules,[2] until this day candidate countries resort to similar pre-departure screening on their borders, as recent reports from Macedonia of the stamping of the passports of their citizens who are likely to claim asylum in Western Europe. Overall, however, cross-European migration has been drawing public attention not because of the fact of migration as such, but rather because arguments concerning the qualities of potential and actual migrants have shaped public debates, policies and regulations across Europe over the past two decades. It is widely acknowledged that migrants are predominantly poor and lacking in opportunities in their home countries and, as such, are in search of better opportunities for social and economic (as opposed to political) advancement.

In recent years, political and societal change has resulted in significantly more diverse societies and has established distinct routes for mediating inter-group conflicts as a result of the integration of European nation-states.[3] Most contemporary European states, however, continue operating on the basis of their residents' relative homogeneity in cultural, ethnic and linguistic terms. Indeed, in many cases issues have arisen about the extent of EU citizens' access to services in the territory of a state. Within this context, it is vital to explore the impact of nation-state building on the understanding of optimal functionality of states prevalent across post-communist, but also increasingly so in the old EU, member-states. Numerous civil society and pressure groups, as well as European governmental bodies, have promoted tolerance and acceptance in European societies of EU citizens moving from one member-state to another. Presented as a part of a self-regulating labour force and financial mobility, the mobility of persons has been presented as a fundamental part of the EU law affecting member-states' citizens and implies equal enjoyment and full protection of fundamental rights, regardless of their place of residence and their decision to migrate.

States' treatment of individuals making the use of their right for mobility appears to evolve around recognition of different, in part conflicting, rationales behind the exercise of free movement. Though the EU offers every citizen the right to reside in any EU member-state for a period of three months without any further stipulation (other than proof of nationality), longer periods of stay need proof of a person not becoming 'a burden on the social assistance system of the host member-state', be it through either employment or availability of adequate financial means.[4] Underlying this assumption is the initial difference in resources that migrants/local communities can tap into—the difference that makes individuals of two groups constituted by their inequalities and questions not only the de facto equality between the EU citizens residing in any country but also the potential equality of citizenship rights guaranteed by their nation-states.

The very nature of socio-economic migration and permissibility of such individual decisions have been used to explain the circular nature of migration from post-communist states.[5] We, however, ask ourselves how far the reluctance of nation-states to accommodate and facilitate the equality of all residents in their countries has resulted in the circulation of people across the borders of European states. Whereas not all members of minority groups from the new states have sought to move into another member-state after national boundaries became but administrative divisions, we should grant particular attention to the movement of minority citizens of the new EU member-states. As virtually no polity remains unaffected by the movement of people, these processes challenge the established categories of national sovereignty, the identity of the nation with their residents and the unity of those at home with those abroad.

Prior to accession, potential recipient states in Western Europe, as well as in North America, have largely relied on sending countries to sanction and control potential migrants before their departure.[6] However, since post-communist states joined the EU, large numbers of people have profited from the freedom of movement within the EU and made use of their right to move without having to justify their objectives.[7] The tension between minority rights protection and non-discrimination have been discussed widely in the context of EU enlargement and the candidate countries' required compliance with and transposition of the Copenhagen Criteria into the domestic legal context.[8] Yet some middle ground in the assessment of policy steps has been found by the EU to ensure good neighbourliness between states and assure that states operate on the basis of policies and political institutions previously put into place and that remained unaltered during the accession process.[9] Strict adherence to principles of underlying sovereignty by states removing citizens of other member-states from their territory, identified for removal mainly, if not solely, on the basis of these individuals' ethnicity, has been cofounded by the principle of good neighbourly relations within and between EU member-states.

Yet EU citizens moving across nation-state borders put pressure on public finance, are perceived as challenging social norms the majority takes for granted and, as such, lend themselves to becoming objects of fierce politicking and are easily presented as profiting from receiving societies. Even more so, because most migrating EU citizens of minority backgrounds exchange unemployment and social marginalisation in their home countries for social exclusion and opportunities for economic integration in receiving states, their status is easily used to justify the view of them benefitting from host states' opportunities at large.

As the legal scholarship has demonstrated, many rights of EU citizenship are of relevance for individual citizens of member-states only once they move abroad, and this is the point that needs to be taken more seriously as we probe the scope of benefits the members of minority communities have gained as they move from their countries of citizenship into another member-state. Especially when the circulation of EU citizens has been framed in terms of the benefit for states of their citizenship either via the return remittances or by dissolving the potential for ethno-political mobilisation and contestation of the existing nation-state policies, the view of citizen circulation across the EU gains a post-national optic.

It is from this vantage point that we need to consider the basic recognition of each EU member-states' citizens as EU citizens *in addition to, rather than in replacement of,* national political membership. The EU treaties implicitly created multi-level citizenship in the EU and thus invited nation-states' displacement of certain responsibilities vis-à-vis their citizens outside their borders. In chapter 3, we suggested that while the scope of inter-state negotiations in the process of EU accession/membership have been different for old and new member-states, opportunities to determine the remit of domestic sovereignty are equally distributed across all member-states. This is in fact the main operational principle of the EU that has been upheld throughout the accession negotiation process. As such, member-states recognise each other's sovereignty and accept other sovereign state's decisions as a fundamental principle underlying inter-state relations in the EU in line with the treaties. Earlier in the book we argued that states across the globe and in the EU specifically recognise citizens of their countries on the basis of their domestic legislation, but ought to acknowledge the authority of other states over their own citizens who decide to move into another nation-state.

Although the human rights system implies that more people are provided with rights, social rights are often withheld, which causes social exclusion.[10] The different kinds of rights and the hierarchy between them thus form a less explicit but certainly not a less severe means of exclusion. Exclusion can thus operate in a subtle way, which also becomes clear in the European social policy of the last couple of decades.[11] This policy emphasizes the autonomous individual, who has to earn his rights by finding a good job and is responsible for his own social justice by using his means in the best way possible. The focus on individuality seems to liberate the citizen of oppressing, interfering policies. Indeed, individuality is a key characteristic of the human rights system. However, it is forgotten that not all people have the same resources to exercise this individual autonomy. In this way, human rights policy can lead to exclusion: 'Not only is the non-European migrant left out, but also the lesser Europeans—those who are unable to exercise and live up to the highest form of life of being productive; those who are stuck in secondary or temporary jobs, and not able to climb the social ladder; and those who face ethnic and religious discrimination in their schooling, in skills-training programmes, and in job applications'.[12]

The constraints put upon relationships between EU member-states as a result of the individual mobility of EU citizens, particularly mobility of EU citizens of minority ethnicity throughout the territory of the Union, has gained attention in the last several years. These developments have been particularly insightful as EU citizens' access to public service provisions has been driving the discussion and has resulted in several 'old' EU member-states imposing conditions on entry by requiring some EU migrants to demonstrate 'good' reasons for movement, having desirable skills and more, and allowing states to judge migrants' potential to contribute, and as such the ability to earn rights. Today's structural context indeed shows an enduring exclusive dynamic, where certain people have no rights or are deprived of certain human rights. Evidence for this is found in the remaining and even aggravated global inequality between non-EU and EU citizens, as well as between asylum seekers and native citizens, and in the increasing demand for highly skilled professionals alongside low-wage workers.[13] The rhetoric of contribution has increasingly come to define states' relationship with citizens from other EU states in the aftermath of the Euro crisis. The question then becomes one of equality of the entitlement to rights and services to all EU citizens as enshrined in EU legal provisions.

Treating EU citizens differently from resident nationals is constrained by the principle of equality for all EU citizens: policymakers' judgement on the treatment of resident non-nationals' EU citizens of other member-states regardless of their formal right of access and abode should be guided by the principle of equality. The stability of societal conditions and the ability of a state to enforce its policy decisions on its territory, however, form the basis for esteem conferred upon member-states in their relationships with one another for the purpose of maintaining good neighbourly relations within the EU. Despite concessions member-states ought to make within the framework of the freedom of movement, it is implicitly acknowledged that each seeks to ensure its own competitiveness and indeed stability of its societal and political conditions.

2. NATION-STATE RESPONSES TO OUT-MIGRATION

States interact not only with one another but also with sub-state agents—that is, majority and minority citizens, citizens of other states and others. They also engage with supra-state bodies such as the EU and UN, multinational corporations and NGOs in the similar way so as to ensure cooperation when dealing with issues of joint interest. Traditionally it has been the political community that defines its members;[14] by joining the EU, post-communist member-states have de facto allowed minority citizens of the state to remove themselves out of the vertical relation with their nationalising state of citizenship. The state-based understanding of citizenship therefore explains why the very term *citizenship* is frequently used synonymously with *nationality*—that is, homeward individual identity. Research on freedom of movement in the EU has underlined that particularly the minority communities have often migrated in pursuit of opportunities unavailable to them at home, a choice that was made easy by them not losing substantial political rights (many of which they could not use in their states of citizenship anyway). Migration from what many members of minorities perceive as a 'nationalising state' adds social and economic rights that were in scarce supply in their states for all citizens and particularly for those who did not make up the state majority community. With this overlapping street-level understanding of citizenship being entrenched in all European societies, it is rather easy for policymakers in the sending countries to tap into its rhetorical toolbox to turn a blind eye onto their own citizens of minority ethnicity, leaving the country to reside in another EU member-state.[15]

While citizenship is generally perceived as a basic category of individual membership in a polity, EU citizenship additionally allows individuals to redefine their relationship with their state by making use of their right for free movement and elude state supervision by moving to another EU member-state where they believe they will be better placed to succeed. It is widely acknowledged that while citizenship in nation-states is indeed filled with national content, EU citizenship provides nothing but the form with rather limited responsibilities that are put on the state where an EU citizen (chooses to) reside. To the extent that states are formally constituted as sovereign polities of majority nations and operate in the context of the EU as good neighbours upholding this very same principle, their means to intervene in the internal affairs of other countries remain very limited.

Although most EU member-states with the exception of Greece and France do not share a vision of their populations as being devoid of any cultural differences, any incorporation of minority issues into the primary law of the EU has failed so far. However, an emphasis on special rights does not offer reasons for discriminating between migrant EU citizens and the local residents, even if belonging to a minority, in terms of access to special rights provided by the member-states.[16] Obviously, the non-discrimination approach implicitly undermines attempts to define the terms of 'minority' deductively within the context of EU institutions, or in domestic legislation. However, built on the primacy of nation-state sovereignty, domestic legislation contains references to minorities in the context of what they are not, as well as what implication belonging to a minority groups entails.[17] In spite of the fact that Muslims are not an ethnic group but a religious minority in the eyes of the EU's Fundamental Rights Agency, this does little to disentangle the 'non-majority' attribute from this group's identity, superimposing a profoundly intertwined scope of institutional effects on the group as a result of not being a part of the majority.[18] As a result, a valuable policy response that addresses needs and prevents the discrimination of non-dominant groups will have important consequences for minority protection in the EU in general.

One negative aspect is related to the position enjoyed by the migrant EU citizens in any host member-state. Should the host member-state have a special minority protection policy in place, it will provide for special rights to be granted to a certain group of local citizens. However, migrants from other member-states cannot be excluded from benefitting from those rights, thus extending the special treatment granted to only a segment of domestic society to non-national residents. This demonstrates that such policies can be of dubious effect, since they cannot be applied to a designated group of EU citizens despite their residence on the territory of the EU member-state. Yet EU citizens seem to be able to adapt well to social and economic realities in their chosen societies, suggesting that instead of political rules of incorporation for new residents, guarantees of basic equality can provide the key to societal integration around the notion of individual interests.[19] Thus, we should turn to the internal view of people who are often portrayed as migrants in the nation-state contexts. Ultimately, Turkish citizens in Germany, migrants from North Africa in France and Russian speakers in the Baltic States are at the same time religious, linguistic and ethnic minorities. Similarly, migrant EU citizens fall within several different minority categories, although discussions of their status does not treat them as such at all, thereby ignoring the tensions that the European integration project generates for nation-states defined in ethno-national terms.

Such limitations point to further limitations of EU citizens' participation in local decision making even if they enjoy free access to employment opportunities in states where they are not nationals.[20] Whereas EU citizens enjoy the unfettered right for equal treatment with the nations of the state where they live and work, third-country nationals are easily singled out as a minority group and are targeted by an array of assimilatory policies, despite the contradictions noted.[21] Needless to say, limitations on EU citizens' political participation are not disconnected from the freedom of movement consistently interpreted as an economic and social right by advocates of national sovereignty, preventing social acceptance and solidarity across the nationality divide.

In the post-Lisbon context in which the Charter of Fundamental Rights of the EU is binding, the relevance of the member-state in determining individual citizens' place and the relationship with the EU has remained as acute as ever.[22] Despite the remarkable activity of the ECJ and a range of recent case law pointing to the gradual emergence of 'the territory of the Union' as a legally binding concept also entailing Union citizenship, nation-states remain reluctant to coordinate a genuine EU-wide approach to minority protection.[23] In this context we need to look into alternative avenues available within the ambit of EU integrative mechanisms to facilitate the representation of minority issues such as via the development in EU citizenship as well as by means of economic integration.

The situation of the majority of Baltic Russians is exemplary in this context. Following intense monitoring prior to EU accession, the Baltic States formally adhered to the Copenhagen Criteria and implemented the *acquis* but failed to assume responsibility over their ethnic minority residents. The ethnic composition of Baltic societies has been challenging from both a political and a social point of view, and successive Estonian and Latvian governments systematically pursued policies to encourage Soviet-era migrants to leave.[24] The Baltic States formalised titular majorities' privileged access to state institutions, enforced public sphere monolingualism in the titular language, offered citizenship rights to those who had pre-Soviet citizenship and left little space for minority rights in their legislative corpus.[25] These policies, however, had a differential impact in each state. In the run-up to independence, Lithuania granted all those willing residents the right of post-Soviet citizenship. This guaranteed full political rights for Lithuania's ethnic Poles and Russians, both accounting for around 7 percent of the population in 1991.[26] Estonia and Latvia issued passports for 'aliens' (in Estonia) and 'non-citizens' (in Latvia) to around 20 and 30 percent of the countries' populations at the time, making wide sections of local populations de jure stateless. Residents of Estonia without domestic citizenship do not have the right to vote in national elections. However, all permanent residents can participate in municipal elections, allowing minority communities some representation at the level of municipalities.[27] Latvia's 'non-citizens' have no voting rights and no opportunity to engage in political decision making at any level of government.[28] Although routes to naturalisation have been made easier in both countries as a result of pressure from the EU, the OSCE, NATO and the CoE, it was at best halting, and today significant sections of society in both countries remain stateless.

Concessions made by governments in Estonia and Latvia during the EU accession period included granting children of stateless parents an automatic right for citizenship, diplomatic protection from the state of residence for 'non-citizens' travelling abroad and equal access to socio-economic opportunities across the EU.[29] In the period between 1999 and 2004, the integration of Russian speakers featured on the agendas of the Estonian and Latvian governments, opening new avenues for naturalisation. Yet after accession in 2004 such interest petered out and, following the meltdown of the local economies in 2008 and 2009, funding for the integration of Russian speakers was cut with dedicated governmental bodies being disbanded by late 2008. Though saving scarce economic resources for cash-strapped governments and mainstreaming of the minority issues to ministries should not have been a bad thing, minority participation that is on a par with that of the majorities is still seen as anathema. All this took place despite the repeated calls at EU official levels for narrowing the gap in the representation of minorities, inclusion of non-citizens into decision making at the national level and enhancing the credibility of state institutions—and as such of the EU—with entire populations they govern. Both Estonia and Latvia have been exposed to virulent criticism for 'provoking' crises in this field. There was the so-called Bronze Soldier crisis in 2007 in the Estonian capital Tallinn and weeklong street protests in Latvia over the transition to increased education in the titular language in 2004.[30] The Russian Federation's heated rhetoric over the discrimination of its 'compatriots' in Estonia and Latvia on both these occasions and overall in the context of these states' membership in the EU as well as NATO lends the minority issue a peculiar status as a challenge for stability not only of these two states but also of the internal EU's minority rights protection as a whole.

Further, rather than supporting societal integration and fostering political stability, the Estonian government put a premium on economic reforms that had an ominously adverse impact on politically, socially and linguistically marginalised segments in society, nearly all of whom are Russian speakers. The fact that the EU opened accession negotiations with Estonia before doing so with any other Baltic State puts the spotlight on the failure of the EU to link limited democratic accountability of the state to resident populations, consistent application of non-discrimination legislation and political participation of local minority residents.[31]

Secondly, the limited coordination of the EU's approach to the rights of non-citizens in Estonia and Latvia reduced considerably the adjustment costs of accession for the two countries. The EU's failure to establish uniform regulation on and of the status of resident non-citizens, their freedom of movement in the EU and support for their rights for participation in the political process at the EU level without granting them access to domestic political participation marked a technocratic, rather than a normative, approach to candidate states during the *acquis* negotiations.[32] In the process of negotiating EU membership, Estonia allowed persons with 'undetermined citizenship' to participate in municipal elections, while in Latvia the issue remains subject to debate.[33] In relation to the use of languages other than the official language (de facto all languages, except eponymous Estonian, Latvian and Lithuanian) in private business, Latvia particularly (but also Estonia and Lithuania to a similar degree) entrenched the role of the state language in the public sphere and state institutions. When the EU pressed Estonia to grant citizenship to children born to stateless parents upon parental application, the Estonian government responded by limiting access to education in languages other than Estonian. Similarly, Lithuania went to great lengths to remove public signs in languages other than Lithuanian, thereby enhancing the state language's visibility in the public sphere.[34]

Many of these steps are understandable from the point of view of domestic legislators and political elites looking back at over forty years of Soviet domination and fears of considerable numbers of European migrants arriving in the region after EU accession in 2004. These fears have yet to materialise. But the impact of countermeasures alienated domestic minorities from both the state where they live and the EU as an institution, able and willing to protect their rights vis-à-vis nationalising states. The shallow understanding of democratic political participation, virulent nation-state building and disengagement of resident populations from politics provide excellent indicators of the Baltic elites' acceptance of EU tutelage, whilst making tokenistic changes to legislation on minorities. Following accession, many of the above-mentioned legal benchmarks were watered down, leading the overwhelming majority of non-citizens to see minorities' disenfranchisement as being part and parcel of the EU's overall project. The EU is widely perceived in the region as a protector of the majority, rather than the minority.[35]

Within this context it would be misleading to follow strictly any of the accepted state-centred definitions of what a minority is. Most important, the EU's approach should necessarily include the global groups that are either invisible or purposefully ignored in the minority rights discourse at the level of the member-states—that is, those created by the Union itself. These include EU citizens residing outside of their country of origin and third-country nationals who are long-term residents in the EU. Although some scholars have attempted to make connections between the member-state-mandated minority categories and these two groups, applying a national understanding of what a minority is to them seems to be unwarranted, if not misleading. So treating third-country nationals as 'new' minorities[36] does not do justice to this group, as a large number of EU residents without EU citizenship have been resident for generations. At the same time, upon the completion of enlargement, the EU lost the ability to influence the policy in the field of minority protection in all the new member-states.[37] As it stands, current legislative provision does not provide the Union with a legal basis to tackle this issue, making its direct intervention in the context of any of the member-states—either 'new' or 'old'—legally impossible.

3. NATION-STATE RESPONSES TO INWARD MIGRATION

Western European nation-states were in general reluctant to open their borders to freedom of movement from the new member-states immediately as these joined the EU in 2004. Initially, only three countries—Ireland, the UK, and Sweden—allowed unrestricted access to economic migrants from the new member-states. By the time Romania and Bulgaria joined the EU in 2007, only ten countries had either dropped or eased restrictions on the movement of EU citizens from the 'new' member-states. Yet the UK announced at the same time that its borders would remain closed to Romanians and Bulgarians until 2014.

This gradual opening of borders to citizens from new EU member-states has simultaneously taken place against the background of expulsion of EU citizens from some states. This additionally serves as a reminder to show that states seek to establish themselves primarily as protectors of the rights of their residents and/or majorities and only as a second step respond to other states' and European concern.[38] Even when it appears that the principle of free movement of member-state citizens and especially the equal treatment of all EU citizens has originated from the 'old' member-states' commitment to fundamental European freedoms, the central role of the nation-state as a sovereign of decision making on its territory has been further reaffirmed as a result of dynamic population movement across the EU. We refer here to the two most prominent examples related to the expulsions of EU citizens from France in the summer of 2009 and the systematic control over EU citizens observed in Italy since the early 2000s.

In the first instance, let us discuss briefly the rhetoric and rationale of France's treatment of its resident non-nationals, EU citizens that caused considerable consternation throughout the entire EU. These followed a shootout in Grenoble in 2010 (in which, however, no migrants were involved) and prompted concerns about societal security as being jeopardised by migrants from the Central Eastern European EU member-states. In the aftermath of the subsequent riot in Grenoble, the incumbent president, Nicolas Sarkozy, delivered what would become an infamous speech in which he claimed that the violence 'highlights a certain kind of behaviour' within travelling communities and established a discursive link between immigration and crime.[39] Roma were connected implicitly to this discussion and were later focussed upon as an 'ethnic minority', though identifying citizens of France in terms of ethnicity contradicted French republican commitment as well as its legal tradition.[40] The combination of the revealed discrimination and the concealment of the fact by French authorities prompted the Commission to start the infringement proceedings against France, focussing specifically on France's failure to transpose the Citizens' Free Movement Directive. With the directive only having been partially applied in national legislation, France was able to legally target EU citizens, who would otherwise be protected from deportation to their 'state of residence', as a result of them being a 'threat to public order' by invoking the 'insufficient [financial] means' of persons in questions to guarantee 'public security'.[41]

While initially an internal analysis of the European Commission stated that Romanian citizens were not discriminated against as an ethnic group, a leaked circular predating the analyses demonstrated that the French authorities used an ethnic denominator to single out Roma on ethnic grounds after the intervention of Sarkozy.[42] What is even more remarkable, the original French circular outlined the rationale for deportation on the basis of individuals' group membership and made it clear that the return of those economically deprived EU citizens to their home countries was akin to humanitarian aid. Thus, not only could the French state appeal to the EU law on the basis of considerations related to public security, but it further points to the precedence of the societal and economic situation of EU citizens in residence over their rights for free movement going in hand with EU citizenship. This is an important point for relationships between states in the EU as precisely in the issue of societal security has the French state appealed to the 'integrity of state' to determine necessary and sufficient reasons for the removal of Roma EU citizens from its territory. If anything, this opened the door for the conditional application of mobility and residence rights to those EU nationals who do not assume, in fact, do not perform their rights and duties akin to those of the resident *national* citizen. Naturally, not all resident national citizens are able to demonstrate similar levels of economic activity or sufficient reasons to be in a territory of their nation-state (for example, when their families reside elsewhere or when unemployed). Yet, as the case of EU citizens' removals from France demonstrates, an inability to demonstrate the required levels of economic, social and political capital, to be treated as a labour force available for the market economy, can lead to suspension of some rights applying to EU citizens at large.

It is in this context that it is necessary to return to the removal of EU citizens from France: in fact, France has long been drawing attention to the economic costs carried by member-states as a result of the limited integration of Roma into labour markets in states sending and receiving Roma migrants. For example, after the second EU Roma Summit in April 2010 and a few months before the expulsions of Romanian and Bulgarian EU citizens, the French secretary of state announced disappointment that the EU was not facing up to the challenges of 'societal security' as a result of poverty in the new member-states.[43] Calling upon Romania and Bulgaria to address issues of poverty in general and Roma integration in particular as a serious social issue here can be largely seen in the context of these two states' imminent accession to the Schengen area.[44]

However, the practice of removing EU citizens to their home countries from France is not limited to the year 2010, when more than ten thousand Roma were deported. In 2009 similar numbers were removed, and around 8,500 Roma were repatriated in 2008. Even before, as early as August 2007 the French authorities issued deportation orders to residents of Roma camps throughout France, building upon the previously devised and perceived as successful system of *Aide au retour humanitaire* in place since December 2006.[45] In practice, these measures applied only to Roma, when from September 2010 French authorities started fingerprinting recipients to prevent individuals from returning and making multiple claims for state aid. Indeed, throughout the period of removing EU citizens from France, the French authorities argued that citizens of new EU member-states put a disproportionate constraint on social security and are perceived to be a threat to public order. In so doing, France as an agent in international forums sought not to privilege its own citizens over others, as is often implied in criticism of contentious rhetoric and practices used during the de facto discriminatory practice against citizens of other EU member-states.

Interestingly, the French government has borrowed much of the rhetoric, policies and practices from experiences made by the Italian government where, too, a single incident of crime lead the Italian government to turn to the widespread perception of 'criminality' as the challenge to societal security.[46] The murder of an Italian by a Romanian in 2007, just a few months after Romania joined the EU, led to a diplomatic spat between Romania and Italy. Following the incident, the Italian government announced the pending expulsions of Romanian citizens 'for imperative reasons of public safety'[47] with immediate effect. Although initially the Romanian government criticised the focus on *Romanians*, compromise was reached between the two heads of state with the emphasis being placed on *Roma* specifically, not on Romanian citizens in general.[48] Whilst both authorities resolved to collaborate with regard to the integration of Roma and stop 'law-breaking behaviour', the Commission and the European Parliament were drawn into the discussion adjudicating the limits of EU rights for free movement and issuing guidelines on implementation. Pushing for the modification of the scope and application of the freedom of movement, the Italian government sought to reduce migration from Romania with similar effects, as was seen in the case of France.

The Security Pact for Rome signed into law by Regional and Provincial authorities further framed (Romanian) Roma as a security issue and encouraged their repatriation with the help of the Romanian government.[49] In the period from 2001 to 2008, the authorities boasted the removal of fifteen thousand Roma from their homes and dealt a prelude to the Ordinances signed by Prime Minister Berlusconi with regard to the 'nomad' community settlements in the Lazio, Campania and Lombardy regions.[50] Giving the state powers to deal with Roma communities, the law transformed the situation of Roma from a 'security threat' to a 'security emergency' on the basis that they cause 'grave social alarm', allowing the expulsions of all undocumented persons.

Setting the precedent for the treatment of EU citizens in their territory in 2008, the Italian authorities offered a blueprint to Roma evictions in several, notably new member-states (Bulgaria, Hungary, Romania and Slovakia) as well as in France, all of which have since engaged in such practices. The assessment of the Fundamental Rights Agency was that segregation is still evident in many EU member-states, sometimes as a result of 'deliberate government policy' in housing policy as well as access to education.[51] Bulgaria, Czech Republic, Hungary, Romania and Slovakia have additionally seen violence targeting Roma on the basis of them lacking official recourse to employment, occupying dilapidated urban dwellings and toiling on the fringes of the official economy.[52] Similar references to Roma in Italian discussion use the term *nomads* while reflecting on criminal activities allegedly typical for the Roma community, 'in order to legitimise the destruction of Roma property, tighten immigration laws, and pre-emptively fingerprint Roma'.[53]

Yet the issue of the Roma presence in Italy is related less to recent migrants from the new EU member-states but rather to refugees mainly from successor states of Yugoslavia and those migrating from Romania *before* the country joined the EU in 2007. The Italian Immigration Law has regulated the status of both of these groups, including on the provision of asylum. As a result, people who fall into these categories are permanently threatened by repatriation to their countries of origin. The situation in Italy differs from that in France not so much because it relates to the time period before the Roma in question were EU citizens. Rather, limited congruence of national policies in Italy throughout the 1990s has granted local solutions high importance and does not allow factoring its impact on relations between EU member-states. In part, this explains the highly localised focus on Roma in Italy as is observed in contemporary scholarship and the specific focus on 'nomadism' as the reason for Roma alienation.[54]

The return of EU citizens to their home countries has been construed by nearly all commentators as a violation of EU freedom of movement and non-discrimination legislation, and also as a restriction on individuals' right of EU citizenship.[55] Not only are these removals of Roma reflected in the public rejection of Roma residents, especially if these are from other states, but in many countries financial remuneration granted for Roma willing to leave additionally taps public opinion that perceives Roma to be scroungers and living off the earnings of the majority. For a variety of reasons, not the least of which is state-sponsored discrimination, the average Roma usually lacks the expertise required even for the lowest-skilled jobs.[56] In reality, given that Roma do not constitute a majority in any EU member-state, there is no reason why either the state of residence or the state of migration should have been concerned about Romani EU citizens in the first place.

However, the actions of governments undertaking removal, and at times actively promoting the return of Romanian and Bulgarian citizens by offering them financial perks, reflects fundamental public hostility to migrants in general, as is increasingly visible across the EU. The fact that 'old' member-states undertook the expulsions of EU citizens points to a further dimension of the relations between states as being structured around the notion of national sovereignty. It relates to a state's capacity to assert its sovereignty over all residents, even in the context of common EU membership.

When assessing the impact of expulsions on relationships between EU member-states, we need to consider the fact that the expelled EU citizens hailed from the new member-states, countries that only recently graduated from candidate to member-state status. During the period of accession, these states had to learn to take cues from the behaviour of 'old' member-states in order to develop policies and consolidate polities that would be similar or at least take existing practice into account. The very nature of candidate status required little reflection from states wishing to be seen as good partners of 'old' EU member-states and to have their ability to comply with the top-down initiatives during the accession period validated in the upgrade of their status to that of member-state. Furthermore, pressures of conditionality have further indicated that new member-states in many respects perform better than the 'old' member-states, but have considerably less leverage in influencing the inter-state relationships.

Taken together, the two above-mentioned factors have had a direct and lasting impact on the perceptions of inter-state relationships between EU member-states and their residents, EU citizens or otherwise. More than anything, political decisions that set the blueprint for interactions between the EU member-states and states with their residents are made by the more established EU member-states that summon considerable economic resources to displace the responsibility for dealing with their own citizens onto sending EU member-states, as witnessed in the case of Roma expulsions.

If anything, we observe here an across-the-board move from consensual to covert, yet coercive, dynamics of settling the rules and negotiating remit of nation-state sovereignty. As such, the principle of nation-state sovereignty over the territory remains a fundamental block on EU integration in general, and the extent to which nation-states can be held accountable to their treatment of resident non-nationals, even if they are EU citizens. This perception fits perfectly with the dominant narrative about the reasons for curtailing migration into the EU and indeed withdrawing state participation in the EU freedom of movement by EU citizens. Similar feelings are widely shared throughout the poorer, usually post-communist member-states' societies who are even more concerned that their nation-states' membership in the EU undermines domestic sovereignty over politics, policy and polity.

CONCLUSION

As discussed throughout the chapter, the EU's commitment to facilitating the freedom of movement for its citizens and long-term resident third-country nationals within its territory has had a number of diverse outcomes. Looking into the future, it appears any existing approach to dealing with minority issues will need to face a harsh reality of the EU as a union of nation-states: regrettably, 'minorities are not determined at the EU level with reference to the entire [Union]'.[57] Obviously, in a community of highly interdependent states that are legally committed to the principle of joint pursuit of common interests, states are likely to be responsive to a wider range of norms we find across the national legislations and in national policies. However, those norms of the EU law, as well as being contingent upon the notion of national sovereignty, are systematically projected into domestic policymaking by neighbouring states, and less formally, by something akin to international public opinion. In this case, collective sensitivity to international norms serves to produce change within the state, but there is no reason to believe that this approach shall prevail in the future without resolving the situations of vulnerable groups in part *created* by EU law.[58]

It is here that demonstrating the sensitivity of nation-states to international recognition need not be reconsidered from a different perspective other than that of governing interactions between states and their nationals. As discussion in this chapter has illustrated, this does not show that states are *not* norm guided, but only that they may tend to respond more to certain normative expectations than to others—for example, the normative expectation held by other member-states, perhaps, that they pursue the national self-interest regardless of the objections of their own or other states' citizens. In the context of minority protection, the politicised process of treaty revisions and increasingly the reluctance of states to delegate further powers to the ECJ, the absolute majority of the post-communist member-states would be ever more reluctant to revise the tenets of national sovereignty. As long as the observed political elites are not acting in any way different from the tyranny of the majority, ethno-national populism is always an option against minority protection. This brings about a reality where the expectations of the citizens, minority groups and the member-states almost never match in the minority protection field, making the EU's further integration an ambitious agenda.

As we have discussed in relation to EU law, nation-states have to take into account developments related to EU states' joint interests with regard to their citizens in line with the expectation that states indeed *ought* to act like sovereign actors. The situation is further complicated by a simple fact that as a whole, the EU member-states are remarkably diverse, boasting numerous recognised as well as *unrecognised* minority groups, making it impossible to distil a unanimously accepted definition of a *majority* for the Union. Indeed, in the absence of a dominant culture, language and historical tradition, every citizen—and resident—of the Union certainly belongs to a minority of sorts. This is particularly true of EU citizens who in recent years have migrated, leaving no doubt about the existence of majorities at the member-state level, not in the EU.

NOTES

1. Patricia Alvarez-Plata, Herbert Brücker, and Boriss Siliverstovs, *Potential Migration from Central and Eastern Europe into the EU-15: An Update* (European Commission, Directorate-General for Employment and Social Affairs, Unit A. 1, 2003).

2. Adam Łazowski, 'And Then They Were Twenty-Seven . . . a Legal Appraisal of the Sixth Accession Treaty', *Common Market Law Review* 44, no. 2 (2007): 401–30.

3. Karen Knop, *Diversity and Self-Determination in International Law* (Cambridge: Cambridge University Press, 2002).

4. Official Journal of the European Union, L158/77, 30.04.2004 Art. 7; also Commission's Guidelines Guidance for Better Transposition of the Directive, COM (2009) 313/4, 8.

5. István Horváth and Remus Gabriel Anghel, 'Migration and Its Consequences for Romania', *Südosteuropa. Zeitschrift Für Politik Und Gesellschaft* 4 (2009): 386–403; Nigel Harris, 'Migration and Development', *Economic and Political Weekly*, 2005, 4591–95.

6. Mit'a Castle-Kanerova, 'Round and Round the Roundabout: Czech Roma and the Vicious Circle of Asylum-Seeking', *Nationalities Papers* 31, no. 1 (2003): 13–25, doi:10.1080/0090599032000058884; Didier Bigo and Elspeth Guild, 'Policing at a Distance: Schengen Visa Policies', in *Controlling Frontiers*, eds. Didier Bigo and Elspeth Guild (Aldershot: Ashgate, 2005), 233–63.

7. Christophe Hillion, 'Enlargement of the European Union—The Discrepancy between Membership Obligations and Accession Conditions as Regards the Protection of Minorities', *Fordham International Law Journal* 27 (2003): 715–40.

8. Antoaneta Dimitrova and Marc Rhinard, 'The Power of Norms in the Transposition of EU Directives', *European Integration Online Papers* 9, no. 16 (2005); James Hughes and Gwendolyn Sasse, 'Monitoring the Monitors: EU Enlargement Conditionality and Minority Protection in the CEECs', *Journal of Ethnopolitics and Minority Issues in Europe*, no. 1 (2003): 1–37.

9. Dmitry Kochenov, *EU Enlargement and the Failure of Conditionality: Pre-Accession Conditionality in the Fields of Democracy and the Rule of Law* (The Hague: Kluwer Law International, 2008); Dimitry Kochenov and Eline De Ridder, 'Democratic Conditionality in Eastern Enlargement: Ambitious Window Dressing', *European Foreign Affairs Review* 16, no. 5 (2011): 589–605.

10. Thomas Faist and Rainer Baubock, *Diaspora and Transnationalism: Concepts, Theories and Methods* (Amsterdam: Amsterdam University Press, 2010).

11. Yasemin Nuhoğlu Soysal, *Limits of Citizenship: Migrants and Postnational Membership in Europe* (Chicago: University of Chicago Press, 1994).

12. Yasemin Nuhoğlu Soysal, 'Citizenship, Immigration, and the European Social Project: Rights and Obligations of Individuality', *British Journal of Sociology* 63, no. 1 (2012): 15.

13. Saskia Sassen, 'A Savage Sorting of Winners and Losers: Contemporary Versions of Primitive Accumulation', *Globalizations* 7, no. 1–2 (2010): 23–50; Mary Nash, John Wong, and Andrew Trlin, 'Civic and Social Integration: A New Field of Social Work Practice with Immigrants, Refugees and Asylum Seekers', *International Social Work* 49, no. 3 (2006): 345–63.

14. W. Rogers Brubaker, 'Citizenship Struggles in Soviet Successor States', *International Migration Review* 26, no. 2 (1992): 269–91; Paul Magnette, 'In the Name of Simplification: Coping with Constitutional Conflicts in the Convention on the Future of Europe', *European Law Journal* 11, no. 4 (2005): 432–51.

15. Bruna Zani and Martyn Barrett, 'Engaged Citizens? Political Participation and Social Engagement among Youth, Women, Minorities, and Migrants', *Human Affairs* 22, no. 3 (2012): 273–82.

16. Kristin Henrard, 'The Interrelationship between Individual Human Rights, Minority Rights and the Right to Self-Determination and Its Importance for the Adequate Protection of Linguistic Minorities', *Ethnopolitics* 1, no. 1 (2001): 41–61.

17. Kristin Henrard, 'An EU Perspective on New versus Traditional Minorities: On Semi-Inclusive Socio-Economic Integration and Expanding Visions of European Culture and Identity', *Columbia Journal of European Law* 17 (2010): 65–67.

18. Gabriel N. Toggenburg, 'The Role of the New EU Fundamental Rights Agency: Debating the "Sex of Angels" or Improving Europe's Human Rights Performance?' *European Law Review*, no. 3 (2008): 385–98.

19. Dora Kostakopoulou, 'The Anatomy of Civic Integration', *Modern Law Review* 73, no. 6 (2010): 933–58.

20. Dimitry Kochenov, 'Free Movement and Participation in the Parliamentary Elections in the Member State of Nationality: An Ignored Link', *Maastricht Journal of European & Comparative Law* 16 (2009): 197; Niamh Nic Shuibhne, 'The Resilience of EU Market Citizenship', *Common Market Law Review* 47, no. 6 (2010): 1597–1628.

21. Although EU law stipulates that as soon as the share of EU citizen non-nationals reaches 20 percent, non-national EU citizens should be granted an automatic right to vote and run in local and EU elections and presently, such derogations are only in force in Luxembourg.

22. Rachel A. Epstein, 'Overcoming "Economic Backwardness" in the European Union', *JCMS: Journal of Common Market Studies* 52, no. 1 (2014): 17–34; Frank Schimmelfennig, Dirk Leuffen, and Berthold Rittberger, 'The European Union as a System of Differentiated Integration: Interdependence, Politicization and Differentiation', *Journal of European Public Policy* 22, no. 6 (2015): 764–82.

23. Dimitry Kochenov, 'EU Citizenship without Duties', *European Law Journal* 20, no. 4 (2014): 482–98.

24. Statistics Estonia counted 1,352,399 residents in Estonia on March 1, 2014, of which over 450,000 individuals are Russian speakers. Of 2,180,442 residents of Latvia on January 1, 2014, 26.9 percent were Russians, 3.4 percent were Belarusians, 2.4 percent were Ukrainians and 2.2 percent were Poles. During the 2011 population census in Lithuania, 6.6 percent declared Polish, 5.8 percent Russian and 1.2 percent Belarusian ethnicity. *Statistical Offices of Estonia, Latvia and Lithuania* (2014). Timofey Agarin, *A Cat's Lick: Democratisation and Minority Communities in the Post-Soviet Baltic* (Amsterdam: Rodopi, 2010).

25. James Hughes, '"Exit" in Deeply Divided Societies: Regimes of Discrimination in Estonia and Latvia and the Potential for Russophone Migration', *Journal of Common Market Studies* 43, no. 4 (2005): 739–69; Dovile Budryte, *Taming Nationalism? Political Community Building in the Post-Soviet Baltic States* (Aldershot: Ashgate, 2005).

26. Dovile Budryte and Vilana Pilinkaite-Sotirovic, 'Lithuania: Progressive Legislation without Popular Support', in *Minority Rights in Central and Eastern Europe*, ed. Bernd Rechel (Oxon: Routledge, 2009), 151–65.

27. On February 1, 2014, there were approximately 83,600 'aliens' in Estonia (6.5 percent of residents), and around 7.25 percent of Estonia's residents carried Russian Federation passports on January 1, 2014. Vello Pettai and Kristina Kallas, 'Estonia: Conditionality amidst a Legal Straightjacket', in *Minority Rights in Central and Eastern Europe*, ed. Bernd Rechel (London: Routledge, 2009), 104–18; Vadim Poleshchuk, *Advice Not Welcomed: Recommendations of the OSCE High Commissioner to Estonia and Latvia and the Response* (Hamburg: LitVerlag, 2001).

28. On January 1, 2014, there were 295,122 'non-citizens' living in Latvia (approximately 14.25 percent of residents), down from approximately 715,000 in 1991; around 1.64 percent of Latvians carried Russian Federation passports on January 1, 2014. See also Nils Muižnieks, ed., *How Integrated Is Latvian Society? An Audit of Achievements, Failures and Challenges* (Riga: University of Latvia Press, 2010); David J. Galbreath and Nils Muižnieks, 'Latvia: Managing Post-Imperial Minorities', in *Minority Rights in Central and Eastern Europe*, ed. Bernd Rechel (London: Routledge, 2009), 135–50.

29. Nils Muižnieks and Ilze Brands-Kehris, 'The European Union, Democratization, and Minorities in Latvia', in *The European Union and Democratization*, ed. Paul J. Kubicek (London: Routledge, 2003), 30–55; Sia Spiliopoulou Akermark et al., eds., *International Obliga-*

tions and National Debates: Minorities around the Baltic Sea (Marienham: The Aland Islands Peace Institute, 2006).

30. Martin Ehala, 'The Bronze Soldier: Identity Threat and Maintenance in Estonia', *Journal of Baltic Studies* 40, no. 1 (2009): 139–58; Iveta Silova, *From Sites of Occupation to Symbols of Multiculturalism: Reconceptualizing Minority Education in Post-Soviet Latvia* (Greenwich, CT: Information Age Publishing, 2006).

31. Timofey Agarin, 'Resident Aliens? Explaining Minority Disaffection with Democratic Politics in the Baltic States', *Ethnopolitics* 12, no. 4 (2013): 331–51, doi:10.1080/174490 57.2012.748247.

32. This additionally impacted the development of the EU-wide regulations on the status of non-citizens in other candidate countries—for example, in the case of Slovenia's 'erased'. Brad K. Blitz, 'Statelessness and the Social (De)Construction of Citizenship: Political Restructuring and Ethnic Discrimination in Slovenia', *Journal of Human Rights* 5 (2006): 453–79.

33. Michele E. Commercio, *Russian Minority Politics in Post-Soviet Latvia and Kyrgyzstan: The Transformative Power of Informal Networks* (Philadelphia: University of Pennsylvania Press, 2010).

34. Tatjana Bulajeva and Gabrielle Hogan-Brun, 'Language and Education Orientations in Lithuania: A Cross-Baltic Perspective Post-EU Accession', *International Journal of Bilingual Education and Bilingualism* 11, no. 3–4 (2008): 396–422.

35. Peter van Elsuwege, *From Soviet Republics to EU Member States. A Legal and Political Assessment of the Baltic States' Accession to the EU* (Leiden: Martinus Nijhoff Publishers, 2008); Priit Järve, 'Soviet Nationalities Policy and Minority Protection in the Baltic States: A Battle of Legacies', in *Institutional Legacies of Communism, Change and Continuities in Minority Protection*, ed. Karl Cordell, Timofey Agarin, and Alexander Osipov (London: Routledge, 2013), 172–85.

36. Henrard, 'An EU Perspective on New versus Traditional Minorities'.

37. Minority protection remains 'an export product and not one for domestic consumption', Bruno de Witte, 'Politics versus Law in the EU's Approach to Ethnic Minorities', in *Europe Unbound: Enlarging and Reshaping the Boundaries of the European Union*, edited by Jan Zielonka (London: Routledge, 2004), 139.

38. Kate Hepworth, 'Abject Citizens: Italian "Nomad Emergencies" and the Deportability of Romanian Roma', *Citizenship Studies* 16, no. 3–4 (2012): 431–49.

39. 'French Divided on Roma Expulsion', *Record*, 19 November 2013, http://www.newsrecord.co/french-divided-on-roma-expulsion/.

40. The French Republic does not gather data on its citizens' ethnicity based on the principle of equal citizenship; yet France's own definition of the Roma population makes innocuous reference to *gens du voyage*—travelling peoples—rather than Roma ethnics. French Republic Act No. 69-3 of January 3, 1969 (relating to the exercise of itinerant trades and the regime applicable to persons travelling without a fixed domicile or residence), Decree No. 2001-569 of 29 June 2001 (on stopping places for Travellers), Act No. 2000-614 of 5 July 2000 (The Reception and Accommodation of Travellers Act, also known as the 'Besson Act'). See also Owen Parker, 'Roma and the Politics of EU Citizenship in France: Everyday Security and Resistance', *JCMS: Journal of Common Market Studies* 50, no. 3 (2012): 475–91, doi:10.1111/ j.1468-5965.2011.02238.x.

41. 'Commission Decided to Start Infringement Proceedings against France'. European Commission, 29 September 2010. http://ec.europa.eu/social/main.jsp?catId=89&langId=en& newsId=902&furtherNews=yes.

42. See particularly, Frank Johannès, 'Le Fichier des Roms du Minstère de L'intérieur', *Le Monde*, 7 October 2010, http://libertes.blog.lemonde.fr/2010/10/07/le-fichier-des-roms-du-ministere-de-linterieur; 'La Circulaire Visant les Roms est "Très Probablement Illégale"', *Le Monde*, 12 September 2010. http://www.lemonde.fr/politique/article/2010/09/12/la-circulaire-visant-les-roms-est-elle-illegale_1410188_82 3448.html.

43. Parker, 'Roma and the Politics of EU Citizenship in France', n. 14; Aidan McGarry and Helen Drake, 'The Politicization of Roma as an Ethnic Other: Security Discourse in France and the Politics of Belonging', in *The Discourses and Politics of Migration in Europe*, edited by Umut Korkut et al. (Houndsmill: Palgrave Macmillan, 2013).

44. Alex Balch, Ekaterina Balabanova, and Ruxandra Trandafoiu, 'A Europe of Rights and Values? Public Debates on Sarkozy's Roma Affair in France, Bulgaria and Romania', *Journal of Ethnic and Migration Studies* 40, no. 8 (2014): 1154–74.

45. Olivier Legros and Tommaso Vitale, 'Les Migrants Roms Dans Les Villes Françaises et Italiennes: Mobilités, Régulations et Marginalités', *Géocarrefour* 86, no. 1 (2011): 3–13.

46. The Italian government's treatment of the so-called nomad emergency inflamed anti-Roma violence, and some politicians openly gauged anti-Roma actions. Special legislation has targeted Roma, declaring their presence in Italy a cause of social harm requiring emergency action. See Nando Sigona, 'Campzenship: Reimagining the Camp as a Social and Political Space', *Citizenship Studies* 19, no. 1 (2015): 1–15, doi:10.1080/13621025.2014.937643; Hepworth, 'Abject Citizens: Italian "Nomad Emergencies" and the Deportability of Romanian Roma'.

47. Human Rights Watch, 'Italy: Expulsion Decree Targets Romanians', www.hrw.org/de/news/2007/11/07/italy-expulsion-decree-targets-romanians; Council of Ministers of the Italian Government, 'Dichiarazione Dello Stato Di Emergenza in Relazione Agli Insediamenti Di Comunita' Nomadi Nel Territorio Delle Regioni Campania, Lazio E Lombardia', 21 May 2008.

48. The Romanian president particularly noted that '[a] crackdown [on Roma and other immigrants] featured heavily in Berlusconi's winning election campaign'. See 'Romanian President Slams Italian Gypsy Rules', Romea.cz, 2 August 2008. http://www.romea.cz/en/news/world/romanian-president-slams-italy-s-gypsy-rules.

49. Prefettura di Roma, Patto per Roma Sicura, European Roma Rights Center, 'Security a La Italiana: Fingerprinting, Extreme Violence and Harassment of Roma in Italy' (Budapest: European Roma Rights Center, 2009).

50. Council of Ministers of the Italian Government, 'Dichiarazione Dello Stato Di Emergenza in Relazione Agli Insediamenti Di Comunita' Nomadi Nel Territorio Delle Regioni Campania, Lazio E Lombardia'.

51. Fundamental Rights Agency, 'Housing Conditions of Roma and Travellers in the EU', 2009, http://fra.europa.eu/en/project/2011/housing-conditions-roma-and-travellers-eu; Amnesty International, 'Submission to the European Commission on the Implementation of the Equality Directives. Index IOR 61/002/2013', 31 January 2013, http://www.amnesty.org/en/library/asset/IOR61/002/2013/en/bbf813ce-2ebf-471f-8fa8-541832eaf4e0/ior610022013en.pdf.

52. Zoë James, 'Hate Crimes against Gypsies, Travellers and Roma in Europe', in *The Routledge International Handbook on Hate Crime*, ed. Nathan Hall et al. (London: Routledge, 2015), 237–48; Margareta Matache, 'The Deficit of EU Democracies: A New Cycle of Violence Against Roma Population', *Human Rights Quarterly* 36, no. 2 (2014): 325–48.

53. Alberto Ronchey, 'L'invasione Dei Nomadi', Corriere Della Sera, 29 September 2007, www.corriere.it/Primo_Piano/Editoriali/2007/09_Settembre/29/ronchey_invasione_nomadi.shtml.

54. Isabella Clough Marinaro and Nando Sigona, 'Introduction: Anti-Gypsyism and the Politics of Exclusion: Roma and Sinti in Contemporary Italy', *Journal of Modern Italian Studies* 16, no. 5 (2011): 583–89, doi:10.1080/1354571X.2011.622467.

55. McGarry and Drake, 'The Politicization of Roma as an Ethnic Other'; Liz Fekete, 'Europe against the Roma', *Race & Class* 55, no. 3 (1 January 2014): 60–70, doi:10.1177/0306396813509196.

56. Maria-Carmen Pantea, 'Policy Implications for Addressing Roma Precarious Migration Through Employment at Home', *International Migration* 51, no. 5 (2013): 34–47, doi:10.1111/imig.12069.

57. Henrard, 'An EU Perspective on New versus Traditional Minorities'.

58. Kyriaki Topidi, *EU Law, Minorities, and Enlargement* (Antwerp: Intersentia, 2010), 98.

Conclusion

Walking Out on Minority Rights?

Our book has engaged with the received wisdom of European Studies as well as minority rights in post-communist Europe. It is our view that it is people, not states, who are the stakeholders of the EU integration process. After having reviewed the processes of change in Central and Eastern Europe since the early 1990s, we have established that post-communist states' EU membership further promoted the ascendancy of the titular nation within the nation-state. With most European states designated national states of the titular majority, perceptions of state-bearing nations about their privileged relationship with 'their' nation-states lie at the heart of state-society, and majority-minority relations in Europe today.

Throughout the book, we have discussed how in the process of the EU accession, best practices of minority protection have been exported to accession countries and have been consolidated into albeit loosely defined, yet normatively ambitious, sets of rules to improve majority-minority relations. Though old member-states have demonstrated only limited preparedness to adapt these regulations domestically, the post-communist states found themselves at the receiving end of these evolving norms. These norms were then diligently transposed into domestic legislations, though were barely understood by minority groups and rarely welcome by the policymakers. Thus, in the process of accession, post-communist countries have found themselves complying with demands for strategic, rather than putatively normative, reasons. These requests for change were first perceived as an external imposition of European norms, and subsequently were affirmed with the reference to post-communist states' commitment to 'return to Europe'. Given the political and social views of minorities being a stumbling block rather than an

asset in nation-state development and democratisation of state-society relations, many changes were re-asserted as ethical concessions, necessary for
becoming more European. As we have indicated in chapters 2–4, the rationale underlining this change could be easily understood as attempted auto-
Orientalisation of post-communist states.

After accession, however, these vaguely defined normative standards of
minority protection have been prone to judicious interpretation by member-
states, 'old' and 'new'. Post-communist EU member-states have found themselves in a position whereby they have had to revise and re-interpret these
norms in the way most acceptable domestically whilst gradually challenging
the overt commitment of the EU to the equality of all citizens. By assuming
their more active role as drivers of change in the European minority rights
regime, post-communist member-states have re-emphasised the central place
of the nation at the heart of their nation-states' integration into the EU. In
more than one sense, therefore, post-communist member-states' engagement
with the European minority rights regime has produced sets of unanticipated
consequences for the regime as a whole and for the EU specifically.

Yet as we write, the issue of minority rights in (post-communist) Europe
has taken a largely unanticipated twist. Since the summer of 2015, the problem of minority-majority relations has been thrown into sharp relief by an
unanticipated consequence of state collapse and civil conflict in the European
neighbourhood, primarily regions affected by war in the Middle East and
Africa. These tectonic shifts have created regional power vacuums, and a
steadily increasing number of people have fled conflict in search of personal
security and opportunities for a better life in Europe. Although refugees have
been arriving from as far as Afghanistan and parts of Sub-Saharan Africa for
many years, the onset of full-scale civil war in Syria in late 2011 is often seen
as the principle reason for ever greater numbers of migrants fleeing to Europe since 2013. Countries in the region bear, of course, the brunt of the
consequences of regional conflicts. Jordan, Lebanon and Turkey host at least
two million Syrian refugees among them. Yet many see no future for themselves in refugee camps and make their way to the EU. While many African
migrants arrive on the coasts of Italy via Libya, migrants from the Middle
East and Asia find themselves principally en route via Turkey, with Greece
being the first port of call in the EU.

The large majority of these migrants head north through the territory of
post-communist member-states. The Dublin Regulations of 1990 stipulate
that it is the responsibility of the state through which asylum seekers first
enter the territory of the EU to offer sanctuary, which further underlines the
relevance of our study of minority situations in Europe for issues salient to
contemporary European politics. Readers of this book will doubtless have
seen footage of people, who have trekked for thousands of miles, attempting
to cross into Hungary and Slovenia in order to reach the outer frontier of the

borderless, Schengen free-travel area. For almost all of these refugees and indeed tens of thousands from elsewhere, including Iraq and Pakistan, their desired point of destination is not necessarily the EU in general. Rather, they seek to reach specific countries, principally Germany and Sweden. However, in order to reach these long-established richer EU member-states, they have to first cross to mainland Greece and then trek through non member-states of the EU, Macedonia and Serbia, before once again reaching the border of the EU in Slovenia, Croatia and Hungary.

Readers who have viewed these scenes will have been disconcerted by the reaction of the Hungarian and other governments in post-communist Europe to the arrival of the migrants. Whereas the response of the Italian, Greek and other West European (EU) member-states may be open to criticism, the reaction of Greek and Italian citizens and the populations of states in Western Europe to the arrival of the refugees has as not yet been one of widespread public hostility. Yet in post-communist Europe, the response of governments and significant sections of society towards immigrants has been more controversial and indicates that the value systems held by governments, political parties and society in general in EU member-states are somewhat differentiated. Without exception, the governments of all post-communist EU member-states, regardless of ideological hue, have expressed deep reservations about hosting refugees.

Admittedly, the EU's founding fathers could scarcely have anticipated the situation that today faces the governments of EU member-states. To cut to the chase, the governments in Slovenia, Croatia, Hungary and Bulgaria have been at the forefront of a campaign that declares to 'preserve the essential character of Europe' by preventing the principally Muslim migrants from beyond Europe's shores from 'irreversibly challenging its Western Christian heritage and culture'. Whereas only Hungary has gone as far as erecting a fence designed to keep migrants out, and although Slovenia might soon follow, the fact of the matter is that there has been little sign of solidarity emanating from post-communist Europe concerning the development of pan-EU solutions to the 'migrant crisis'. Rather than offering sanctuary, their 'answer' seems to be either to simply shunt as many refugees as possible elsewhere or to put forward exculpatory reasons as to why said refugees should not be settled in post-communist Europe. In their defence, there is some credence to the argument that they simply lack the infra and opportunity structures to cope with economic pressures, be it from the largely idle domestic labour force, many of whom are under- or unemployed, or from large numbers of migrants. We can further note that within post-communist Europe, domestic opposition to the immigration policies of incumbents seems geared towards the preservation of the national integrity of the nation-state. In other words, rhetoric to one side, there is no commitment to multiculturalism, no matter how defined.

As the discerning reader will note, such atavism is not confined to post-communist Europe and points to the rise of radical right and populist movements in a number of long-established EU member-states. For example, the Sweden Democrats, the United Kingdom Independence Party (UKIP), the True Finns, the National Front in France and Patriotic Europeans Against the Islamisation of the Occident (PEGIDA) in Germany all convey concerns for the future identity of their state and its constituent nation. Such groups are increasingly powerful in Western Europe. Yet while in Western Europe migrants are to some degree protected by prominent civil society groups and a liberal centre-left, neither of these exists to any great degree in post-communist Europe, leaving migrants dependent upon a mix of grudging state aid, NGOs and flimsy domestic support networks. But the determination of the Hungarian state to reduce—or at the very minimum to regulate—migration flows by erecting border fences with its post-communist neighbours should not be viewed in isolation. Successive governments in the UK have sought to move its border with the Schengen zone to Calais on the French side of the English Channel, while the Spanish government has razor-wired the perimeter of its African exclaves of Ceuta and Melilla to the same effect.

There is, however, a difference in the terms of the debate on immigration that allows us to distinguish between public views in long-established EU member-states and attitudes on the subject held in post-communist member-states. The difference lies in the fact that hostility towards immigrants appears to be more mainstream in the latter than in the former. This is not to deny that migration is not controversial in the longer-established liberal democracies of Western and Northern Europe. It is a contentious issue, and, if anything, it promises to become more so in the near future. The difference between the two parts of the EU lies in the fact that there is widespread consensus in post-communist Europe that both in- and out-migration damages the political, economic and social fabric of society. Therefore, the 'national' fabric of society is held to be particularly vulnerable to immigrants. This phenomenon is ubiquitous to all member-states, but governments in post-communist states often argue that Muslim immigrants specifically are incapable of integrating within their societies, appreciating their host countries' Christian heritage and integrating into the national mould. Further, as we have demonstrated throughout chapters 4–7, these perceptions are shaped not so much by the (ethno-)nationalism as by the reverence for and ownership of the nation-state by the majority across the post-communist member-states.

The reactions of governments in post-communist Europe indicate that what lies at the root of their response is the desire to ensure that the current ethnic status quo is not called into question. Given the number of people who since 2004 have migrated from countries such as Latvia, Lithuania, Poland, Hungary and Romania to Western European EU member-states, we are in the

curious situation in which it appears that certain governments and their supporters regard the right of their citizens to migrate as sacrosanct. Yet they
simultaneously proclaim that their countries are not countries of 'immigration' and as such should not be perceived as destinations for immigrants in
general and Muslim refugees in particular. In essence, the argument put
forward is that the national sovereignty of the country and cultural distinc-
tiveness of its people are under threat as a consequence of inward migration
on the part of people who are ethnically and culturally different from the
majority nation. In fact, we have previously heard similar arguments from
nearly all post-communist countries when during the process of the EU
membership negotiations greater respect for domestic minorities—social,
ethnic, linguistic and sexual—was stipulated as a precondition for accession.
Of course, the European minority rights regime was not designed with even
half an eye toward the current and largely unforeseen situation. Yet the
invocation of history—for example, ancestral memories of Ottoman rule or
Soviet dominance—coupled with a perception that there be no (further) concessions that might result in the ethno-national character of the nation-state
being in some way (further) diluted, tells us that throughout the post-communist member-states, up to twelve years of EU membership has done little to
change attitudes towards the 'Other' among either political elites or the wider
general public.

This response to the 'migrant crisis' illustrates a wider point made by us
in this book. Namely, although post-communist EU member-states have acceded to a wide range of international agreements and are possessed of a
political class that rhetorically claims to support minority rights, members of
non-dominant groups, whether migrants or (indigenous) minorities, are still
treated with a degree of suspicion. All find themselves subject to pressure
exerted by conservative political forces that speak on behalf of elements of
the titular nation. This applies to 'indigenous' groups such as the Polish
minority in Lithuania and the German minority in Poland, 'socialist migrants' such as Russian speakers in the Baltic States and Vietnamese in the
Czech Republic, or indeed Roma across the post-communist area. The Roma
find themselves in the worst situation of all: they have little economic power,
low social status and no kin-state to lend the group any advocacy in European forums. In fact, given the collapse of semi- and unskilled job markets
that formerly provided limited opportunities for Roma, their situation today
is probably worse than it was in 1989.

The questions we ask throughout the book are why the governments in
the new member-states in particular have acted in the manner negligent of
minority rights protection, and what their reaction to recent social and political challenges teaches us about the success of the European minority rights
regime in the propagation of the value system that underpins it. The Copenhagen Criteria and the general process of pre-accession conditionality were

as much as anything else designed to popularise and inculcate shifts in post-communist consciousness, encouraging what we might loosely call 'new values' with regards to nation, ethnicity and identity. In short, during the accession phase the EU promoted candidate countries' minority rights policies fostering intergroup tolerance while neglecting the much more fundamental task of exposing intolerance among post-communist publics. Respect for minority rights and equality were predicated upon acceptance that members of an entity that seeks to move toward 'ever closer union' would see the European Union as a social and political space open to all its citizens. However, as we observe in the case of the Danish People's Party, which has held office in coalition, and Geert Wilders's Party for Freedom, which propped up the government in the Netherlands, advocacy for restrictive policies with regards to both immigration and naturalisation has been on the rise throughout the entire continent. In other words, intolerance towards migrants among the populace and the surge of the radical right political rhetoric in 'old' member-states has only supported the prior understandings of ethno-national belonging and indeed the sense of entitlement among the national majorities of the 'new' member-states.

Although internal EU migration challenges the endeavour of EU member-states to assimilate all non-core populations into the national mould, the EU's focus on equality of all EU citizens on the whole territory of the Union de facto supports the aspiration of mobile Europeans to retain their national cultures by putting them at an advantage vis-à-vis those Europeans who are not mobile. This unusual phenomenon poses a particular challenge to the territorially bound views of nations endowed with territories of their own, where they can enjoy the ultimate decision-making power. If we return to the theme of newly arrived non-European migrants, given the lack of empathy in post-communist Europe to resident minority groups who have been living in these territories since medieval times, the prospect of sustained inward migration from outside the EU does not bode well. Those migrants who do settle in countries such as Slovenia, Hungary, the Czech Republic, Slovakia, Poland, Lithuania, Latvia or Estonia are likely to be subject to extreme social exclusion with little prospect of obtaining redress.

This is where our book moves beyond narrow concerns with minorities and their rights and addresses the contemporary crisis of the Union often described as a 'crisis of solidarity' in the light of external migrations: EU member-states are under no obligation to ensure third-country nationals'—be they refugees, labour or economic migrants—equality, and therefore often press for their assimilation, undermining the scope of application of minority rights to these groups. While practical and normative problems with assimilating third-country nationals abound in the EU, policies aimed at migrant integration are likely to co-opt migrants into the view of the state that favours the ethno-national majority and tacitly maintains the perception that popula-

tions of nation-states are internally homogeneous and as such can be distin-
guished from one another by virtue of their differentiated characteristics.
Minority protection, therefore, has been a paramount tool for ensuring peace
and stability in relationships between nation-states in Europe, and has proven
to be the most effective means to avoid social tensions from turning into
violent conflicts in both domestic and regional politics. The evidence presented throughout our book underlines that nation-states continue to serve the
interests of the titular majority, despite the continuing process of supranational integration.

Our book highlights the persistent marginalisation of minorities across
post-communist Europe, the continuous neglect of the situation of Roma and
exclusion of extra-European migrants from participation in governance
across the EU. It underlines all but the rhetoric commitment of individual
member-states and the EU as an entity to guarantee equality. It is in this
context, we find the great danger of 'Orientalising' the eastern part of the
continent by the savvy Western observers. Of course, political elites in post-
communist member-states submerge their different visions of Europe in ano-
dyne talk of 'a community of universal values'. Our book calls for a straightforward acknowledgement that nation-states in post-communist Europe
endow their citizens with views on questions of identity and migration that
differ from those of the 'Brussels consensus'. This is precisely because the
European Union has not developed from a unilinear past. The fact is that
post-communist governments continue to find it difficult to reconcile their
recovered nation-state-bound identities with EU's discourse on 'unity in diversity' and 'ever closer union'. Until these differences are acknowledged for
what they are and not dismissed as being in some way retrograde or reaction-
ary, many of the problems we have identified in this book are likely to
remain unresolved.

Within this context, we can note that the creation of some kind of civic
European identity, the grander designs of the 'European project', is yet to be
met. This truism applies to all EU member-states. Among the steps to take in
order to avoid what may prove to be an existential threat to its current
configuration, the EU needs to address the persistent (in post-communist
member-states) and the resurfacing (in the 'old' member-states) conflation
between competing allegiances to the state and the nation. Those who hold
high office need to take cognisance of how and why the attempt to re-fashion
attitudes in post-communist Europe towards questions of national and ethnic
identity has not been met with more success. On the one hand, this entails
acknowledging that more attention needs to be paid to how institutional
designs shape the mind-set and expectations of people whom nation-states
serve. On the other, it requires recognition of the fact that, like it or not,
political institutions of member-states in post-communist Europe have historical trajectories radically different from those of their Western European

counterparts. Although post-communist countries are fully fledged EU member-states with a right—and indeed, the obligation—to shape, educate and socialise their citizens into democratic publics, their inherited political institutions will for some time still produce radically different expectations of whom and how the state should serve first and foremost.

Throughout the book, we have discussed post-communist political institutions' shaping policies towards minorities and why these are understood by political leaders and publics alike as a necessary step for bringing the nation-states up to speed with the 'West'. However, the relationship between states and societies, as well as majorities and minorities, has not been framed on the basis of presumed 'common standards' believed useful in overcoming post-communist legacies as the 'past of the West'. It remains clear, however, that in the future all EU member-states, post-communist or not, will find it easier to walk out on minority rights as long as the institutions of nation-states maintain their pivotal role in finessing solutions on a case-by-case basis rather than yielding greater coordinating and policymaking capacity to the EU.

Bibliography

Aalberts, Tanja E. 'The Future of Sovereignty in Multilevel Governance Europe: A Constructivist Reading'. *JCMS: Journal of Common Market Studies* 42, no. 1 (2004): 23–46.

Adshead, Maura. 'Europeanization and Changing Patterns of Governance in Ireland'. *Public Administration* 83, no. 1 (2005): 159–78. doi:10.1111/j.0033-3298.2005.00442.x.

Agadjanian, Alexander. 'Revising Pandora's Gifts: Religious and National Identity in the Post-Soviet Societal Fabric'. *Europe-Asia Studies* 53, no. 3 (2001): 473–88.

Agarin, Timofey. 'Angels with Dirty Faces? European Identity, Politics of Representation and Recognition of Romani Interests'. *Ethnicities* 14, no. 6 (1 December 2014): 849–60. doi:10.1177/1468796814542186.

Agarin, Timofey. *A Cat's Lick: Democratisation and Minority Communities in the Post-Soviet Baltic*. Amsterdam: Rodopi, 2010.

Agarin, Timofey. 'Civil Society versus Nationalizing State? Advocacy of Minority Rights in the Post-Socialist Baltic States'. *Nationalities Papers* 39, no. 2 (2011): 181–203.

Agarin, Timofey. 'Cooptation as Integration? National Programme "Integration of Society in Latvia" on Minority Participation'. In *Minority Integration in Central Eastern Europe: Between Ethnic Diversity and Equality*, edited by Timofey Agarin and Malte Brosig, 199–223. Amsterdam: Rodopi, 2009.

Agarin, Timofey. 'The Dead Weight of the Past? Institutional Change, Policy Dynamics and the Communist Legacy in Minority Protection'. In *Institutional Legacies of Communism: Change and Continuities in Minority Protection*, edited by Karl Cordell, Timofey Agarin, and Alexander Osipov, 14–30. London: Routledge, 2013.

Agarin, Timofey. 'Flawed Premises and Unexpected Consequences: Support of Regional Languages in Europe'. *Nationalism and Ethnic Politics* 20, no. 3 (2014): 349–69. doi:10.1080/13537113.2014.937629.

Agarin, Timofey. 'Nation-State Building with the Bear in Mind: The Impact of the Russian Federation in Post-Soviet "Breakaway" Regions'. In *Extraterritorial Citizenship in Postcommunist Europe*, edited by Timofey Agarin and Ireneusz Pawel Karolewski, 109–34. Lanham, MD: Rowman & Littlefield, 2015.

Agarin, Timofey. 'Resident Aliens? Explaining Minority Disaffection with Democratic Politics in the Baltic States'. *Ethnopolitics* 12, no. 4 (2013): 331–51. doi:10.1080/17449057.2012.748247.

Agarin, Timofey. 'The Root Cause of Romani Exclusion and the European National Roma Integration Strategies'. In *When Stereotype Meets Stereotypes: Antiziganism in European Societies*, by Timofey Agarin, 223–43. Hanover, Germany: Ibidem-Verlag, 2014.

Agarin, Timofey. 'Travelling without Moving? Limits of European Governance for Romani Inclusion'. *Ethnicities* 14, no. 6 (2014): 737–55. doi:10.1177/1468796814542184.

Agarin, Timofey, and Ada-Charlotte Regelmann. 'Status Quo Multiculturalism: The Crux of Minority Policies in Central Eastern Europe's EU Member-States'. *Journal of Minority Studies* 5, no. 3 (2011): 69–98.

Agarin, Timofey, and Ada-Charlotte Regelmann. 'Which Is the Only Game in Town? Minority Rights Issues in Estonia and Slovakia during and after EU Accession'. *Perspectives on European Politics and Society* 13, no. 4 (2012): 443–61. doi:10.1080/15705854 .2012.731934.

Ahrens, Geert-Hinrich. *Diplomacy on the Edge: Containment of Ethnic Conflict and the Minorities Working Group of the Conferences on Yugoslavia*. Baltimore: Johns Hopkins University Press, 2007.

Akermark, Sia Spiliopoulou, Leena Huss, Stefan Oeter, and Alastair Walker, eds. *International Obligations and National Debates: Minorities around the Baltic Sea*. Marienham: The Aland Islands Peace Institute, 2006.

Alvarez-Plata, Patricia, Herbert Brücker, and Boriss Siliverstovs. *Potential Migration from Central and Eastern Europe into the EU-15: An Update*. European Commission, Directorate-General for Employment and Social Affairs, Unit A. 1, 2003.

Amnesty International. 'Submission to the European Commission on the Implementation of the Equality Directives. Index IOR 61/002/2013'. 31 January 2013. https://www.amnesty.org/ en/documents/ior61/002/2013/en/.

Arias, Aimee Kanner, and Mehmet Gurses. 'The Complexities of Minority Rights in the European Union'. *International Journal of Human Rights* 16, no. 2 (2012): 321–36.

Arraiza, Jose-Maria. 'Good Neighbourliness as a Limit to Extraterritorial Citizenship: The Case of Hungary and Slovakia'. In *Good Neighbourliness in the European Legal Context*, edited by Dimitry Kochenov and Elena Basheska. Leiden: Brill Nijhoff, 2015.

Atikcan, Ece Ozlem. 'European Union and Minorities: Different Paths of Europeanization?' *Journal of European Integration* 32, no. 4 (2010): 375–92.

Attwell, Katie. 'Ethnocracy without Groups: Conceptualising Ethnocratiser States without Reifying Ethnic Categories'. *Ethnopolitics* (22 April 2015): 1–16. doi:10.1080/17449057 .2015.1035559.

Balch, Alex, Ekaterina Balabanova, and Ruxandra Trandafoiu. 'A Europe of Rights and Values? Public Debates on Sarkozy's Roma Affair in France, Bulgaria and Romania'. *Journal of Ethnic and Migration Studies* 40, no. 8 (2014): 1154–74.

Bancroft, Angus. *Roma and Gypsy-Travellers in Europe: Modernity, Race, Space and Exclusion*. Aldershot: Ashgate Publishing, 2005.

Banducci, Susan A., Todd Donovan, and Jeffrey A. Karp. 'Minority Representation, Empowerment, and Participation'. *Journal of Politics* 66, no. 2 (2004): 534–56.

Barany, Zoltan. 'Politics and the Roma in State-Socialist Eastern Europe'. *Communist and Post-Communist Studies* 33, no. 4 (2000): 421–37.

Barnes, Samuel H., and Janos Simon. *Popular Conceptions of Democracy in Postcommunist Europe*. Budapest: Erasmus Foundation, 1998.

Barrington, Lowell W., Erik S. Herron, and Brian D. Silver. 'The Motherland Is Calling: Views of Homeland among Russians in the Near Abroad'. *World Politics* 55, no. 2 (2003): 290–313. doi:10.1353/wp.2003.0008.

Basheska, Elena. 'The Good Neighbourliness Condition in EU Enlargement'. *Contemporary Southeastern Europe* 1, no. 1 (2014): 92–111.

Bauböck, Rainer. 'Morphing the Demos into the Right Shape: Normative Principles for Enfranchising Resident Aliens and Expatriate Citizens'. *Democratization* 22, no. 5 (2015): 820–39. doi:10.1080/13510347.2014.988146.

Beblavý, Miroslav, and Emília Sičáková-Beblavá. 'The Changing Faces of Europeanisation: How Did the European Union Influence Corruption in Slovakia Before and After Accession?' *Europe-Asia Studies* 66, no. 4 (2014): 536–56. doi:10.1080/09668136.2014.899767.

Beissinger, Mark R. *Nationalist Mobilization and the Collapse of the Soviet State*. Cambridge: Cambridge University Press, 2002.

Bell, M. 'The Implementation of European Anti-Discrimination Directives: Converging towards a Common Model?' *Political Quarterly* 79, no. 1 (2008): 36–44.

Berg, Eiki. 'Ethnic Mobilisation in Flux: Revisiting Peripherality and Minority Discontent in Estonia'. *Space and Polity* 5, no. 1 (2001): 5–26.

Berg, Eiki, and Wim van Meurs. 'Borders and Orders in Europe: Limits of Nation and State-Building in Estonia, Macedonia and Moldova'. *Journal of Communist Studies and Transition Politics* 18, no. 4 (2002): 51–74.

Berger, Maria, Christian Galonska, and Ruud Koopmans. 'Political Integration by a Detour? Ethnic Communities and Social Capital of Migrants in Berlin'. *Journal of Ethnic and Migration Studies* 30, no. 3 (2004): 491–507.

Bickerton, Chris J. *European Integration: From Nation-States to Member States*. Oxford: Oxford University Press, 2012.

Bickerton, Chris J., Bastien Irondelle, and Anand Menon. 'Security Co-Operation beyond the Nation-State: The EU's Common Security and Defence Policy'. *JCMS: Journal of Common Market Studies* 49, no. 1 (2011): 1–21.

Bieber, Florian. 'Building Impossible States? State-Building Strategies and EU Membership in the Western Balkans'. *Europe-Asia Studies* 63, no. 10 (2011): 1783–1802. doi:10.1080/09668136.2011.618679.

Bigo, Didier, and Elspeth Guild. 'Policing at a Distance: Schengen Visa Policies'. In *Controlling Frontiers*, edited by Didier Bigo and Elspeth Guild, 233–63. Aldershot: Ashgate, 2005.

Blitz, Brad K. 'Statelessness and the Social (De)Construction of Citizenship: Political Restructuring and Ethnic Discrimination in Slovenia'. *Journal of Human Rights* 5 (2006): 453–79.

Bochsler, Daniel, and Edina Szöcsik. 'Building Inter-Ethnic Bridges or Promoting Ethno-Territorial Demarcation Lines? Hungarian Minority Parties in Competition'. *Nationalities Papers* 41, no. 5 (2013): 761–79. doi:10.1080/00905992.2013.801411.

Bochsler, Daniel, and Edina Szöcsik. 'The Forbidden Fruit of Federalism: Evidence from Romania and Slovakia'. *West European Politics* 36, no. 2 (2013): 426–46.

Böhmelt, Tobias, and Tina Freyburg. 'The Temporal Dimension of the Credibility of EU Conditionality and Candidate States' Compliance with the *Acquis Communautaire*, 1998–2009'. *European Union Politics* 14, no. 2 (2013): 250–72.

Börzel, Tanja, Tobias Hofmann, and Diana Panke. 'Policy Matters But How? Explaining Non-Compliance Dynamics in the EU'. KFG Working Paper 24, Free University Berlin, 2011.

Börzel, Tanja, and Thomas Risse. 'When Europeanisation Meets Diffusion: Exploring New Territory'. *West European Politics* 35, no. 1 (2012): 192–207.

Bourne, Angela K. 'European Integration and Conflict Resolution in the Basque Country, Northern Ireland and Cyprus'. *Perspectives on European Politics and Society* 4, no. 3 (2003): 391–415.

Brosig, Malte. 'The Challenge of Implementing Minority Rights in Central Eastern Europe'. *Journal of European Integration* 32, no. 4 (1 July 2010): 393–411. doi:10.1080/07036331003797539.

Brosig, Malte. 'No Space for Constructivism? A Critical Appraisal of European Compliance Research'. In *Trajectories of Minority Rights Issues in Europe: The Implementation Trap?*, edited by Timofey Agarin and Malte Brosig, 6–23. Oxon: Routledge, 2015.

Brubaker, W. Rogers. 'Citizenship Struggles in Soviet Successor States'. *International Migration Review* 26, no. 2 (1992): 269–91.

Brubaker, Rogers. 'The "Diaspora" Diaspora'. *Ethnic and Racial Studies* 28, no. 1 (2005): 1–19.

Brubaker, Rogers. 'Ethnicity without Groups'. *European Journal of Sociology* 43, no. 2 (2003): 163–89.

Brubaker, Rogers. 'Language, Religion and the Politics of Difference'. *Nations and Nationalism* 19, no. 1 (2013): 1–20.

Brubaker, Rogers. 'Migration, Membership, and the Modern Nation-State: Internal and External Dimensions of the Politics of Belonging'. *Journal of Interdisciplinary History* 41, no. 1 (2010): 61–78.

Brubaker, Rogers. *Nationalism Reframed: Nationhood and the National Question in the New Europe*. Cambridge: Cambridge University Press, 1996.

Brubaker, Rogers, and David D. Laitin. 'Ethnic and Nationalist Violence'. *American Review of Sociology* 24 (1998): 423–52.

186 *Bibliography*

Buček, Jan. 'Responding to Diversity: Solutions at the Local Level in Slovakia'. In *Diversity in Action: Local Public Management of Multi-Ethnic Communities in Central and Eastern Europe*, edited by Anna Mária Bíró and Petra Kovács, 273–306. Budapest: Open Society Institute, 2002.

Budryte, Dovile. *Taming Nationalism? Political Community Building in the Post-Soviet Baltic States*. Aldershot: Ashgate, 2005.

Budryte, Dovile, and Vilana Pilinkaite-Sotirovic. 'Lithuania: Progressive Legislation without Popular Support'. In *Minority Rights in Central and Eastern Europe*, edited by Bernd Rechel, 151–65. Oxon: Routledge, 2009.

Bulajeva, Tatjana, and Gabrielle Hogan-Brun. 'Language and Education Orientations in Lithuania: A Cross-Baltic Perspective Post-EU Accession'. *International Journal of Bilingual Education and Bilingualism* 11, no. 3–4 (2008): 396–422.

Bunce, Valerie. 'Rethinking Recent Democratization: Lessons from the Postcommunist Experience'. *World Politics* 55, no. 2 (2003): 167–92.

Capoccia, Giovanni, and R. Daniel Kelemen. 'The Study of Critical Junctures: Theory, Narrative, and Counterfactuals in Historical Institutionalism'. *World Politics* 59, no. 3 (2007): 341–69.

Carey, Sean. 'Undivided Loyalties: Is National Identity an Obstacle to European Integration?' *European Union Politics* 3, no. 4 (2002): 387–413.

Castle-Kanerova, Mit'a. 'Round and Round the Roundabout: Czech Roma and the Vicious Circle of Asylum-Seeking'. *Nationalities Papers* 31, no. 1 (2003): 13–25. doi:10.1080/0090599032000058884.

Cederman, Lars-Erik. 'Nationalism and Bounded Integration: What It Would Take to Construct a European Demos'. *European Journal of International Relations* 7, no. 2 (2001): 139–74.

Cederman, Lars-Erik, Andreas Wimmer, and Brian Min. 'Why Do Ethnic Groups Rebel? New Data and Analysis'. *World Politics* 62, no. 1 (2010): 87–119.

Celinska, Katarzyna, and Agnieszka Gutkowska. 'The Polish Roma: From a Persecuted to a Protected Minority'. *International Journal of Comparative and Applied Criminal Justice* 38, no. 2 (2014): 157–71.

Center for Interethnic Dialog and Tolerance, AMALIPE. 'The Council of Ministers Adopted the National Strategy for Roma Integration'. *News*, 22 December 2011. http://amalipe.com/index.php?nav=news&id=1010&lang=2.

Checkel, Jeffrey T. 'International Institutions and Socialization in Europe'. *Arena Working Papers* WP 01/11 (2001).

Checkel, Jeffrey T. 'Why Comply? Social Learning and European Identity Change'. *International Organization* 55, no. 3 (2001): 553–88.

Chinn, Jeff, and Robert J. Kaiser. *Russians as the New Minority: Ethnicity and Nationalism in the Soviet Successor States.* Boulder, CO: Westview Press, 1996.

Chiru, Mihail, and Sergiu Gherghina. 'Parliamentary Sovereignty and International Intervention: Elite Attitudes in the First Central European Legislatures'. *East European Politics* 30, no. 1 (2014): 21–33. doi:10.1080/21599165.2013.858627.

Cholewinski, Ryszard. 'Migrants as Minorities: Integration and Inclusion in the Enlarged European Union'. *JCMS: Journal of Common Market Studies* 43, no. 4 (2005): 695–716.

'La Circulaire Visant les Roms est "Très Probablement Illégale"'. *Le Monde*, 12 September 2010. http://www.lemonde.fr/politique/article/2010/09/12/la-circulaire-visant-les-roms-est-elle-illegale_1410188_82 3448.html.

Clough Marinaro, Isabella, and Nando Sigona. 'Introduction: Anti-Gypsyism and the Politics of Exclusion: Roma and Sinti in Contemporary Italy'. *Journal of Modern Italian Studies* 16, no. 5 (2011): 583–89. doi:10.1080/1354571X.2011.622467.

Cohen, Shari J. *Politics without a Past: The Absence of History in Postcommunist Nationalism.* London: Duke University Press, 1999.

Coman, Ramona. 'Strengthening the Rule of Law at the Supranational Level: The Rise and Consolidation of a European Network'. *Journal of Contemporary European Studies* (24 July 2015): 1–18. doi:10.1080/14782804.2015.1057482.

Commercio, Michele E. *Russian Minority Politics in Post-Soviet Latvia and Kyrgyzstan: The Transformative Power of Informal Networks*. Philadelphia: University of Pennsylvania Press, 2010.

'Commission Decided to Start Infringement Proceedings against France'. European Commission, 29 September 2010. http://ec.europa.eu/social/main.jsp?catId=89&langId=en&newsId=902&furtherNews=yes.

Connor, Walker. *Ethnonationalism: The Quest for Understanding*. Princeton, NJ: Princeton University Press, 1994.

Connor, Walker. 'Nation-Building or Nation-Destroying?' *World Politics* 24, no. 3 (1972): 319–55.

Conversi, Daniele. 'Majoritarian Democracy and Globalization versus Ethnic Diversity?' *Democratization* 19, no. 4 (2011): 789–811. doi:10.1080/13510347.2011.626947.

Cordell, Karl, ed. *Ethnicity and Democratisation in the New Europe*. London: Routledge, 1999.

Cordell, Karl, ed. 'The Ideology of Minority Protection during the Post-Communist Transition in Europe'. In *Institutional Legacies of Communism, Change and Continuities in Minority Protection*, edited by Karl Cordell, Timofey Agarin, and Alexander Osipov, 77–89. London: Routledge, 2013.

Cordell, Karl, Timofey Agarin, and Alexander Osipov, eds. *Institutional Legacies of Communism: Change and Continuities in Minority Protection*. London: Routledge, 2013.

Cordell, Karl, and Stefan Wolff. *Ethnic Conflict: Causes, Consequences, and Responses*. Cambridge: Polity, 2009.

Cordell, Karl, and Stefan Wolff. 'Germany as a Kin-State: The Development and Implementation of a Norm-Consistent External Minority Policy towards Central and Eastern Europe'. *Nationalities Papers* 35, no. 2 (2007): 289–315.

Council of Ministers of the Italian Government. 'Dichiarazione Dello Stato Di Emergenza in Relazione Agli Insediamenti Di Comunita' Nomadi Nel Territorio Delle Regioni Campania, Lazio E Lombardia'. 21 May 2008.

Crawford, Beverly, and Arend Lijphart, eds. *Liberalization and Leninist Legacies: Comparative Perspectives on Democratic Transitions*. Berkeley: International and Area Studies, 1997.

Csaba, Laszlo. 'From Sovietology to Neo-Institutionalism'. *Post-Communist Economies* 21, no. 4 (2009): 383–98.

Csepeli, Gyorgy, and David Simon. 'Construction of Roma Identity in Eastern and Central Europe: Perception and Self-Identification'. *Journal of Ethnic and Migration Studies* 30, no. 1 (2004): 129–50.

Csergo, Zsuzsa. 'Beyond Ethnic Division: Majority-Minority Debate About the Postcommunist State in Romania and Slovakia'. *East European Politics and Societies* 16, no. 1 (2002): 1–29.

Csergo, Zsuzsa. *Talk of the Nation: Language and Conflict in Romania and Slovakia*. London: Cornell University Press, 2007.

Cullet, Philippe. 'Differential Treatment in International Law: Towards a New Paradigm of Inter-State Relations'. *European Journal of International Law* 10, no. 3 (1999): 549–82.

Daskalovski, Zhidas. 'Democratic Consolidation and the "Stateness" Problem: The Case of Macedonia'. *Global Review of Ethnopolitics* 3, no. 2 (2004): 52–66. doi:10.1080/147 18800408405165.

Davy, Richard. 'Helsinki Myths: Setting the Record Straight on the Final Act of the CSCE, 1975'. *Cold War History* 9, no. 1 (2009): 1–22.

'Decade of Roma Inclusion 2005–2015: Terms of Reference'. 2005. http://www.romadecade.org/cms/upload/file/9292_file1_terms-of-reference.pdf.

'Decade Watch: Roma Activists Assess the Progress of the Decade of Roma Inclusion, 2005–2006'. 2007. http://siteresources.worldbank.org/PGLP/Resources/NadirRedzepi DecadeWatchBackgroundPaper.pdf.

Deegan-Krause, Kevin. 'Uniting the Enemy: Politics and the Convergence of Nationalisms in Slovakia'. *East European Politics & Societies* 18, no. 4 (2004): 651–96.

Deegan-Krause, Kevin, and Tim Haughton. 'Toward a More Useful Conceptualization of Populism: Types and Degrees of Populist Appeals in the Case of Slovakia'. *Politics & Policy* 37, no. 4 (2009): 821–41.

Deets, Stephen, and Sherrill Stroschein. 'Dilemmas of Autonomy and Liberal Pluralism: Examples Involving Hungarians in Central Europe'. *Nations and Nationalism* 11, no. 2 (2005): 285–305.

Delreux, Tom, and Bart Kerremans. 'How Agents Weaken Their Principals' Incentives to Control: The Case of EU Negotiators and EU Member States in Multilateral Negotiations'. *Journal of European Integration* 32, no. 4 (2010): 357–74.

de Witte, Bruno. 'Politics versus Law in the EU's Approach to Ethnic Minorities'. In *Europe Unbound: Enlarging and Reshaping the Boundaries of the European Union*, edited by Jan Zielonka, 139. London: Routledge, 2004.

Dimitrova, Antoaneta, and Geoffrey Pridham. 'International Actors and Democracy Promotion in Central and Eastern Europe: The Integration Model and Its Limits'. *Democratization* 11, no. 5 (2004): 91–112.

Dimitrova, Antoaneta, and Mark Rhinard. 'The Power of Norms in the Transposition of EU Directives'. *European Integration Online Papers* 9, no. 16 (2005).

Djokic, Dejan, and James Ker-Lindsay, eds. *New Perspectives on Yugoslavia: Key Issues and Controversies*. London: Routledge, 2010.

Drake, Anna, and Allison McCulloch. 'Deliberating and Learning Contentious Issues: How Divided Societies Represent Conflict in History Textbooks'. *Studies in Ethnicity and Nationalism* 13, no. 3 (2013): 277–94. doi:10.1111/sena.12045.

Džankić, Jelena, Simonida Kacarska, Nataša Pantić, and Jo Shaw. 'The Governance of Citizenship Practices in the Post-Yugoslav States: The Impact of Europeanisation'. *European Politics and Society* 16, no. 3 (2015): 337–46. doi:10.1080/23745118.2015.1061744.

Earnest, David C. 'The Enfranchisement of Resident Aliens: Variations and Explanations'. *Democratization* 22, no. 5 (29 July 2015): 861–83. doi:10.1080/13510347.2014.979162.

Easterly, William. 'Can Institutions Resolve Ethnic Conflict?' *Economic Development and Cultural Change* 49, no. 4 (2001): 687–706.

Ehala, Martin. 'The Bronze Soldier: Identity Threat and Maintenance in Estonia'. *Journal of Baltic Studies* 40, no. 1 (2009): 139–58.

Engström, Jenny. 'The Power of Perception: The Impact of the Macedonian Question on Inter-Ethnic Relations in the Republic of Macedonia'. *Global Review of Ethnopolitics* 1, no. 3 (2002): 3–17. doi:10.1080/14718800208405102.

Epstein, Rachel A. 'Overcoming "Economic Backwardness" in the European Union'. *JCMS: Journal of Common Market Studies* 52, no. 1 (2014): 17–34.

Epstein, Rachel A., and Ulrich Sedelmeier. 'Beyond Conditionality: International Institutions in Postcommunist Europe after Enlargement'. *Journal of European Public Policy* 15, no. 6 (2008): 795–805.

European Commission. 'Council Directive 2000/43/EC of 29 June 2000 Implementing the Principle of Equal Treatment between Persons Irrespective of Racial or Ethnic Origin'. 2000. http://eur-lex.europa.eu/LexUriServ/LexUriServ.do?uri=CELEX:32000L0043:en:HTML.

European Commission. 'Council Directive 2000/78/EC of 27 November 2000 Establishing a General Framework for Equal Treatment in Employment and Occupation'. 2000. http://eur-lex.europa.eu/LexUriServ/LexUriServ.do?uri=CELEX:32000L0078:en:HTML.

European Commission. 'An EU Framework for National Roma Integration Strategies up to 2020 (EC/COM/2011/173 Final)'. 2011. http://eur-lex.europa.eu/LexUriServ/LexUriServ.do?uri=COM:2011:0173:FIN:EN:PDF.

European Commission. 'National Roma Integration Strategies: A First Step in the Implementation of the EU Framework. COM/2012/133'. 2012. http://ec.europa.eu/justice/discrimination/files/com2012_226_en.pdf.

European Commission. 'Roma Integration: First Findings of Roma Task Force and Report on Social Inclusion EC/MEMO/10/701'. 2010. http://europa.eu/rapid/press-release_MEMO-10-701_en.htm.

European Parliament. 'European Parliament Resolution on the Situation of the Roma in the European Union, P6_TA(2005)0151'. 2005. http://www.europarl.europa.eu/sides/getDoc. do?pubRef=-//EP//TEXT+TA+P6-TA-2005-0151+0+DOC+XML+V0//EN.

European Roma Rights Center. 'Security a La Italiana: Fingerprinting, Extreme Violence and Harassment of Roma in Italy'. Budapest: European Roma Rights Center, 2009.

Faist, Thomas, and Rainer Baubock. *Diaspora and Transnationalism: Concepts, Theories and Methods*. Amsterdam: Amsterdam University Press, 2010.

Fearon, James, and David D. Laitin. 'Ordinary Language and External Validity: Specifying Concepts in the Study of Ethnicity'. Annual Meetings of the American Political Science Association, 2000.

Featherstone, Kevin. '"Europeanization" and the Centre Periphery: The Case of Greece in the 1990s'. *South European Society and Politics* 3, no. 1 (1998): 23–39.

Fekete, Liz. 'Europe against the Roma'. *Race & Class* 55, no. 3 (1 January 2014): 60–70. doi:10.1177/0306396813509196.

Franco-Guillén, Núria. 'Selfishness of the Affluent? Stateless Nationalist and Regionalist Parties and Immigration'. *Journal of Ethnic and Migration Studies* (21 September 2015): 1–13. doi:10.1080/1369183X.2015.1082287.

Fraser, Nancy, and Axel Honneth. *Redistribution or Recognition? A Political-Philosophical Exchange*. London: Verso Books, 2003.

Frėjutė-Rakauskienė, Monika. 'The Impact of the EU Membership on Ethnic Minority Participation: Parties of Lithuanian Ethnic Minorities in the European Parliament Elections'. *Politikos Mokslų Almanachas* 10 (2011): 7–30.

'French Divided on Roma Expulsion'. *Record*, 19 November 2013. http://www.newsrecord.co/ french-divided-on-roma-expulsion/.

Freyburg, Tina, Sandra Lavenex, Frank Schimmelfennig, Tatiana Skripka, and Anne Wetzel. 'EU Promotion of Democratic Governance in the Neighbourhood'. *Journal of European Public Policy* 16, no. 6 (2009): 916–34.

Freyburg, Tina, and Solveig Richter. 'National Identity Matters: The Limited Impact of EU Political Conditionality in the Western Balkans'. *Journal of European Public Policy* 17, no. 2 (2010): 263–81.

Friedland, Roger, and Robert R. Alford. 'Bringing Society Back in: Symbols, Practices and Institutional Contradictions'. In *The New Institutionalism in Organizational Analysis*, edited by Walter W. Powell and Paul J. DiMaggio, 232–63. Chicago: University of Chicago Press, 1991.

Friedman, Eben. 'The Ethnopolitics of Territorial Division in the Republic of Macedonia'. *Ethnopolitics* 8, no. 2 (2009): 209–21. doi:10.1080/17449050802243418.

Fumagalli, Matteo. 'Framing Ethnic Minority Mobilisation in Central Asia: The Cases of Uzbeks in Kyrgyzstan and Tajikistan'. *Europe-Asia Studies* 59, no. 4 (2007): 567–90.

Fundamental Rights Agency. 'Housing Conditions of Roma and Travellers in the EU'. 2009. http://fra.europa.eu/en/project/2011/housing-conditions-roma-and-travellers-eu.

Fundamental Rights Agency. 'The Situation of Roma in 11 EU Member States'. May 2012. http://fra.europa.eu/en/publication/2012/situation-roma-11-eu-member-states-survey-results-glance.

Fundamental Rights Agency. 'The Situation of Roma EU Citizens Moving to and Settling in Other EU Member States'. European Union Fundamental Rights Agency, 9 November 2009. http://fra.europa.eu/en/publication/2012/situation-roma-eu-citizens-moving-and-settling-other-eu-member-states.

Gadjanova, Elena. 'What Is an Ethnic Appeal? Policies as Metonymies for Ethnicity in the Political Rhetoric of Group Identity'. *Ethnopolitics* 12, no. 3 (2013): 307–30. doi:10.1080/ 17449057.2012.730261.

Galbreath, David J. 'European Integration through Democratic Conditionality: Latvia in the Context of Minority Rights'. *Journal of Contemporary European Studies* 14, no. 1 (2006): 69–87.

Galbreath, David J. 'Securitizing Democracy and Democratic Security: A Reflection on Democratization Studies'. *Democracy and Security* 8, no. 1 (2012): 28–42. doi:10.1080/ 17419166.2012.653737.

Galbreath, David J., and Jeremy W. Lamoreaux. 'The Baltic States as "Small States": Negotiating the "East" by Engaging the "West"'. *Journal of Baltic States* 39, no. 1 (2008).

Galbreath, David J., and Joanne McEvoy. 'European Integration and the Geopolitics of National Minorities'. *Ethnopolitics* 9, no. 3–4 (2010): 357–77.

Galbreath, David J., and Joanne McEvoy. *The European Minority Rights Regime: Towards a Theory of Regime Effectiveness*. Basingstoke: Palgrave, 2011.

Galbreath, David J., and Nils Muižnieks. 'Latvia: Managing Post-Imperial Minorities'. In *Minority Rights in Central and Eastern Europe*, edited by Bernd Rechel, 135–50. London: Routledge, 2009.

Ganev, Venelin I. 'Post-Accession Hooliganism: Democratic Governance in Bulgaria and Romania after 2007'. *East European Politics & Societies* 27, no. 1 (2013): 26–44.

Gehring, Thomas, Sebastian Oberthür, and Marc Mühleck. 'European Union Actorness in International Institutions: Why the EU Is Recognized as an Actor in Some International Institutions, but Not in Others'. *JCMS: Journal of Common Market Studies* 51, no. 5 (2013): 849–65. doi:10.1111/jcms.12030.

Gherghina, Sergiu, and George Jiglau. 'Explaining Ethnic Mobilisation in Post-Communist Countries'. *Europe-Asia Studies* 63, no. 1 (2011): 49–76. doi:10.1080/09668136.2011.534302.

Gijberts, Mérove, Louk Hagendoorn, and Peer Scheepers, eds. *Nationalism and Exclusion of Migrants: Cross-National Comparisons*. Aldershot: Ashgate, 2004.

Gill, Graeme. 'Nationalism and the Transition to Democracy: The Post-Soviet Experience'. *Demokratizatsiya: The Journal of Post-Soviet Democratization* 14, no. 4 (2006): 613–26.

Glenn, John K. 'From Nation-States to Member-States: Accession Negotiations as an Instrument of Europeanization'. *Comparative European Politics* 2 (2004): 3–28.

Gorenburg, Dmitry. *Minority Ethnic Mobilization in the Russian Federation*. Cambridge: Cambridge University Press, 2003.

Grabbe, Heather. 'European Union Conditionality and the "Acquis Communautaire"'. *International Political Science Review* 23, no. 3 (2002): 249–68.

Grabbe, Heather. *The EU's Transformative Power: Europeanization through Conditionality in Central and Eastern Europe*. Basingstoke: Palgrave Macmillan, 2006.

Grabbe, Heather. 'How Does Europeanization Affect CEE Governance? Conditionality, Diffusion and Diversity'. *Journal of European Public Policy* 8, no. 6 (2001): 1013–31.

Grigorescu, Alexandru. 'Transferring Transparency: The Impact of European Institutions of East-Central Europe'. In *Norms and Nannies, The Impact of International Organizations on the Central and East European States*, edited by Ronald H. Linden, 59–90. Lanham, MD: Rowman & Littlefield, 2002.

Grimm, Sonja, and Okka Lou Mathis. 'Stability First, Development Second, Democracy Third: The European Union's Policy towards the Post-Conflict Western Balkans, 1991–2010'. *Europe-Asia Studies* 67, no. 6 (3 July 2015): 916–47. doi:10.1080/09668136.2015.1055237.

Grzymala-Busse, Anna M. *Redeeming the Communist Past: The Regeneration of Communist Parties in East Central Europe*. Cambridge: Cambridge University Press, 2002.

Guibernau, Montserrat. *Catalan Nationalism: Francoism, Transition and Democracy*. London: Routledge, 2004.

Guiraudon, Virginie. 'Equality in the Making: Implementing European Non-Discrimination Law'. *Citizenship Studies* 13, no. 5 (1 October 2009): 527–49. doi:10.1080/13621020903174696.

Guy, Will. 'EU Initiatives on Roma: Limitations and Ways Forward'. In *Romani Politics in Contemporary Europe: Poverty, Ethnic Mobilization, and the Neo-Liberal Order*, edited by Nidhi Trehan and Nando Sigona. Basingstoke: Palgrave, 2010.

Haas, Peter M. 'Introduction: Epistemic Communities and International Policy Coordination'. *International Organization* 46, no. 1 (1992): 1–34.

Halász, Iván. 'Models of Kin Minority Protection in Central and Eastern Europe'. In *Beyond Sovereignty: From Status Law to Transnational Citizenship?* edited by Osamu Ieda, 255–79. Sapporo: Slavic Research Center, Hokkaido University, 2006.

Hale, Henry E. 'The Parade of Sovereignties: Testing Theories of Secession in the Soviet Setting'. *British Journal of Political Science* 30 (2000): 31–56.

Halikiopoulou, Daphne, Kyriaki Nanou, and Sofia Vasilopoulou. 'The Paradox of Nationalism: The Common Denominator of Radical Right and Radical Left Euroscepticism'. *European Journal of Political Research* 51, no. 4 (2012): 504–39. doi:10.1111/j.1475-6765.2011.02050.x.

Hall, Peter A., and Rosemary C. R. Taylor. 'Political Science and the Three New Institutionalisms'. *Political Studies* 44, no. 5 (1996): 936–57.

Hammarberg, T., Commissioner for Human Rights. 'Human Rights of Roma and Travellers in Europe'. Council of Europe, 2012.

Han, Enze, Joseph O'Mahoney, and Christopher Paik. 'External Kin, Economic Disparity and Minority Ethnic Group Mobilization'. *Conflict Management and Peace Science* 31, no. 1 (1 February 2014): 49–69. doi:10.1177/0738894213501762.

Hanrieder, Tine. 'Gradual Change in International Organisations: Agency Theory and Historical Institutionalism'. *Politics* 34, no. 4 (2014): 324–33. doi:10.1111/1467-9256.12050.

Harlig, Jeffrey. 'National Consolidation vs. European Integration: The Language Issue in Slovakia'. *Security Dialogue* 28, no. 4 (1997): 479–91. doi:10.1177/0967010697028004008.

Harris, Nigel. 'Migration and Development'. *Economic and Political Weekly*, 2005, 4591–95.

Haughton, Tim. 'Exit, Choice and Legacy: Explaining the Patterns of Party Politics in Post-Communist Slovakia'. *East European Politics* 30, no. 2 (2014): 1–20. doi:10.1080/21599165.2013.867255.

Haughton, Tim. 'Half Full but Also Half Empty: Conditionality, Compliance and the Quality of Democracy in Central and Eastern Europe'. *Political Studies Review* 9, no. 3 (2011): 323–33. doi:10.1111/j.1478-9302.2010.00220.x.

Haughton, Tim. 'When Does the EU Make a Difference? Conditionality and the Accession Process in Central and Eastern Europe'. *Political Studies Review* 5, no. 2 (2007): 233–46.

Haverland, Markus. 'Does the EU *Cause* Domestic Developments? Improving Case Selection in Europeanisation Research'. *West European Politics* 29, no. 1 (2006): 134–46.

Heinen, Jacqueline. 'Public/Private: Gender—Social and Political Citizenship in Eastern Europe'. *Theory and Society* 26, no. 4, Special Issue on Recasting Citizenship (1997): 577–97.

Heintze, Hans-Joachim. 'Contradictory Principles in the Helsinki Final Act?' *OSCE Yearbook*, 2004.

Henderson, Karen. 'Slovakia and the Democratic Criteria for EU Accession'. *Back to Europe: Central and Eastern Europe and the European Union*. Abbington: Taylor and Francis, 1999.

Henderson, Karen. *Slovakia: The Escape from Invisibility*. London: Routledge, 2002.

Henrard, Kristin. 'An EU Perspective on New versus Traditional Minorities: On Semi-Inclusive Socio-Economic Integration and Expanding Visions of European Culture and Identity'. *Columbia Journal of European Law* 17 (2010): 57–99.

Henrard, Kristin. 'The Interrelationship between Individual Human Rights, Minority Rights and the Right to Self-Determination and Its Importance for the Adequate Protection of Linguistic Minorities'. *Ethnopolitics* 1, no. 1 (2001): 41–61.

Hepworth, Kate. 'Abject Citizens: Italian "Nomad Emergencies" and the Deportability of Romanian Roma'. *Citizenship Studies* 16, no. 3–4 (2012): 431–49.

High Level Advisory Group. 'Report of the High Level Advisory Group of Experts on the Social Integration of Ethnic Minorities and Their Full Participation in the Labour Market'. Brussels, 2007.

Hillion, Christophe. 'Enlargement of the European Union—The Discrepancy between Membership Obligations and Accession Conditions as Regards the Protection of Minorities'. *Fordham International Law Journal* 27 (2003): 715–40.

Honneth, Axel. *The I in We: Studies in the Theory of Recognition*. Cambridge: Polity, 2012.

Horowitz, Donald L. 'Democracy in Divided Societies'. In *Nationalism, Ethnic Conflict, and Democracy*, edited by Larry Diamond and Marc F. Plattner. London: Johns Hopkins University Press, 1994.

Horváth, István, and Remus Gabriel Anghel. 'Migration and Its Consequences for Romania'. *Südosteuropa. Zeitschrift Für Politik Und Gesellschaft* 4 (2009): 386–403.

Hughes, James. '"Exit" in Deeply Divided Societies: Regimes of Discrimination in Estonia and Latvia and the Potential for Russophone Migration'. *Journal of Common Market Studies* 43, no. 4 (2005): 739–69.

Hughes, James, and Gwendolyn Sasse. 'Monitoring the Monitors: EU Enlargement Conditionality and Minority Protection in the CEECs'. *Journal of Ethnopolitics and Minority Issues in Europe*, no. 1 (2003): 1–37.

Hughes, James, Gwendolyn Sasse, and Claire Gordon. 'Conditionality and Compliance in the EU's Eastward Enlargement: Regional Policy and the Reform of Sub-National Government'. *Journal of Common Market Studies* 42, no. 3 (2004): 523–51.

Human Rights Watch. 'Italy: Expulsion Decree Targets Romanians'. 7 November 2007. http://www.hrw.org/de/news/2007/11/07/italy-expulsion-decree-targets-romanians.

Hurrell, Andrew, and Anand Menon. 'Politics Like Any Other? Comparative Politics, International Relations and the Study of the EU'. *West European Politics* 19, no. 2 (1996): 386–402.

Huszka, Beáta. 'Framing National Identity in Independence Campaigns: Secessionist Rhetoric and Ethnic Conflict'. *Nationalism and Ethnic Politics* 20, no. 2 (2014): 153–73. doi: 10.1080/13537113.2014.909153.

Ieda, Osamu, ed. *Beyond Sovereignty: From Status Law to Transnational Citizenship?* Sapporo: Slavic Research Center, Hokkaido University, 2006.

Imig, Douglas R., and Sydney Tarrow. 'Political Contention in a Europeanising Polity'. *West European Politics* 23, no. 4 (2000): 73–93.

Ishiyama, John T. 'Ethnopolitical Parties and Democratic Consolidation in Post-Communist Eastern Europe'. *Nationalism and Ethnic Politics* 7, no. 3 (2001): 25–45.

Jackson-Preece, Jennifer. *National Minorities and the European Nation-States System*. Oxford: Oxford University Press, 1998.

Jackson-Preece, Jennifer. 'National Minority Rights vs. State Sovereignty in Europe: Changing Norms in International Relations?' *Nations and Nationalism* 3, no. 3 (1997).

Jakoubek, Marek, and Tomáš Hirt. *Romové: Kulturologické Etudy*. Plzeň: Aleš Čeněk, 2004.

James, Zoë. 'Hate Crimes against Gypsies, Travellers and Roma in Europe'. In *The Routledge International Handbook on Hate Crime*, edited by Nathan Hall, Abbee Corb, Paul Giannasi, and John G.D. Grieve, 237–48. London: Routledge, 2015.

Järve, Priit. 'Soviet Nationalities Policy and Minority Protection in the Baltic States: A Battle of Legacies'. In *Institutional Legacies of Communism: Change and Continuities in Minority Protection*, edited by Karl Cordell, Timofey Agarin, and Alexander Osipov, 172–85. London: Routledge, 2013.

Jenne, Erin K. *Ethnic Bargaining. The Paradox of Minority Empowerment*. London: Cornell University Press, 2007.

Jenne, Erin K., and Florian Bieber. 'Situational Nationalism: Nation-Building in the Balkans, Subversive Institutions and the Montenegrin Paradox'. *Ethnopolitics* 13, no. 5 (2014): 431–60. doi:10.1080/17449057.2014.912447.

Jeram, Sanjay, Arno van der Zwet, and Verena Wisthaler. 'Friends or Foes? Migrants and Sub-State Nationalists in Europe'. *Journal of Ethnic and Migration Studies* (15 September 2015): 1–13. doi:10.1080/1369183X.2015.1082286.

Johannès, Frank. 'Le Fichier des Roms du Minstère de L'intérieur'. *Le Monde*, 7 October 2010, http://libertes.blog.lemonde.fr/2010/10/07/le-fichier-des-roms-du-ministere-de-linterieur.

Johns, Michael. '"Do as I Say, Not as I Do": The European Union, Eastern Europe and Minority Rights'. *East European Politics and Societies* 17, no. 4 (2003): 682–99.

Johns, Michael. 'Quiet Diplomacy, the European Union and Conflict Prevention: Learning from the HCNM on Issues of Social Cohesion'. *International Journal on Minority and Group Rights* 19, no. 3 (2012): 243–65. doi:10.1163/15718115-01903006.

Jowitt, Ken. *New World Disorder: The Leninist Extinction*. Berkeley: University of California Press, 1993.

Jubulis, Mark A. 'The External Dimension of Democratization in Latvia: The Impact of European Institutions'. *International Relations* 13, no. 3 (1996): 59–73.

Kacarska, Simonida. 'The Representation of Minorities in the Public Sector in the EU Accession Process'. In *Institutional Legacies of Communism: Change and Continuities in Minority Protection*, edited by Karl Cordell, Timofey Agarin, and Alexander Osipov, 217–31. London: Routledge, 2013.

Kanemoto, Yoshitsugu, and W. Bentley MacLeod. 'The Ratchet Effect and the Market for Secondhand Workers'. *Journal of Labor Economics* 10, no. 1 (1992): 85–98.

Kapralski, Slawomir. 'Symbols and Rituals in the Mobilisation of the Romani National Ideal'. *Studies in Ethnicity and Nationalism* 12, no. 1 (2012): 64–81. doi:10.1111/j.1754-94 69.2012.01152.x.

Karolewski, Ireneusz Pawel. 'Constitutionalization of the European Union as a Response to the Eastern Enlargement: Functions versus Power'. *Journal of Communist Studies and Transition Politics* 23, no. 4 (2007): 501–24.

Karolewski, Ireneusz Pawel. 'The Polish Charter: Extraterritorial Semi-Citizenship and Soft Power'. In *Extraterritorial Citizenship in Postcommunist Europe*, edited by Timofey Agarin and Ireneusz Pawel Karolewski, 65–88. Lanham, MD: Rowman & Littlefield, 2015.

Kaufmann, Eric P. *Rethinking Ethnicity: Majority Groups and Dominant Minorities*. London: Routledge, 2004.

Keil, Soeren. 'Europeanization, State-Building and Democratization in the Western Balkans'. *Nationalities Papers* 41, no. 3 (2013): 343–53.

Kelley, Judith G. *Ethnic Politics in Europe: The Power of Norms and Incentives*. Oxford: Princeton University Press, 2004.

Kemp, Walter A. *Nationalism and Communism in Eastern Europe and the Soviet Union: A Basic Contradiction*. New York: St. Martin's Press, 1999.

King, Charles. *Extreme Politics: Nationalism, Violence, and the End of Eastern Europe*. Oxford: Oxford University Press, 2009.

King, Charles, and Neil J. Melvin. *Nations Abroad: Diaspora Politics and International Relations in the Former Soviet Union*. Boulder, CO: Westview Press, 1998.

Klandermans, Bert. 'New Social Movements and Resource Mobilization: The European and the American Approach Revisited'. *International Journal of Mass Emergencies and Disasters* 4, no. 2 (1986): 13–37.

Knop, Karen. *Diversity and Self-Determination in International Law*. Cambridge: Cambridge University Press, 2002.

Kochenov, Dimitry. 'EU Citizenship without Duties'. *European Law Journal* 20, no. 4 (2014): 482–98.

Kochenov, Dimitry. *EU Enlargement and the Failure of Conditionality: Pre-Accession Conditionality in the Fields of Democracy and the Rule of Law*. The Hague: Kluwer Law International, 2008.

Kochenov, Dimitry. 'Free Movement and Participation in the Parliamentary Elections in the Member State of Nationality: An Ignored Link'. *Maastricht Journal of European & Comparative Law* 16 (2009): 197.

Kochenov, Dimitry. 'The Internal Aspects of Good Neighbourliness in the EU: Loyalty and Values'. In *Good Neighbourly Relations in the European Legal Context*, edited by Dmitry Kochenov and Elena Basheska. Nijhoff: Brill, 2015.

Kochenov, Dimitry, and Eline De Ridder. 'Democratic Conditionality in Eastern Enlargement: Ambitious Window Dressing'. *European Foreign Affairs Review* 16, no. 5 (2011): 589–605.

Kochenov, Dmitry, Vadim Poleshchuk, and Aleksejs Dimitrovs. 'Do Professional Linguistic Requirements Discriminate? A Legal Analysis: Estonia and Latvia in the Spotlight'. In *European Yearbook of Minority Issues*, 10:137–87. Nijhoff: Brill, 2013.

Kohler-Koch, Beate. 'The Strength of Weakness: The Transformation of Governance in the EU'. *The Future of the Nation State. Essays on Cultural Pluralism and Political Integration*, 1996.

Kohler-Koch, Beate, and Berthold Rittberger. 'The "Governance Turn" in EU Studies'. *Journal of Common Market Studies* 44, no. 1 (2006): 27–49.

Koinova, Maria. 'Challenging Assumptions of the Enlargement Literature: The Impact of the EU on Human and Minority Rights in Macedonia'. *Europe-Asia Studies* 63, no. 5 (2011): 807–32. doi:10.1080/09668136.2011.576023.

Koinova, Maria. *Ethnonationalist Conflict in Postcommunist States. Varieties of Governance in Bulgaria, Macedonia, and Kosovo*. Philadelphia: University of Pennsylvania Press, 2013.

Koinova, Maria. 'Why Do Ethnonational Conflicts Reach Different Degrees of Violence? Insights from Kosovo, Macedonia, and Bulgaria during the 1990s'. *Nationalism and Ethnic Politics* 15, no. 1 (2009): 84–108.

Koktsidis, Pavlos I. 'How Conflict Spreads: Opportunity Structures and the Diffusion of Conflict in the Republic of Macedonia'. *Civil Wars* 16, no. 2 (3 April 2014): 208–38. doi:10.1080/13698249.2014.927703.

Koktsidis, Pavlos I. 'Nipping an Insurgency in the Bud—Part I: Theory and Practice of Non-Military Coercion in FYR Macedonia'. *Ethnopolitics* 12, no. 2 (2013): 183–200.

Kolstø, Pål. 'Nation-Building in the Former USSR'. *Journal of Democracy* 7, no. 1 (1996): 118–32.

Kolstø, Pål. *Political Construction Sites: Nation-Building in Russia and the Post-Soviet States*. Boulder, CO: Westview Press, 2000.

Koneska, Cvete. 'Ethnic Power-Sharing in Bosnia and Macedonia: Institutional Legacies of Communism'. In *Institutional Legacies of Communism, Change and Continuities in Minority Protection*, edited by Karl Cordell, Timofey Agarin, and Alexander Osipov, 124–38. London: Routledge, 2013.

Kostadinova, Galina. 'Minority Rights as a Normative Framework for Addressing the Situation of Roma in Europe'. *Oxford Development Studies* 39, no. 2 (2011): 163–83.

Kostakopoulou, Dora. 'The Anatomy of Civic Integration'. *Modern Law Review* 73, no. 6 (2010): 933–58.

Kostakopoulou, Dora. 'Thick, Thin and Thinner Patriotisms: Is This All There Is?' *Oxford Journal of Legal Studies* 26, no. 1 (2006): 73–106.

Kovács, Mária M. 'Standards of Self-Determination and Standards of Minority-Rights in the Post-Communist Era: A Historical Perspective'. *Nations and Nationalism* 9, no. 3 (1 July 2003): 433–50. doi:10.1111/1469-8219.00105.

Kuzio, Taras. '"Nationalising" States or Nation-Building? A Critical Review of the Theoretical Literature and Empirical Evidence.' *Nations and Nationalism* 7, no. 2 (2001): 135–54.

Kymlicka, Will. 'Categorizing Groups, Categorizing States: Theorizing Minority Rights in a World of Deep Diversity'. *Ethics & International Affairs* 23, no. 4 (2009): 371–88.

Kymlicka, Will. *Multicultural Citizenship: A Liberal Theory of Minority Rights*. Oxford: Clarendon Press, 1995.

Kymlicka, Will. *Multicultural Odysseys: Navigating the New International Politics of Diversity*. Oxford: Oxford University Press, 2007.

Laitin, David D. *Identity in Formation: The Russian-Speaking Populations in the Near Abroad*. Ithaca London: Cornell University Press, 1998.

Lajcakova, Jarmila. 'Advancing Empowerment of the Roma in Slovakia through a Non-Territorial National Autonomy'. *Ethnopolitics* 9, no. 2 (2010): 171–96.

Lajcakova, Jarmila. 'The Uneasy Road towards Remedying the Economic and Cultural Disadvantage of the Roma in Slovakia'. *International Journal on Minority and Group Rights* 14, no. 1 (2007): 59–83.

Lane, Thomas. *Lithuania: Stepping Westward*. London: Routledge, 2002.

LaPorte, Jody, and Danielle N. Lussier. 'What Is the Leninist Legacy? Assessing Twenty Years of Scholarship'. *Slavic Review* 70, no. 3 (2011): 637–54.

Lavenex, Sandra, and Frank Schimmelfennig. 'Relations with the Wider Europe'. *Journal of Common Market Studies* 45, no. s1 (2007): 143–62.

Lavenex, Sandra, and Nicole Wichmann. 'The External Governance of EU Internal Security'. *European Integration* 31, no. 1 (2009): 83–102.

Łazowski, Adam. 'And Then They Were Twenty-Seven . . . a Legal Appraisal of the Sixth Accession Treaty'. *Common Market Law Review* 44, no. 2 (2007): 401–30.

Lederach, John Paul. *Building Peace: Sustainable Reconciliation in Divided Societies*. Washington, DC: United States Institute of Peace Press, 1997.

Legros, Olivier, and Tommaso Vitale. 'Les Migrants Roms Dans Les Villes Françaises et Italiennes: Mobilités, Régulations et Marginalités'. *Géocarrefour* 86, no. 1 (2011): 3–13.

Levitz, Philip, and Grigore Pop-Eleches. 'Why No Backsliding? The European Union's Impact on Democracy and Governance Before and After Accession'. *Comparative Political Studies* 43, no. 4 (2010): 457–85.

Linz, Juan J. 'State Building and Nation Building'. *European Review* 1, no. 4 (1993): 355–69.

Linz, Juan J., and Alfred Stepan. *Problems of Democratic Transition and Consolidation: Southern Europe, South America, and Post-Communist Europe*. Baltimore: Johns Hopkins, 1996.

Linz, Juan J., and Alfred Stepan. 'Toward Consolidated Democracies'. *Journal of Democracy* 7, no. 2 (1996): 14–33.

Ma, Shu-Yun. 'Taking Evolution Seriously, or Metaphorically? A Review of Interactions between Historical Institutionalism and Darwinian Evolutionary Theory'. *Political Studies Review*, 1 July 2014. doi:10.1111/1478-9302.12059.

Magnette, Paul. 'In the Name of Simplification: Coping with Constitutional Conflicts in the Convention on the Future of Europe'. *European Law Journal* 11, no. 4 (2005): 432–51.

Mahoney, James, and Kathleen Thelen. 'A Theory of Gradual Institutional Change'. In *Explaining Institutional Change: Ambiguity, Agency, and Power*, edited by James Mahoney and Kathleen Thelen, 1–37. Cambridge: Cambridge University Press, 2010.

Maletz, Donald J. 'Tocqueville's Tyranny of the Majority Reconsidered'. *Journal of Politics* 64, no. 3 (2002): 741–63.

Malloy, Tove H. *National Minority Rights in Europe*. Oxford: Oxford University Press, 2005.

Marko, Joseph. 'The Concept of "Nation"'. *European Yearbook of Minority Issues Online* 5, no. 1 (2005): 141–46.

Martin, Terry. 'Borders and Ethnic Conflict: The Soviet Experiment in Ethno-Territorial Proliferation'. *Jahrbücher Für Geschichte Osteuropas* 47 (1999): 538–55.

Marushiakova, Elena, and Vesselin Popov. 'The Shades of Incomplete'. In *Roma Education in Europe: Practices, Policies and Politics*, edited by Maja Miskovic, 135–46. London: Routledge, 2013.

Mason, David S. *Revolution and Transition in East-Central Europe*. Boulder, CO: Westview Press, 1992.

Matache, Margareta. 'The Deficit of EU Democracies: A New Cycle of Violence Against Roma Population'. *Human Rights Quarterly* 36, no. 2 (2014): 325–48.

Matras, Yaron. 'Scholarship and the Politics of Romani Identity: Strategic and Conceptual Issues'. *European Yearbook of Minority Issues* 10 (2013): 211–47.

Mayrgündter, Tanja. 'The Implementation of the ECRML in Slovakia under Construction: Structural Preconditions, External Influence and Internal Obstacles'. *Perspectives on European Politics and Society* 13, no. 4 (1 December 2012): 480–96. doi:10.1080/15705854.2012.731936.

McBride, Cillian. 'Democratic Participation, Engagement and Freedom'. *British Journal of Politics & International Relations* 15, no. 4 (2013): 493–508. doi:10.1111/j.1467-856X.2012.00516.x.

McDonald, Christina, and Katy Negrin. *No Data—No Progress: Country Findings: Data Collection in Countries Participating in the Decade of Roma Inclusion 2005–2015*. Budapest: Open Society Foundations, 2010.

McGann, Anthony J. 'The Tyranny of the Supermajority: How Majority Rule Protects Minorities'. *Journal of Theoretical Politics* 16, no. 1 (2004): 53–77.

McGarry, Aidan. 'The Dilemma of the European Union's Roma Policy'. *Critical Social Policy* 32, no. 1 (2012): 126–36.

McGarry, Aidan, and Timofey Agarin. 'Unpacking the Roma Participation Puzzle: Presence, Voice and Influence'. *Journal of Ethnic and Migration Studies* 40, no. 12 (20 March 2014): 1972–90. doi:10.1080/1369183X.2014.897599.

McGarry, Aidan, and Helen Drake. 'The Politicization of Roma as an Ethnic Other: Security Discourse in France and the Politics of Belonging'. In *The Discourses and Politics of Migration in Europe*, edited by Umut Korkut, Gregg Bucken-Knapp, Aidan McGarry, Jonas Hinnfors, and Helen Drake, 73–91. Houndmills: Palgrave Macmillan, 2013.

McMahon, Simon. 'Assessing the Impact of European Union Citizenship: The Status and Rights of Romanian Nationals in Italy'. *Journal of Contemporary European Studies* 20, no. 2 (1 June 2012): 199–214. doi:10.1080/14782804.2012.685391.

Merkel, Wolfgang, and Brigitte Weiffen. 'Does Heterogeneity Hinder Democracy?' *Comparative Sociology* 11, no. 3 (2012): 387–421.

Meyer-Sahling, Jan-Hinrik. 'Varieties of Legacies: A Critical Review of Legacy Explanations of Public Administration Reform in East Central Europe'. *International Review of Administrative Sciences* 75, no. 3 (2009): 509–28.

Michalowski, Ines. 'Required to Assimilate? The Content of Citizenship Tests in Five Countries'. *Citizenship Studies* 15, no. 6–7 (2011): 749–68.

Mikulova, Kristina, and Michal Simecka. 'Norm Entrepreneurs and Atlanticist Foreign Policy in Central and Eastern Europe: The Missionary Zeal of Recent Converts'. *Europe-Asia Studies* 65, no. 6 (12 July 2013): 1192–1216. doi:10.1080/09668136.2013.813681.

Ministerski Savet na Republika Balgarija. 'Nacionalna Strategija Na Republika Balgarija Za Integrirane Na Romite (2012–2020)'. 2012. http://www.nccedi.government.bg/page.php?category=125.

Ministerski Savet na Republika Balgarija. 'Ramkova Programa Za Ravnopravno Integrirane Na Romite v Balgarskoto Obshtestvo'. April 1999. http://www.ncedi.government.bg/en/index.html.

Miskovic, Maja. *Roma Education in Europe: Practices, Policies and Politics*. London: Routledge, 2013.

Mitzen, Jennifer. 'Ontological Security in World Politics: State Identity and the Security Dilemma'. *European Journal of International Relations* 12, no. 3 (2006): 341–70.

Mole, Richard C. M. *The Baltic States from the Soviet Union to the European Union: Identity, Discourse and Power in the Post-Communist Transition of Estonia, Latvia and Lithuania*. London: Routledge, 2012.

Moravcsik, Andrew. 'The Origins of Human Rights Regimes: Democratic Delegation in Postwar Europe'. *International Organization* 52, no. 2 (2000): 729–52.

Moravcsik, Andrew, and Milada A. Vachudova. 'National Interests, State Power, and EU Enlargement'. *East European Politics and Societies* 17, no. 1 (2003): 42–58.

Muižnieks, Nils, ed. *How Integrated Is Latvian Society? An Audit of Achievements, Failures and Challenges*. Riga: University of Latvia Press, 2010.

Muižnieks, Nils, and Ilze Brands-Kehris. 'The European Union, Democratization, and Minorities in Latvia'. In *The European Union and Democratization*, edited by Paul J. Kubicek, 30–55. London: Routledge, 2003.

Munck, Gerardo L., and Carol Skalnik Leff. 'Modes of Transition and Democratization'. *Journal of Democracy* 29, no. 3 (1997): 343–62.

Mušinka, A. et al. *Atlas of Roma Communities in Slovakia 2013*. Bratislava: UNDP Europe and the CIS, Bratislava Regional Centre, 2014.

Mylonas, Harris, Adria Lawrence, and Erica Chenoweth. 'Assimilation and Its Alternatives: Caveats in the Study of Nation-Building Policies'. *Journal of Southern Europe and the Balkans* 2, no. 2 (2000): 141–48.

Nagel, Joane, and Susan Olzak. 'Ethnic Mobilization in New and Old States: An Extension of the Competition Model'. *Social Problems* 30, no. 2 (1982): 127–41.

Nancheva, Nevena. *Between Nationalism and Europeanisation: Narratives of National Identity in Bulgaria and Macedonia*. Colchester: ECPR Press, 2015.

Nancheva, Nevena. 'Imagining Policies: European Integration and the European Minority Rights Regime'. *Journal of Contemporary European Studies* (13 July 2015): 1–17. doi:10.1080/14782804.2015.1056725.

Nash, Mary, John Wong, and Andrew Trlin. 'Civic and Social Integration: A New Field of Social Work Practice with Immigrants, Refugees and Asylum Seekers'. *International Social Work* 49, no. 3 (2006): 345–63.

Nedelsky, Nadya. 'Constitutional Nationalism's Implications for Minority Rights and Democratization: The Case of Slovakia'. *Ethnic and Racial Studies* 26, no. 1 (2003): 102–28.

Nic Shuibhne, Niamh. 'The Resilience of EU Market Citizenship'. *Common Market Law Review* 47, no. 6 (2010): 1597–1628.

Nimni, Ephraim. 'National–Cultural Autonomy as an Alternative to Minority Territorial Nationalism'. *Ethnopolitics* 6, no. 3 (2007): 345–64.

Norwich, Liora. 'Fighting by the Rules: A Comparative Framework for Exploring Ethnic Mobilization Patterns in Democratic Contexts'. *Ethnopolitics* 14, no. 4 (2015): 354–81. doi:10.1080/17449057.2015.1015323.

Noutcheva, Gergana. 'Fake, Partial and Imposed Compliance: The Limits of the EU's Normative Power in the Western Balkans'. *Journal of European Public Policy* 16, no. 7 (2009): 1065–84.

Noutcheva, Gergana, and Senem Aydin-Düzgit. 'Lost in Europeanisation: The Western Balkans and Turkey'. *West European Politics* 35, no. 1 (2012): 59–78.

Noutcheva, Gergana, and Dimitar Bechev. 'The Successful Laggards: Bulgaria and Romania's Accession to the EU'. *East European Politics & Societies* 22, no. 1 (2008): 114–44.

Novagrockiene, Jurate. 'The Development and Consolidation of the Lithuanian Political Party System'. *Journal of Baltic Studies* 32, no. 2 (2001): 141–55.

O'Brennan, John. '"Bringing Geopolitics Back In": Exploring the Security Dimension of the 2004 Eastern Enlargement of the European Union'. *Cambridge Review of International Affairs* 19, no. 1 (1 March 2006): 155–69. doi:10.1080/09557570500501911.

O'Dwyer, Conor. *Runaway State-Building: Patronage Politics and Democratic Development.* Baltimore: Johns Hopkins University Press, 2006.

O'Nions, Helen. *Minority Rights Protection in International Law: The Roma of Europe.* Aldershot: Ashgate, 2007.

Olzak, Susan. 'Ethnic Protest in Core and Periphery States'. *Ethnic and Racial Studies* 21, no. 2 (1998): 187–217.

Olzak, Susan. *The Global Dynamics of Racial and Ethnic Mobilization.* Stanford: Stanford University Press, 2006.

OSCE. 'Statement on Roma and Sinti at the Working Sessions 6 and 7 of the Annual Human Dimension Implementation Meeting of the OSCE-ODIHR, Warsaw, September 2007 HDIM IO/205/07'. HDIM IO/205/07, 2007. http://www.osce.org/odihr/27315.

Osipov, Alexander. 'Implementation Unwanted? Symbolic vs. Instrumental Policies in the Russian Management of Ethnic Diversity'. *Perspectives on European Politics and Society* 13, no. 4 (1 December 2012): 425–42. doi:10.1080/15705854.2012.731933.

Palermo, Francesco, and Natalie Sabanadze, eds. *National Minorities in Inter-State Relations.* Leiden: Martinus Nijhoff Publishers, 2011.

Panke, Diana. 'Good Instructions in No Time? Domestic Coordination of EU Policies in 19 Small States'. *West European Politics* 33, no. 4 (2010): 770–90.

Pantea, Maria-Carmen. 'Policy Implications for Addressing Roma Precarious Migration through Employment at Home'. *International Migration* 51, no. 5 (2013): 34–47. doi:10.1111/imig.12069.

Parker, Owen. 'Roma and the Politics of EU Citizenship in France: Everyday Security and Resistance'. *JCMS: Journal of Common Market Studies* 50, no. 3 (2012): 475–91. doi:10.1111/j.1468-5965.2011.02238.x.

Pereira, Alexius. 'Does Multiculturalism Recognise or "Minoritise" Minorities?' *Studies in Ethnicity and Nationalism* 8, no. 2 (2008): 349–56.

Pero, Davide, and John Solomos. 'Introduction: Migrant Politics and Mobilization: Exclusion, Engagements, Incorporation'. *Ethnic and Racial Studies* 33, no. 1 (2010): 1–18.

Petsinis, Vassilis. 'Croatia's Framework for Minority Rights: New Legal Prospects within the Context of European Integration'. *Ethnopolitics* 12, no. 4 (2013): 352–67.

Petsinis, Vassilis. 'Ethnic Relations, the EU, and Geopolitical Implications: The Cases of Estonia and Croatia'. *Ethnopolitics* (4 March 2015): 1–15. doi:10.1080/17449057 .2015.1017317.

Pettai, Vello, and Kristina Kallas. 'Estonia: Conditionality amidst a Legal Straightjacket'. In *Minority Rights in Central and Eastern Europe*, edited by Bernd Rechel, 104–18. London: Routledge, 2009.

Phillips, Anne. *Multiculturalism without Culture.* Princeton, NJ: Princeton University Press, 2007.

Phillips, Anne, and Seyla Benhabib. 'From Inequality to Difference: A Severe Case of Displacement?' *New Left Review*, no. 224 (1997): 143–53.

Phillips, Deborah. 'Minority Ethnic Segregation, Integration and Citizenship: A European Perspective'. *Journal of Ethnic and Migration Studies* 36, no. 2 (2010): 209–25.

Phinnemore, David. 'And We'd Like to Thank . . . Romania's Integration into the European Union, 1989–2007'. *Journal of European Integration* 32, no. 3 (2010): 291–308.

Piasere, Leonardo. *I Rom d'Europa: Una Storia Moderna*. Roma: Laterza, 2004.

Poleshchuk, Vadim. *Advice Not Welcomed: Recommendations of the OSCE High Commissioner to Estonia and Latvia and the Response*. Hamburg: LitVerlag, 2001.

Popescu, Diana Elena. 'Moral Exclusion and Blaming the Victim: The Deligitimising Role of Antiziganism'. In *When Stereotype Meets Prejudice: Antiziganism in European Societies*, edited by Timofey Agarin, 171–200. Stuttgart: ibidem, 2014.

Popovski, Vesna. *National Minorities and Citizenship Rights in Lithuania, 1988–1993*. Houndmills: Palgrave, 2000.

Prefettura di Roma, Patto per Roma Sicura, European Roma Rights Center. 'Security a La Italiana: Fingerprinting, Extreme Violence and Harassment of Roma in Italy'. Budapest: European Roma Rights Center, 2009.

Pridham, Geoffrey. 'The EU's Political Conditionality and Post-Accession Tendencies: Comparisons from Slovakia and Latvia'. *JCMS: Journal of Common Market Studies* 46, no. 2 (2008): 365–87.

Pridham, Geoffrey. 'Securing the Only Game in Town: The EU's Political Conditionality and Democratic Consolidation in Post-Soviet Latvia'. *Europe-Asia Studies* 61, no. 1 (2009): 51–84.

Pridham, Geoffrey. 'The Slovak Parliamentary Election of September 2002: Its Systemic Importance'. *Government and Opposition* 38, no. 3 (2003): 333–56.

Prieto-Flores, Oscar, and Teresa Sordé-Martí. 'The Institutionalization of Panethnicity from the Grassroots Standpoint in a European Context: The Case of Gitanos and Roma Immigrants in Barcelona'. *Ethnicities* 11, no. 2 (2011): 202–17.

Radaelli, Claudio M. 'How Does Europeanization Produce Domestic Policy Change? Corporate Tax Policy in Italy and the United Kingdom'. *Comparative Political Studies* 30, no. 5 (1997): 553–75.

Ram, Melanie H. 'Interests, Norms and Advocacy: Explaining the Emergence of the Roma onto the EU's Agenda'. *Ethnopolitics* 9, no. 2 (2010): 197–217.

Ram, Melanie H. 'Legacies of EU Conditionality: Explaining Post-Accession Adherence to Pre-Accession Rules on Roma'. *Europe-Asia Studies* 64, no. 7 (September 2012): 1191–1218. doi:10.1080/09668136.2012.696813.

Ram, Melanie H. 'Romania: From Laggard to Leader?' In *Minority Rights in Central and Eastern Europe*, edited by Bernd Rechel, 180–94. London: Routledge, 2009.

Raunio, Tapio. 'Holding Governments Accountable in European Affairs: Explaining Cross-National Variation'. *Journal of Legislative Studies* 11, no. 3–4 (2005): 319–42.

Razsa, Maple, and Nicole Lindstrom. 'Balkan Is Beautiful: Balkanism in the Political Discourse of Tudman's Croatia'. *East European Politics and Societies* 18, no. 4 (2004): 628–50.

Rechel, Bernd. *Minority Rights in Central and Eastern Europe*. London: Routledge, 2009.

Regelmann, Ada-Charlotte. *Minority Integration and State-Building: Post-Communist Transformations*. London: Routledge, 2016.

Resler, Tamara J. 'Dilemmas of Democratisation: Safeguarding Minorities in Russia, Ukraine and Lithuania'. *Europe-Asia Studies* 49, no. 1 (1997): 89–106.

Ringold, Dena, Mitchell Alexander Orenstein, and Erika Wilkens. *Roma in an Expanding Europe: Breaking the Poverty Cycle*. Washington, DC: World Bank Publications, 2005.

Risse, Thomas. 'Neofunctionalism, European Identity, and the Puzzles of European Integration'. *Journal of European Public Policy* 12, no. 2 (2005): 291–309.

Risse, Thomas, and Kathryn Sikkink. 'The Socialization of International Human Rights Norms into Domestic Practices: Introduction'. *Cambridge Studies in International Relations* 66 (1999): 1–38.

Roe, Paul. 'Securitization and Minority Rights: Conditions of Desecuritization'. *Security Dialogue* 35, no. 3 (2004): 279–94.

Roeder, Philip G. 'Secessionism, Institutions, and Change'. *Ethnopolitics* 13, no. 1 (2014): 86–104. doi:10.1080/17449057.2013.844437.

Romanian President Slams Italian Gypsy Rules'. Romea.cz, 2 August 2008. http://www.romea.cz/en/news/world/romanian-president-slams-italy-s-gypsy-rules.

Ronchey, Alberto. 'L'invasione Dei Nomadi'. Corriere Della Sera, 29 September 2007. http://www.corriere.it/Primo_Piano/Editoriali/2007/09_Settembre/29/ronchey_invasione_nomadi.shtml.

Rosas, Allan, Jan E. Helgesen, and Diane Goodman. *The Strength of Diversity: Human Rights and Pluralist Democracy*. Dordrecht: Martinus Nijhoff, 1992.

Rostas, Iulius, and Andrew Ryder. 'EU Framework for National Roma Integration Strategies: Insights into Empowerment and Inclusive Policy Development'. In *Gypsies and Travellers: Empowerment and Inclusion in British Society*, edited by Andrew Ryder and Joanna Richardson. Bristol: Policy Press, 2012.

Roughneen, Dualta. *The Right to Roam: Travellers and Human Rights in the Modern Nation-State*. Newcastle: Cambridge Scholars Publishing, 2010.

Russinov, Rumyan. 'The Bulgarian Framework Programme for Equal Integration of Roma: Participation in the Policy-Making Process'. *Roma Rights, Journal of the European Roma Rights Centre* (2001).

Sabatier, Paul A. 'Top-Down and Bottom-Up Approaches to Implementation Research: A Critical Analysis and Suggested Synthesis'. *Journal of Public Policy* 6, no. 1 (2008): 21–48.

Sasse, Gwendolyn. 'The Politics of EU Conditionality: The Norm of Minority Protection during and beyond EU Accession'. *Journal of European Public Policy* 15, no. 6 (2008): 842–60.

Sasse, Gwendolyn. 'Securitization or Securing Rights? Exploring the Conceptual Foundations of Policies towards Minorities and Migrants in Europe'. *JCMS: Journal of Common Market Studies* 43, no. 4 (2005): 673–93.

Sasse, Gwendolyn. 'Tracing the Construction and Effects of EU Conditionality'. In *Minority Rights in Central and Eastern Europe*, edited by Bernd Rechel, 17–31. London, New York: Routledge, 2009.

Sassen, Saskia. 'A Savage Sorting of Winners and Losers: Contemporary Versions of Primitive Accumulation'. *Globalizations* 7, no. 1–2 (2010): 23–50.

Schimmelfennig, Frank. 'Strategic Calculation and International Socialization: Membership Incentives, Party Constellations, and Sustained Compliance in Central and Eastern Europe'. *International Organization* 59, no. 4 (2005): 827–60.

Schimmelfennig, Frank, and Arista Maria Cirtautas. 'Europeanisation Before and After Accession: Conditionality, Legacies and Compliance'. *Europe-Asia Studies* 62, no. 3 (2010): 421–41.

Schimmelfennig, Frank, Stefan Engert, and Heiko Knobel. 'Costs, Commitment and Compliance: The Impact of EU Democratic Conditionality on Latvia, Slovakia and Turkey'. *Journal of Common Market Studies* 41, no. 3 (2003): 495–518.

Schimmelfennig, Frank, Dirk Leuffen, and Berthold Rittberger. 'The European Union as a System of Differentiated Integration: Interdependence, Politicization and Differentiation'. *Journal of European Public Policy* 22, no. 6 (2015): 764–82

Schmidt, Vivien A., and Claudio M. Radaelli. 'Policy Change and Discourse in Europe: Conceptual and Methodological Issues'. *West European Politics* 27, no. 2 (2004): 183–210.

Schulze, Jennie L. 'Estonia Caught between East and West: EU Conditionality, Russia's Activism and Minority Integration'. *Nationalities Papers* 38, no. 3 (2010): 361–92.

Schwellnuss, Guido. 'Anti-Discrimination Legislation'. In *Minority Rights in Central and Eastern Europe*, edited by Bernd Rechel, 32–45. Oxon: Routledge, 2009.

Schwellnus, Guido. 'Reasons for Constitutionalization: Non-Discrimination, Minority Rights and Social Rights in the Convention on the EU Charter of Fundamental Rights'. *Journal of European Public Policy* 13, no. 8 (2006): 1265–83.

Sedelmeier, Ulrich. 'After Conditionality: Post-Accession Compliance with EU Law in East Central Europe'. *Journal of European Public Policy* 15, no. 6 (September 2008): 806–25. doi:10.1080/13501760802196549.

Sedelmeier, Ulrich. 'Is Europeanisation through Conditionality Sustainable? Lock-In of Institutional Change after EU Accession'. *West European Politics* 35, no. 1 (2012): 20–38.

Shin, To-Ch'ol, and Jason Wells. 'Is Democracy the Only Game in Town?' *Journal of Democracy* 16, no. 2 (2005): 88–101.

Shulman, Stephen. 'Nationalist Sources of International Economic Integration'. *International Studies Quarterly* 44, no. 3 (2000): 365–90.

Sigona, Nando. 'Campzenship: Reimagining the Camp as a Social and Political Space'. *Citizenship Studies* 19, no. 1 (2015): 1–15. doi:10.1080/13621025.2014.937643.

Sigona, Nando, and Peter Vermeersch. 'The Roma in the New EU: Policies, Frames and Everyday Experiences'. *Journal of Ethnic and Migration Studies* 38, no. 8 (2012): 1189–93.

Silova, Iveta. *From Sites of Occupation to Symbols of Multiculturalism: Reconceptualizing Minority Education in Post-Soviet Latvia*. Greenwich, CT: Information Age Publishing, 2006.

Skogly, Sigrun. *Beyond National Borders: States' Human Rights Obligations in International Cooperation*. Cambridge: Cambridge University Press, 2006.

Slater, Wendy, and Andrew Wilson. *The Legacy of the Soviet Union*. Houndmills: Palgrave, 2004.

Slezkine, Yuri. 'The USSR as a Communal Appartment, or How a Socialist State Promoted Ethnic Particularism'. *Slavic Review* 53, no. 2 (1994): 414–52.

Smith, Jackie. 'Exploring Connections between Global Integration and Political Mobilization'. *Journal of World Systems Research* 10, no. 1 (2004): 255–85.

Smith, Karen E. 'The European Union at the Human Rights Council: Speaking with One Voice but Having Little Influence'. *Journal of European Public Policy* 17, no. 2 (2010): 224–41.

Söderbaum, Fredrik, and Luk Van Langenhove. 'Introduction: The EU as a Global Actor and the Role of Interregionalism'. *European Integration* 27, no. 3 (2005): 249–62.

Soysal, Yasemin Nuhoğlu. 'Citizenship, Immigration, and the European Social Project: Rights and Obligations of Individuality'. *British Journal of Sociology* 63, no. 1 (2012): 1–21.

Soysal, Yasemin Nuhoğlu. *Limits of Citizenship: Migrants and Postnational Membership in Europe*. Chicago: University of Chicago Press, 1994.

Spencer, Philip, and Howard Wollman. 'Nationalism and Democracy in the Transition from Communism in Eastern Europe'. *Contemporary Politics* 3, no. 2 (1997): 171–88.

Spendzharova, Aneta B., and Milada Anna Vachudova. 'Catching Up? Consolidating Liberal Democracy in Bulgaria and Romania after EU Accession'. *West European Politics* 35, no. 1 (2012): 39–58.

Spiro, Peter J. 'A New International Law of Citizenship'. *American Journal of International Law* 105, no. 4 (October 2011): 694–746. doi:10.5305/amerjintelaw.105.4.0694.

Spirova, Maria, and Darlene Budd. 'The EU Accession Process and the Roma Minorities in New and Soon-to-Be Member States'. *Comparative European Politics* 6, no. 1 (2008): 81–101. doi:10.1057/palgrave.cep.6110123.

Steunenberg, Bernard, and Mark Rhinard. 'The Transposition of European Law in EU Member States: Between Process and Politics'. *European Political Science Review* 2, no. 3 (2010): 495–520.

Stoddard, Edward. 'Between a Rock and a Hard Place? Internal–External Legitimacy Tensions and EU Foreign Policy in the European Periphery'. *Journal of European Integration* 37, no. 5 (24 March 2015): 553–70. doi:10.1080/07036337.2015.1019487.

Stroschein, Sherrill. *Ethnic Struggle, Coexistence, and Democratization in Eastern Europe*. Cambridge: Cambridge University Press, 2012.

Tesser, Lynn. *Ethnic Cleansing and the European Union: An Interdisciplinary Approach to Security, Memory and Ethnography*. Basingstoke: Palgrave Macmillan, 2013.

Tesser, Lynn M. 'The Geopolitics of Tolerance: Minority Rights under EU Expansion in East-Central Europe'. *East European Politics and Societies* 17, no. 3 (2003): 483–532.

Thomas, Daniel C. 'The Helsinki Accords and Political Change in Eastern Europe'. *Cambridge Studies in International Relations* 66 (1999): 205–33.

Tilly, Charles. *From Mobilization to Revolution*. Reading, MA: Addison-Wesley, 1978.

Toggenburg, Gabriel N. 'The Role of the New EU Fundamental Rights Agency: Debating the "Sex of Angels" or Improving Europe's Human Rights Performance?' *European Law Review*, no. 3 (2008): 385–98.

Tolz, Vera. 'Conflicting "Homeland Myths" and Nation-State Building in Postcommunist Russia'. *Slavic Review* 57, no. 2 (1998): 267–94.

Topidi, Kyriaki. *EU Law, Minorities, and Enlargement*. Antwerp: Intersentia, 2010.

Toshkov, Dimiter, and Elitsa Kortenska. 'Does Immigration Undermine Public Support for Integration in the European Union?' *JCMS: Journal of Common Market Studies* 53, no. 4 (1 July 2015): 910–25. doi:10.1111/jcms.12230.

Trehan, Nidhi, and Nando Sigona, eds. *Romani Politics in Contemporary Europe: Poverty, Ethnic Mobilization, and the Neo-Liberal Order.* Basingstoke: Palgrave, 2010.

Triadafilopoulos, Triadafilos. 'Illiberal Means to Liberal Ends? Understanding Recent Immigrant Integration Policies in Europe'. *Journal of Ethnic and Migration Studies* 37, no. 6 (2011): 861–80.

Turcu, Anca, and R. Urbatsch. 'Diffusion of Diaspora Enfranchisement Norms: A Multinational Study'. *Comparative Political Studies* 48, no. 4 (1 March 2015): 407–37. doi:10.1177/0010414014546331.

Udrea, Andreea. 'A Kin-State's Responsibility: Cultural Identity, Recognition, and the Hungarian Status Law'. *Ethnicities* 14, no. 2 (1 April 2014): 324–46. doi:10.1177/1468796812472145.

Underdal, Arild. 'Strategies in International Regime Negotiations: Reflecting Background Conditions or Shaping Outcomes?' *International Environmental Agreements: Politics, Law and Economics* 12, no. 2 (2012): 129–44.

Vachudova, Milada Anna. *Europe Undivided: Democracy, Leverage, and Integration After Communism.* Oxford: Oxford University Press, 2005.

van Baar, Huub. *The European Roma: Minority Representation, Memory, and the Limits of Transnational Governmentality.* Eigen Beheer. Amsterdam, 2011.

van Duin, Pieter, and Zuzana Polackova. 'Democratic Renewal and the Hungarian Minority Question in Slovakia'. *European Societies* 2, no. 3 (2000): 335–60.

van Elsuwege, Peter. *From Soviet Republics to EU Member States. A Legal and Political Assessment of the Baltic States' Accession to the EU.* Leiden: Martinus Nijhoff Publishers, 2008.

van Elsuwege, Peter. 'Good Neighbourliness as a Condition for Accession to the European Union: Finding the Balance between Law and Politics'. In *Good Neighbourliness in the European Legal Context,* edited by Dimitry Kochenov and Elena Basheska, 217–34. Leiden: Nijhoff, 2015.

Vašečka, Michal, ed. *Čačipen Pal O Roma. Súhrnná Správa O Rómoch Na Slovensku.* Bratislava: IVO, 2002.

Vasilev, George. 'EU Conditionality and Ethnic Coexistence in the Balkans: Macedonia and Bosnia in a Comparative Perspective'. *Ethnopolitics* 10, no. 1 (2011): 51–76. doi:10.1080/17449057.2010.535701.

Vermeersch, Peter. 'Ethnic Mobilisation and the Political Conditionality of European Union Accession: The Case of the Roma in Slovakia'. *Journal of Ethnic and Migration Studies* 28, no. 1 (2002): 83–101.

Vermeersch, Peter. 'Reframing the Roma: EU Initiatives and the Politics of Reinterpretation'. *Journal of Ethnic and Migration Studies* 38, no. 8 (2012): 1195–1212.

Vermeersch, Peter. *The Romani Movement: Minority Politics and Ethnic Mobilization in Contemporary Central Europe.* Oxford: Berghahn Books, 2006.

Vihalemm, Triin. 'Crystallizing and Emancipating Identities in Post-Communist Estonia'. *Nationalities Papers* 35, no. 3 (2007): 477–502.

Vitikainen, Annamari. 'Liberal Multiculturalism Group Membership and Distribution of Cultural Policies'. *Ethnicities* 9, no. 1 (2009): 53–74.

Vollebaek, Knut. 'The Bolzano/Bozen Recommendations on National Minorities in Inter-State Relations & Explanatory Note'. OSCE HCNM, June 2008.

Vollebaek, Knut. 'The International Politics of Minority Issues: Could the Early 1990s Return?' London School of Economics and Political Science. 7 May 2009. http://www.lse.ac.uk/publicEvents/events/2009/20090312t0911z001.aspx.

Voller, Yaniv. 'Contested Sovereignty as an Opportunity: Understanding Democratic Transitions in Unrecognized States'. *Democratization* 22, no. 4 (7 June 2015): 610–30. doi:10.1080/13510347.2013.856418.

von dem Knesebeck, Julia. *The Roma Struggle for Compensation in Post-War Germany.* Hatfield: University of Hertfordshire Press, 2011.

Waever, Ole. 'Identity, Integration and Security: Solving the Sovereignty Puzzle in EU Studies'. *Journal of International Affairs* 48, no. 2 (1995).

Warleigh, Alex. 'Learning from Europe? EU Studies and the Re-Thinking of "International Relations"'. *European Journal of International Relations* 12, no. 1 (2006): 31–51.

Waterbury, Myra A. *Between State and Nation: Diaspora Politics and Kin-State Nationalism in Hungary*. Houndmills: Palgrave Macmillan, 2010.

Waterbury, Myra A. 'Uncertain Norms, Unintended Consequences: The Effects of European Union Integration on Kin-State Politics in Eastern Europe'. *Ethnopolitics* 7, no. 2–3 (2008): 217–38.

Waters, Mary C., Van C. Tran, Philip Kasinitz, and John H. Mollenkopf. 'Segmented Assimilation Revisited: Types of Acculturation and Socioeconomic Mobility in Young Adulthood'. *Ethnic and Racial Studies* 33, no. 7 (2010): 1168–93.

Wiener, Antje. 'Making Sense of the New Geography of Citizenship: Fragmented Citizenship in the European Union'. *Theory and Society* 26, no. 4 (1997): 529–60.

Wimmer, Andreas. 'Does Ethnicity Matter? Everyday Group Formation in Three Swiss Immigrant Neighbourhoods'. *Ethnic and Racial Studies* 27, no. 1 (2003): 1–36.

Wimmer, Andreas. 'Elementary Strategies of Ethnic Boundary Making'. *Ethnic and Racial Studies* 31, no. 6 (2008): 1025–55. doi:10.1080/01419870801905612.

Wimmer, Andreas. 'The Making and Unmaking of Ethnic Boundaries: A Multilevel Process Theory'. *American Journal of Sociology* 113, no. 4 (2008): 970–1022.

Wolff, Jonas. 'Democracy Promotion, Empowerment, and Self-Determination: Conflicting Objectives in US and German Policies towards Bolivia'. *Democratization* 19, no. 3 (1 June 2012): 415–37. doi:10.1080/13510347.2012.674356.

Wolff, Stefan. '"Bilateral" Ethnopolitics after the Cold War: The Hungarian Minority in Slovakia, 1989–1999'. *Perspectives on European Politics and Society* 2, no. 2 (2001): 159–95.

Wolff, Stefan. *Ethnic Conflict: A Global Perspective*. Oxford: Oxford University Press, 2006.

Wolff, Stefan. 'The Institutional Structure of Regional Consociations in Brussels, Northern Ireland, and South Tyrol'. *Nationalism and Ethnic Politics* 10, no. 3 (2004): 387–414.

Wright, Richard, Mark Ellis, and Virginia Parks. 'Immigrant Niches and the Intrametropolitan Spatial Division of Labour'. *Journal of Ethnic and Migration Studies* 36, no. 7 (2010): 1033–59.

Zani, Bruna, and Martyn Barrett. 'Engaged Citizens? Political Participation and Social Engagement among Youth, Women, Minorities, and Migrants'. *Human Affairs* 22, no. 3 (2012): 273–82.

Zavadskaya, Margarita, and Christian Welzel. 'Subverting Autocracy: Emancipative Mass Values in Competitive Authoritarian Regimes'. *Democratization* 22, no. 6 (19 September 2015): 1105–30. doi:10.1080/13510347.2014.914500.

Zellner, Wolfgang. *On the Effectiveness of the OSCE Minority Regime: Comparative Case Studies on Implementation of the Recommendations of the High Commissioner on National Minorities of the OSCE*. Hamburg: Hamburger Beiträge zur Friedensforschung und Sicherheitspolitik, 1999.

Zielonka, Jan, ed. *Europe Unbound: Enlarging and Reshaping the Boundaries of the European Union*. London: Routledge, 2004.

Zuber, Christina Isabel, and Edina Szöcsik. 'Ethnic Outbidding and Nested Competition: Explaining the Extremism of Ethnonational Minority Parties in Europe'. *European Journal of Political Research*, 1 July 2015. doi:10.1111/1475-6765.12105.

Index

30848293R00130

Printed in Great
Britain
by Amazon